MOTOPIA

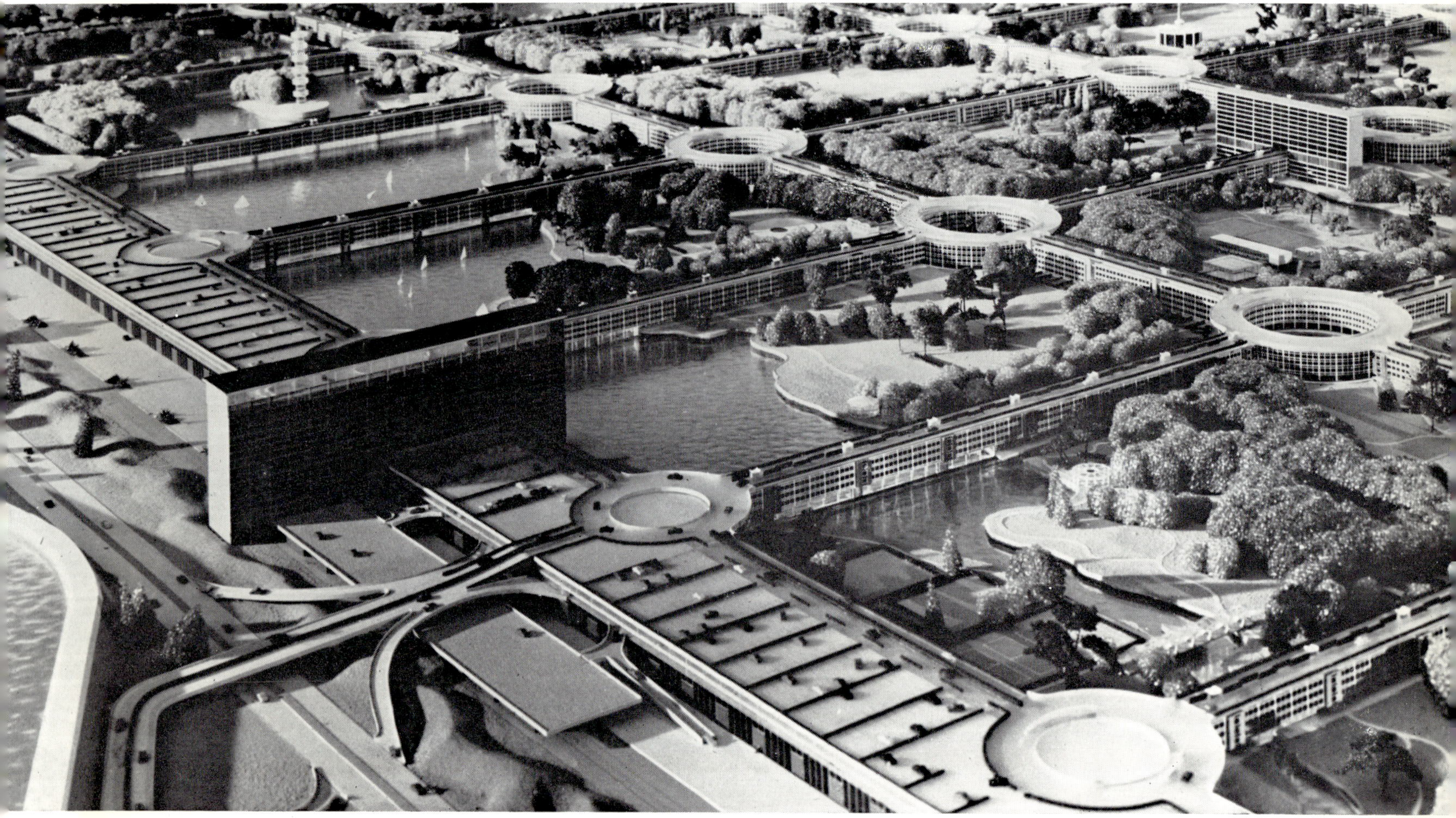

MOTOPIA

A Study in the Evolution of Urban Landscape

G. A. Jellicoe

Studio Books

To JOHN GLOAG

Acknowledgements

Motopia is the diagram of an idea only and should not be taken literally either in regard to its site, which is in the Green Belt round London, or in the severity of its geometry, which in reality would be complex.

The project was initiated by the Glass Age Development Committee of Messrs Pilkington Brothers Limited, St Helens, Lancashire, the members of which were Mr Ove Arup, Mr Edward Mills and myself. The design was worked out in detail by Miss June Colwill, of the office of Jellicoe, Ballantyne & Coleridge, and the model was made by Messrs Thorp. The Publishers and I are indebted to Messrs Pilkington Brothers for permission to reproduce the photographs of the model and the colour illustrations by Gordon Cullen.

The pedigree of Motopia has been collected by my wife from many sources, to all of whom I am most grateful, but there are four that require special mention: The New Landscape *by Gyorgy Kepes,* Europe from the Air *by E. E. and H. R. Muller,* The Things we see—Gardens *by Lady Allen of Hurtwood and Susan Jellicoe, and the various works of M. le Corbusier.*

First published by Studio Books, Longacre Press Ltd,
161 Fleet Street, London EC4, and printed and bound
in England by W & J Mackay & Co Ltd, Chatham, Kent
Design and typography by Anthony Adams

CONTENTS

The *Utopia* of Sir Thomas More was first published in 1516, and gave a new word to the English language. Utopias generally come to the fore when there is social discontent, and have the advantage of crystallizing the ideals of the time: that is to say that, all else being equal, they express the state or city in which we should most like to live. Motopia is such an idea, and arises not so much from normal discontent as from the realization that our present physical conditions are being thrown into chaos by the advent of one car per family and even one per person. Man has always been preoccupied with inventions to increase his mobility beyond the use of his own two legs, but except for the horse and the ship, no great transformation took place until the coming of the railways in the first half of the nineteenth century. Even then the railways did not interfere with the ways of the society of the time, which continued to develop and eventually to reach a climax in the middle of the century that was the wonder of the world. The railway did not in fact obtrude itself upon the domestic life of the middle- and upper-class individual.

The shapes of our towns and cities are today built on centuries of history, some having marked characteristics of one age, some of another. Some have grown from tiny hamlets and field tracks; some from fortifications; some from the formal layouts of the Renaissance; some from industry; and the later ones, known as garden cities, as a return to nature. But all these dispositions have one thing in common: they are planned for the pedestrian and the horse-drawn vehicle. The railways, when they were added, were confined within certain limits, and because of their nature, were automatically segregated from the path of the pedestrian.

The advent of the internal combustion engine at the beginning of the century may prove to be as significant to man's material way of life as anything that had happened before, except perhaps the invention of printing. Printing disseminated ideas and was, of course, the fore-runner of television. The car is a metal shell which man has grown around himself. By this means he is able to propel himself at will to distances and at speeds that were certainly never the intention of nature. If all the slow-moving molluscs on the sea rocks were suddenly to acquire self-propulsion twenty times their present rate, we can imagine the collisions and disasters that would befall them. Man's condition is somewhat similar, because although he has had 60 years to adapt himself personally, he has omitted to adapt his environment as well. It is for this reason that he finds himself today bewildered by circumstances which he alone has created, in times of peace and prosperity, and of his own free will. The purpose of this study is not to attempt to alleviate the major problem of existing cities (which is no more than that of putting new wine into old bottles), but of designing a new setting unencumbered by what already exists. This will at least help us to get the issues clear; to determine whether we are in perpetuity condemned to the presence of noise, dirt, smell, and a permanent sense of danger; or whether there is an ideal environment that would give us the best of all worlds.

To do this we must dig deep into the origins and make-up of modern man.

At a certain moment in the world's history, one of the species of animals who roamed its surface turned in upon itself and was able to contemplate. It was certainly a decisive moment, for the species was ultimately to take control of the earth, and for all we know, of the planets as well. But however far this power of contemplation could take him, he would nevertheless remain an animal. His body would remain the same, except that he became upright and lost his tail; and he would remain dependent upon his five senses. The environment in which he first appeared and took shape was probably in a warm climate, and almost certainly within a canopy of trees. It must, paradoxically, have been both friendly and hostile, for danger lurked everywhere. The shaping took many hundreds of thousands of years, and was so in harmony with the natural surroundings that just as we say today that a building and its landscape is one comprehensive design, so it may be said that the original *Homo sapiens* was part of his natural landscape. He was adapted to it and could not easily live without it. Because his intellect was low, his instincts, like those of any other animal, were acutely developed. Some instincts, such perhaps, as telepathy, may have diminished so much in the course of time that we are no longer aware of their past existence; others, especially those concerned with the preservation of the individual, the family, and the species, are still paramount.

In comparatively recent times and only a few thousand years ago, man had so far developed beyond the animal as to put on record his observations of the world around him. These are the rock paintings, the most famous of which are at Lascaux in southern France. What concerns us most about these drawings is that they display a sensitivity of feeling which has not been surpassed by even the great periods of civilization, and beside which twentieth-century man appears something of a boor. It seems strange that 'feeling' as we understand the word has not increased with education and learning; that in fact it has deteriorated. It is in all probability a quality that exists between animal and animal, and animal and environment, and is based upon an acute perception of all the senses. His environment, which had shaped his body, shaped his mind also. These drawings are not naturalistic as we understand the word, for they portray the idea or essence of the object, and this is much more significant.

In due time man began to extend his art and to make the first patterns on the surface of the earth to reflect his aspirations. If we now transfer him to England, we see the patterns of the circles of Stonehenge and Dartmoor. We can follow him through the Middle Ages, continuously rationalizing his way of life, especially in regard to food and shelter. But all this time he remains subsidiary to his natural environment, in which the two qualities of hostility and affection are still curiously blended. Feeling, rather than intellect, has created a deep faith in a world beyond the visual world, and his emotions are expressed in cathedrals and churches whose art is apparently based on observation of the surrounding world, but which are in fact the pure creation of his imagination.

By the middle of the sixteenth century the forests were cleared, printing had been invented, a new learning was spreading from the Mediterranean, and *Utopia* was published. Something under two centuries later a revolution took place in the outlook on landscape and it is from this point, the first half of the eighteenth century, that the evolution of Motopia properly begins.

The new learning from Rome and Greece had brought with it an outlook towards nature that was one of the conqueror. Man had found his power, and a symbol of this was the ordering and regimenting of nature into classical and geometric shape, and more particularly into the grand avenue developed so splendidly under the French. These avenues became fashionable in England, until quite suddenly the native genius asserted itself in a way never before experienced except perhaps in prehistoric times. The Englishman decided that if he were to live within the geometry of a house (and at that time he favoured the high geometry of Palladio), he wished his environment to be a free and not an ordered landscape. In this way came about the English School of Landscape Gardening, whose art was similar to that of the cave-man in as much as it was based again upon acute observation of nature passed, as it were, through the aesthetic digestive process. We have therefore the first major step taken by Western civilization to separate the geometric arts from the biological arts, and to give each their proportionate value. It is interesting that China had reached such a balance over a thousand years previously, and it was her recently discovered art (together with that of the painters) which partly provided the precedent and rules of the design of the English park.

In the country this separation of geometry and biology created the Palladian villa in its broad and boundless environment. In the town it developed still further the squares that enclosed parts of the country within the urban scene, such as the Inns of Court, and later blossomed into an association of landscape and architecture that is famous. The most splendid examples are of course St James's Park, Regent Street and Regent's Park in London; and the shapely terraces, crescents, and circus at Bath.

Until the early nineteenth century, therefore, the English seemed to have reconciled quite contentedly their love of town with their pronounced love of country. The industrial age altered this balance, and we are now ashamed of the huge agglomerations of slums which were built with no thought but the need to man the machines. It is true that the terrace and landscape tradition was still developing, as at Holland Park, but by and large the urge was dying and for some reason the great Victorian squares of the middle and upper class do not interest us as did those of the previous age; perhaps because the plantations of the square had become out of harmony with the ponderous neo-classical architecture in which they were set. This solid classicism developed parallel with the fantastic development of the structural and mechanical sciences, sciences which were backed by the boldness of conception which produced the Crystal Palace in 1851, and the Inner Circle underground railway in 1863. By the end of the century, the majority of people lived in conditions entirely dominated by the machine and by the system which the machine had created. A second landscape revolution then took place, but one that was slower to develop because its beginnings were altruistic and concerned an inarticulate class. Cadburys built the first garden village, Bournville, and from this sprang the garden city movement, a movement that was in fact a return to nature. Since that time almost the entire public housing effort has been directed towards giving each family a semi-detached house and garden. So powerful and fresh is the memory of the long urban terraces of slums, and so strong has been the prejudice against them that the ideal became the English country village, its cottages set about the village green, or placed among trees and flowers and protected by a trim hedgerow from the quiet road. Just as the English School of Landscape Gardening provided an original contribution to the art of the world, so did the English garden village in its highest form, as at Hampstead Garden Suburb or Welwyn Garden City. It is of profound significance that while we must give pride of place to European countries in the geometric arts, it is England that has the keenest sense of the country. The Chelsea Flower Show of the Royal Horticultural Society, for instance, has no equal anywhere.

In due course, and after the last war, England put forth yet another prodigious effort in the creation of New Towns. The garden city movement was carried to the next stage, one in which the country was to be brought more consciously within the urban area, and where for the first time serious notice was taken of the problem of traffic. Shopping centres were made precincts; pedestrian ways were developed throughout the town so far as possible; the architecture was romantic, diversified, and in scale with trees. Occasionally a tall building broke the skyline, but generally the idea of the village was extended to areas covering several square miles, the units broken down agreeably as in agricultural countryside.

Fifteen years ago it was calculated that there would be one car for every ten houses; today the figure is one car per house. The sense of village is disrupted, and in any case it becomes inadequate as a functioning organism. Let us now examine what has happened, what history advises us to be our true instincts, and on what premises an entirely new environment may be created.

(a) The predicament is that while we want the best of both worlds, the mechanical and the biological, nothing will stop us achieving the first at the cost of the second. Man has two passions behind this: the first is to increase his own mobility, the second is to live up to his neighbour. While happiness may be in his own garden, he will rarely believe it is not somewhere else where his car can now take him; and we must assume, therefore (and beyond possible doubt), that short of economic catastrophe or further invention, the car is with us indefinitely.

(b) This mobile shell in which we encase ourselves is lethal soon after it begins to move. Usually it hurls itself along a street designed for slow-moving horse carriages, and is separated from the pedestrian by a six-inch curb only; both pedestrian and driver are acting mainly on the sub-conscious, for otherwise no power on earth could keep the accidents as low as they are. It can make undesirable noises and when in motion perpetually emits an odour as disagreeable as that of a skunk, able to kill plants at three feet and permanently retard growth for a considerable area around. It requires space at home equal to that of half the living room, and demands aggressively an equal amount wherever it may terminate its journey.

(c) Despite these criticisms, however, it represents an increase in man's stature which is a tribute to his intellectual achievements, and as such should fill us with a sense of pride and dignity. That it does not do so is because we rarely see it in the context to which it properly belongs. This context is one belonging wholly to the mechanical arts, whose laws derive mainly from the geometry of the universe. Whenever this machine is loosed upon the biological world, it is destructive to man and plant alike.

(d) Therefore the ideal town would seem to be one in which the traffic circulation were piped like drainage and water; out of sight and mind, to go as fast as it likes, to smell as it wants, and to make noises. It cannot do this on the same level as the ground, and therefore it must either go underground or overhead. It cannot go underground like the railways, because the cost would be prodigious and our town must essentially be economic; and in a garden village it would be monstrous to place it on stilts, where in any case it would not fulfil the basic requirement of being out of sight and mind.

(e) We must therefore conceive a town on wholly different lines from those at present adopted. Let us cause the last century and a half to dissolve, and continue where John Nash left off at Regent's Park; that period when the landscape architects were doing everything in their power to reduce by illusion all dreary matters such as drives and approach roads from their conception of landscape. Let us observe the long lines of terraces, their height, and relation to trees and open spaces. Let us observe how old-fashioned are the high pitched roofs with their chimneys, and how more orderly is the modern terrace with its flueless heating and its concrete flat roof; and then let us reflect what would happen if we quite simply took the road, placed it on the roof which fits it so admirably in regard to breadth, and then left the whole of the land free to do with it what we will—walk and run and play, breathe deeply, and associate with trees and flowers unspoiled by petrol fumes.

II

When you come out of the sky upon Motopia, your first view is of a geometric framework of rectangles with circles at the intersection. This frame appears to lie lightly upon the natural landscape extending northwards from the Thames. Except for the gardens and canals, the approach road, and the obvious association with the great embankments of the reservoirs at Staines, there is no apparent connexion between the frame and the ground. It might be accidental, and in this way the view we are observing is somewhat similar to that seen looking upon landscape through the panes of a Georgian window. Open the window and theoretically at least you would get a continuous and flowing scenery. In a single glance, therefore, we can comprehend the social idea of Motopia: the separation of mechanical and biological man. A few minutes later our plane lands at London Airport, and our car whistles on the new road extension up and over and up the Motopia fly-over, along the roof roads, down the circle ramp and into the mews road to stop at the covered entrance to our own block of dwellings. Here we cast off our shell and descend as human beings to our home. It is here (and if it is summer, on the balcony) that we can ponder upon this new environment; what it is, why it is and if it is going to answer our needs. (If we are interested in the past, we can recall that once before at a critical moment of history two totally dissimilar worlds had been merged to harmonize fairly satisfactorily. In historic Greece, the full impact of the gods of the ancient world, led by the goddess of fertility, and emerging as it were from the soil, met and intermingled with Zeus and his company descending from the skies on Mount Olympus. The impact of these two ideas might well have dislocated the Greeks as we are being dislocated today, and it is a tribute to the classical world that not only were the forces reconciled, but they were combined to give extraordinary power to the development of western civilization.)

Before us, from our balcony, lies a rectangle enclosed by terraces five storeys in height, so wide and full of trees that the farther side is confused; we have seen something of this in Lincoln's Inn or Russell Square, the largest squares in London. On the ground are a proportion of all the open spaces normally required of a town of thirty thousand and contained within them are the associated buildings: schools, clubs of all kinds, cafés and restaurants, and so forth. Here too are the churches, ordered and geometrical and set among trees. The rectangles are large enough to contain luxuriant indigenous forest trees and we observe three informal belts of hardwood trees drifting across the full landscape from north to south; here, we are told, there are continuous forest paths and children can play wildly as they do on Hampstead Heath. Trees as well as plants do well, because the buildings (to use a phrase of Thomas More) are well set against the wind. The soil, which is not wasted, is among the best in England and growth should excel that in the neighbouring Kew Gardens, which is retarded by gas and other fumes. Rivers also cross from north to south and these have their own riverside scenery. But what interests us in the landscape most of all are great areas of lakes on which yachts are gaily sailing. We are told that these lakes were made from waste gravel pits, and are particularly popular because we are by nature a water-loving and sea-faring nation, and until these were developed and moorings provided, the crowding on the Thames (especially of moorings) had been overwhelming. We learn, too, that there is nothing new in this idea, for it appears that the greatest of the English playgrounds, the Norfolk Broads, was originally made by the extraction of peat in the Middle Ages, and not, as many think, by nature.

We find this view from the balcony of unending and changing interest. Apparently the landscape of no rectangle repeats another, and as at times it passes beneath the buildings, it is possible to have so many walks within the confines of Motopia that an hour's stroll on Sunday, from door back to door, need not repeat itself for a year. We watch from above, too, the owners of the private gardens, of which there are over a thousand and without which no

English town would be complete. The gardens are quite long and it is entertaining to see how the ends of the plots invariably vanish under trees, for the Englishman above all likes his privacy. Far away, also, we see a gaily coloured water bus moving along one of the canals, until it passes into one of the circles preparatory to taking passengers to the shopping centre. Altogether we enjoy these moments intensely, and then we realize that the perception of the scene we are watching has been intensified by natural smells and country sounds. Indeed, we are told that so powerful is the sound of birds that many new dwellers from the towns suffered at first from the novelty of natural sounds, especially at dawn. Somehow the mechanical world in nearly all its horrid manifestations has been excluded. Helicopters, for instance, are forbidden overhead, and must land on the extremities of the roof roads, fold their wings, and proceed to their house garage like a car. (We do not mind the drone of a plane over ten thousand feet above us.) But there are other sights and sounds, such as moving cars and wireless, and to see how these have been suppressed and the pleasures of sound regained we must now turn to a study of the buildings.

From our vantage point we have already seen how the terraces frame the open spaces as they do in the London Squares. One facade stands on pilotis and this arcade gives a continuous covered walk throughout the town. A model of the original scheme (now displayed in the town centre) had shown severity in regard to facade and to outline. In practice the long terrace facades have been designed by different architects working on certain basic standard units, and we now observe them to be inventive and entertaining, more perhaps like the manifold inventiveness at Brighton than the single inventiveness of Nash in Regent's Park. The basic plan of each bay conforms to the standard overall dimensions. These are deeper back to front than a traditional terrace, because of course Motopia is air-conditioned and the service rooms and storage are in what is normally the dark centre of the dwelling. Stairs and lifts are established; but after this a prospective client may rent, lease, or purchase as many units as he wishes. He then adjusts the interior according to his tastes, which is traditional practice; but he is also allowed to adjust the exterior, which is not. Grave concern was first expressed about this departure from normal elevational control, but in practice the overall architectural frame is so strong that errors of taste in regard to fragments are really very engaging. From where we sit we particularly enjoy the complex of projecting balconies, each in different colours and patterns and of course eloquent with flowers; reminiscent of huge hanging flower boxes. They are reflected, as are both the landscape and passing clouds, in the highly polished surfaces between the structural ribs, and the windows. Within a general freedom of expression there are of course rigid codes of practice in regard, for instance, to overshadowing, and also to garden watering. Most people in Motopia are satisfied with the balcony gardens which are easy to maintain, but for a long time could not get used to this idea of hanging gardens, as in Babylon. The silhouette from our viewpoint is unusual and rather tranquil and beautiful in the summer light. The actual summit line is a clipped evergreen hedge, behind which the moving cars are quite invisible. This line is occasionally broken by some gay balcony top, while the facade as a whole is continuously broken by the full-grown trees. The architects had studied the eighteenth-century terraces of London with great care, and had concluded that the uneasy silhouette of chimneys, dormers, etc. did in fact enhance the peacefulness of the terrace facade itself. Provide an unending flat roof and the result may be boring and severe. They had no hesitation therefore in encouraging a broken skyline rising from the central verge of the double tracks in the top decks, whether it was the tops of the lift chambers, or the bushes in between.

We can now appreciate how it is that sound and smell of the roof-road cars are dissipated into the air. More difficult to overcome were the noises and fumes of the mews road; the former were reduced to normal country sounds by an acoustic ceiling, the latter rely on cross-ventilation. A scheme to provide a giant baffle for children's playgrounds was abandoned when it was found how many persons enjoy such occasional liveliness. We have suddenly realized, also, that on this summer's day there are no wireless sounds, and we find the solution to this normal pest of urban existence is that when the wireless is on the double windows must be closed. This is possible with artificial ventilation, but not otherwise. The insulation between houses is excellent; and in fact even the scholar can work sealed against all forms of compelling noises.

We now turn in upon the cell, the home which must be individual to each family and which must have absolute privacy. One might have expected a roar and vibration from overhead traffic (especially in a top flat) but what the engineers foretold has proved correct: there is no problem of sound. In any case all cars, including delivery vans, run on pneumatic tyres, and their effect upon the structure by braking is negligible. The horn should never be used, and the only serious sound is revving in the mews road, but there is no question of sound transmission to the structure below. Sounds of this nature are absorbed by normal acoustic precautions in the ceiling.

Further examination of the dwelling, or apartment, showed that in all cases except the one-room flat, the outlook was double: either east and west, or north and south. The English preference tends towards the former and this fixed the shape and alignment of the Motopian rectangle. The windows occupy the whole end-wall space, which can be opened fully in summer upon the balcony. A form of Venetian blind reduces glare, and gives a greater sense of enclosure in winter; double glazing prevents heat loss, which in any case is counteracted by thermostatic air-conditioning. The centre of the apartment, which is artificially lit, is given over to services such as kitchen and bathroom, all equipped with every mechanical device. Power is supplied electrically from nuclear energy, and we take some pleasure in discovering a small store of candles, matches, and sufficient oil fuel to subsist independently for a week. The furniture is modern, the fabrics are beautiful, there are flowers in the rooms as well as on the balconies, there are books of all kinds and modern paintings in evidence, and a concealed T.V. set. In short we have a cell in which the external world is brought in as never before, and where it is possible for a family to be self-sufficient, if need be.

Let us now leave this cell and open the front door upon the stairs and lift. Downwards leads into the landscape world we have already described, and through this on foot to all parts of the town. The tempo is pedestrian and related to one's physical abilities. We were interested to learn that it is possible to live a full and happy life in Motopia without a car, and it is very suitable to old persons who especially appreciate the ground floor garden flats. In good weather, the walk to the town centre threads through the landscape, but it can also be reached by walking under cover along the arcades. The only public transport provided is that of the water buses, which can be reached under cover and in a few minutes from the most extreme dwelling. The frequency of the service has increased to one every few minutes, and the sensation is very reminiscent of Venice. The service is popular with housewives, because the conditions, unlike those of a motorbus, are essentially friendly, social, unhurried, and quiet.

But it is time we took a tour on the roof tops.

On emerging from the lift we find ourselves in the mews road, the level below the rooftops. This is a one-way street with specific parking space for one car per dwelling, and two or three visitors' cars per staircase. There is space, too, for one stopping delivery van. We learn that in practice the whole economy and dimensions of Motopia are calculated upon the capacity and use of the mews road, for the roof roads for such a small town are if anything too generous as residential roads. We are told that the margin for the unexpected is somewhat small; for instance, on a Saturday afternoon, when all domestic cars are parked, when visitors arrive, and when vans may also be delivering, there is a certain congestion reminiscent of the usual conditions in London itself. But there is more discipline, and the one way flow allows offside curb parking in an emergency. A family requiring two cars either rents the space of a neighbour who has none, or takes space in the nearest neighbourhood circle. Generally we are glad to see how small is the average car and how it has adapted itself to its new conditions. Certainly the mews are immaculately clean and we learn that cars are cleaned, rather like shoes, overnight; this covered entrance to our home reminds us of that of many hotels and commercial buildings, where the approach is direct from an underground car park, and where seemliness is essential.

Our car drives slowly along the mews road and curls up the ramp round the circle. We notice that strict white lines prevent us from cutting immediately across oncoming traffic and that rather than take an immediate left turn we must weave round a full circle. Even in the rush hour, however, the traffic flow of the average circle is so small as to cause no anxiety in regard to danger or continuous flow. These circles are second only in importance to the mews road in fixing the design of Motopia, and we must therefore digress a moment before we proceed to the town centre.

The gridiron plan was selected for the first example of Motopia because throughout history and even today it is the engineer's simplest layout for a town. The modern problem, apart from aesthetics, lies at the junction: whether there shall be 'lights', a roundabout, or some variety of fly-over. In the design of Motopia the road is regarded as a service unit and as such has been played down; the important question was as to which possibility was the most agreeable for the residential pattern. The fly-over was cumbersome and expensive; the straight junction with lights meant the normal difficulty of a residential square, i.e. the juxtaposition of two houses in the corner, and the problem of the dark centre. A circle provides a charming residential solution, for it not only solves the outlook problem, but provides an internal architectural court that is in contrast to the open space of the rectangle. This circle is founded on English history; we find it at the Globe theatre, and of course later in Bath, Edinburgh, and elsewhere. It must be sufficiently large not to appear like a well, and not unreasonably large for traffic circulation above. The dwellings are approached by access balconies and look outwards only. The internal court is the centre of its neighbourhood, and is alternatively a local shopping centre or a water bus station. It contains the local club and public house, the essential shops, the infants' school, and so forth. The court is paved and each receives a market once a fortnight. It is a natural theatre arena and travelling amateur and professional companies of music and drama are encouraged to come here from time to time. The ground floor exits can be sealed by glass against wind, and in an emergency tarpaulins can be spread over those spectators who are not in the surrounding galleries. There can be hubbub without disturbance to the surrounding residences.

Our car now sets course along a roof road. Above us is the sky. On our left is a continuous clipped hedge of a nature chosen to survive petrol fumes, set in a high concrete curb. On our right is the central verge on which great care has been expended to make it interesting. The background is rich and mainly evergreen foliage, but interspersed ingeniously with this are tubs of shrubs in full flower. These are changed constantly and provide the motorist with continuous pleasure. At night there is no dazzle, for the lighting is from the curb upon the surface of the road, a system that has been found satisfactory provided there are no pedestrians. Pedestrians and dogs are forbidden absolutely. The tracks are sufficiently wide to allow for the breakdown or the passing of cars, but normally all cars travel at the maximum permitted speed of 40 m.p.h.

The single huge structure of the Town Centre, a mile in length, is actually placed at the entrance to Motopia rather than in the centre. The reason is that such centres serve a surrounding population at least five times that of the town itself, and it was essential to keep this traffic, and service traffic, from using the roof roads. The centre allows for approach by road, rail and helicopter. The roof parking areas are based on the American experiments of shoppers' markets, and access is by the continuous vertical lift (developed in Germany) called the Paternoster. The principle of the design is that of a linear shopping street, one side containing two levels of shops, and the other overlooking the splendid adjoining landscape. Here too are cinemas and at least one theatre, but the uses of the interior can be interchanged at will. It is air-conditioned and under one cover. The broad mall has moving bands for customers in a hurry, but the main purpose of this street is not one of hurry but of leisure and enjoyment. Its counterpart in history is the Stoa of Attalos in the Agora of Athens, recently reconstructed, beneath whose colonnades it is now possible to envisage the considerable part it played in the life of the city. In much the same way the Stoa of Motopia is a centre for meeting friends and for leisurely discussion; and is complementary to the individuality of the home.

We now end our visit to Motopia by ascending the tall office block, let out to various firms, and survey the scene from the Council suite on the top floor. Here, too, is the watchful eye of the traffic administrator, and it is with him that our final deliberations are concerned. Is Motopia worth while, and what are the errors of this first design? Quite clearly the road engineers would have to tackle the entrance, especially the roundabouts, which gives a feeling of the congestion of a bottle neck; and yet even in the rush hour of cars leaving for work in London, it is calculated that at the most only three thousand cars per hour would pass into the main arterial road, and congestion here is negligible in comparison to the London approaches. A car requires for safety its own length in front for every 10 m.p.h. of speed. The traffic administrator says that once the residential traffic has reached the distributive roads, there is no difficulty. Because of this, indeed, the town could expand almost indefinitely. His fear lies in the unpredictable outside traffic to the shopping centre meeting the predictable rush-hour traffic of the town itself. He enjoys discoursing on the flexibility of the two-level gridiron pattern. For instance, if a resident invites five hundred guests to a wedding in one of the landscape churches, he can by previous notice to the administrator seal off any section as a car park, since alternative routes are easily provided. Fire fighting presents no difficulty. He admits that of course it is quite impossible wholly to exclude vehicular traffic from the ground landscape. Existing roads have in fact been retained, and extra service roads added as required; the conditions are the same as for Hampstead Heath, which also requires service roads. The essential point is that only the authorized have access, and the speed limit is low; the pedestrian is paramount. When we ask him about cyclists, he gives us an answer that we do not like at all: that the cycle is a form of traction midway between pedestrian and car, is an anachronism in the modern world, and requires very costly special facilities. No cycles are allowed in Motopia, but parking facilities are provided conveniently near the entrance, and thereafter the cyclist becomes a pedestrian.

We are taking this last comprehensive view from a point that is not advantageous to the views of the town, for the scenery is designed to be seen from a low level and the several parts to unfold gradually. Nevertheless the simplicity is such that it does not strike us as strange that the total cost of the residential areas compares favourably with those of a similar population housed in fourteen-storey towers. There is no structural problem and the methods of mass production have been employed to the full. Admittedly the shopping centre is expensive, but the cost per cube is no more than that already spent by the great stores. We ask the final question that has been bothering us. It is a middle-income group town with rentals of £100 per person, and must therefore pay for itself without subsidy and with profit: how did it come to be built when the whole tradition of English speculative building is based on trial and error, and when it is clear that at least one-third of the 10,000 dwellings must be built in a single effort before it can be worth while? The answer is that the scale of modern finance has no parallel in history. Motopia was built (and will no doubt be extended) not by a single company, but by a consortium of companies. The word 'consortium' was first used in the English language in 1881, and is peculiarly expressive of the pooling of resources of a number of great firms for a particular objective. It is this method that is behind the programme of Nuclear Power stations, for a single such station costs as much as the whole of Motopia.

TOWN GEOMETRY

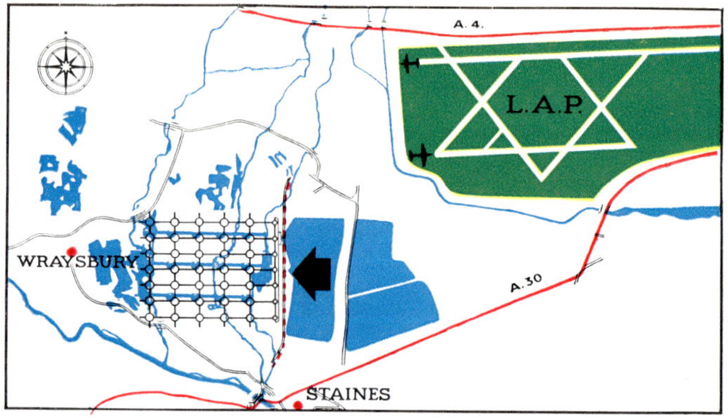

1a **The land pattern of Motopia**

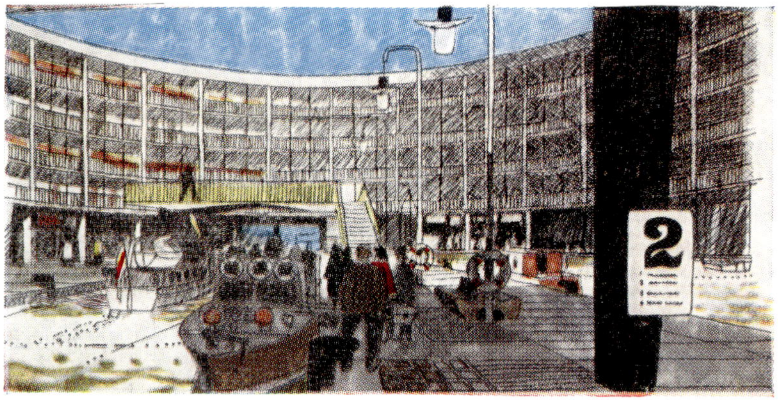

1b **The line and the circle in Motopia**
Drawing by Gordon Cullen

In the beginning, and out of chaos, geometry preceded biology as a phenomenon of the universe. The gases solidified and became balls swirling in mathematical circles. Then, as we are told, the envelope of the earth became covered with minute cells, still geometric and exactly similar one to another. After a considerable number of millions of years these cells, under different conditions, broke and became vegetation and animals, and the biological sciences began. In due course appears *Homo sapiens*, a curious creature having on the one hand a constant urge towards lifting itself by means of the mathematical sciences above its animal state; and on the other, encompassed by the indisputable fact that it is still an animal. Prehistoric man was concerned with great and everlasting monuments and the value placed on house and home was transitory; modern man, no longer fearful of his environment, is preoccupied almost wholly with daily affairs. As we proceed through history we can deduce exactly his way of thought from the patterns he leaves upon the envelope of the earth. The three patterns of the Motopia landscape express the highest artificial mobility yet achieved (London Airport), the planned conservation of water for the animal needs (Staines Reservoirs), and the framework of geometry placed upon the natural landscape (his home).

Patterns of Carnac and Stonehenge are simplified versions of such grand landscapes as those of ancient Egypt and Mesopotamia, but it was in the Meander Valley in Asia Minor that the idea of the modern town plan was first evolved and executed in Miletus and Priene. Here is a juxtaposition of buildings that is eminently agreeable rather than overwhelming—the so-called gridiron plan is laid out with the greatest skill for the interest and dignity of the individual. Set against hills on either side of what was once the broad estuary of a river, whose very name provokes meditation, we have a relationship between geometry and landscape that is beautifully balanced for the conditions of the time. For a long period, during the dark ages, the cities of western man were dominated by the expediency of war and social conditions arising from lack of learning. Rye is a typical medieval town whose charm to us today is irresistible because it is far removed from the mechanical planning from which we shrink. Nevertheless, it is a retrograde step to consider that our future should be influenced by an outlook that is now purely one of sentiment. It is revealing to turn to the adjoining town of Winchelsea, and observe how Edward I in 1280 laid out the only new medieval town in England on lines that were as scientific as those of Miletus or Motopia.

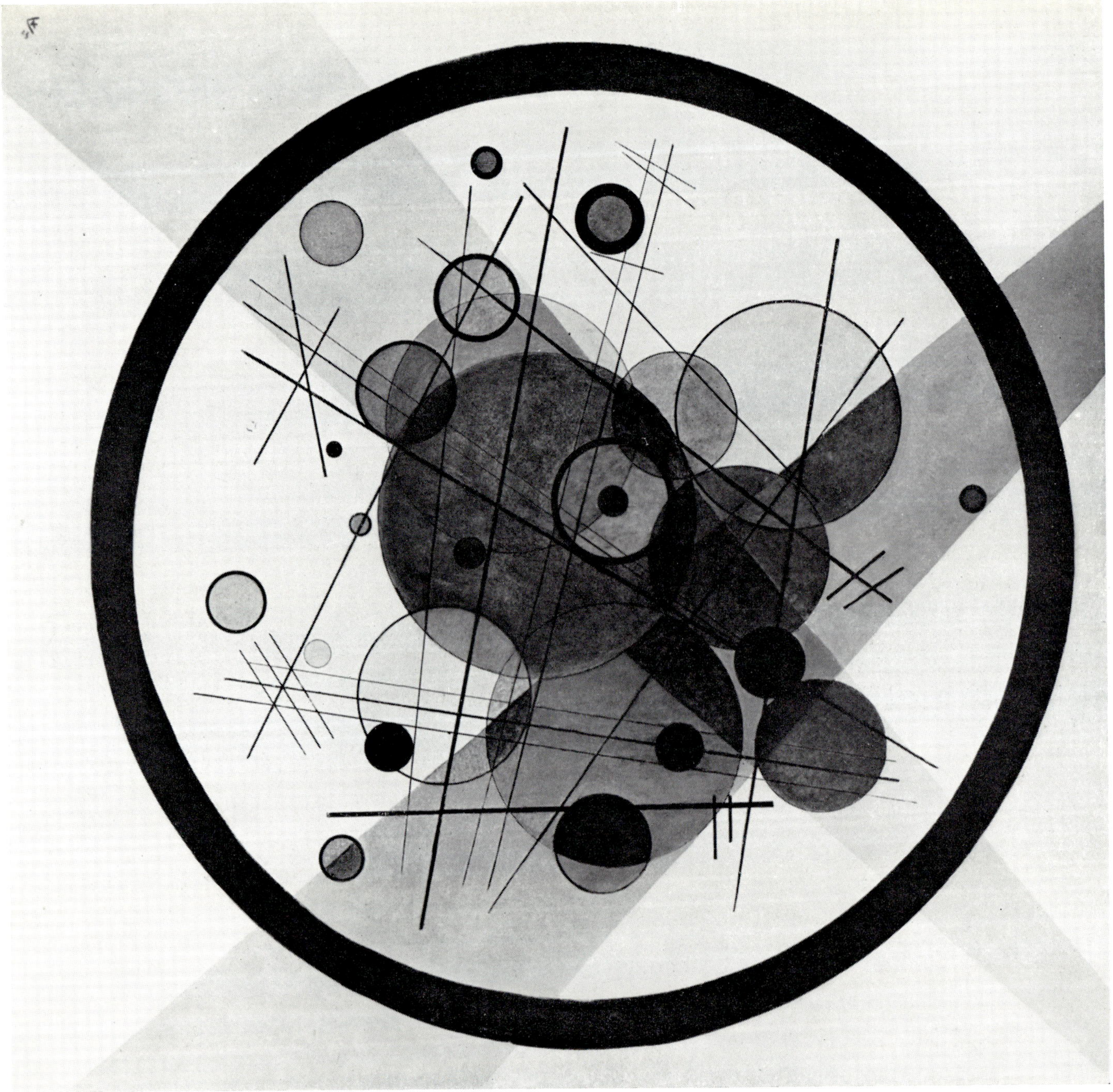

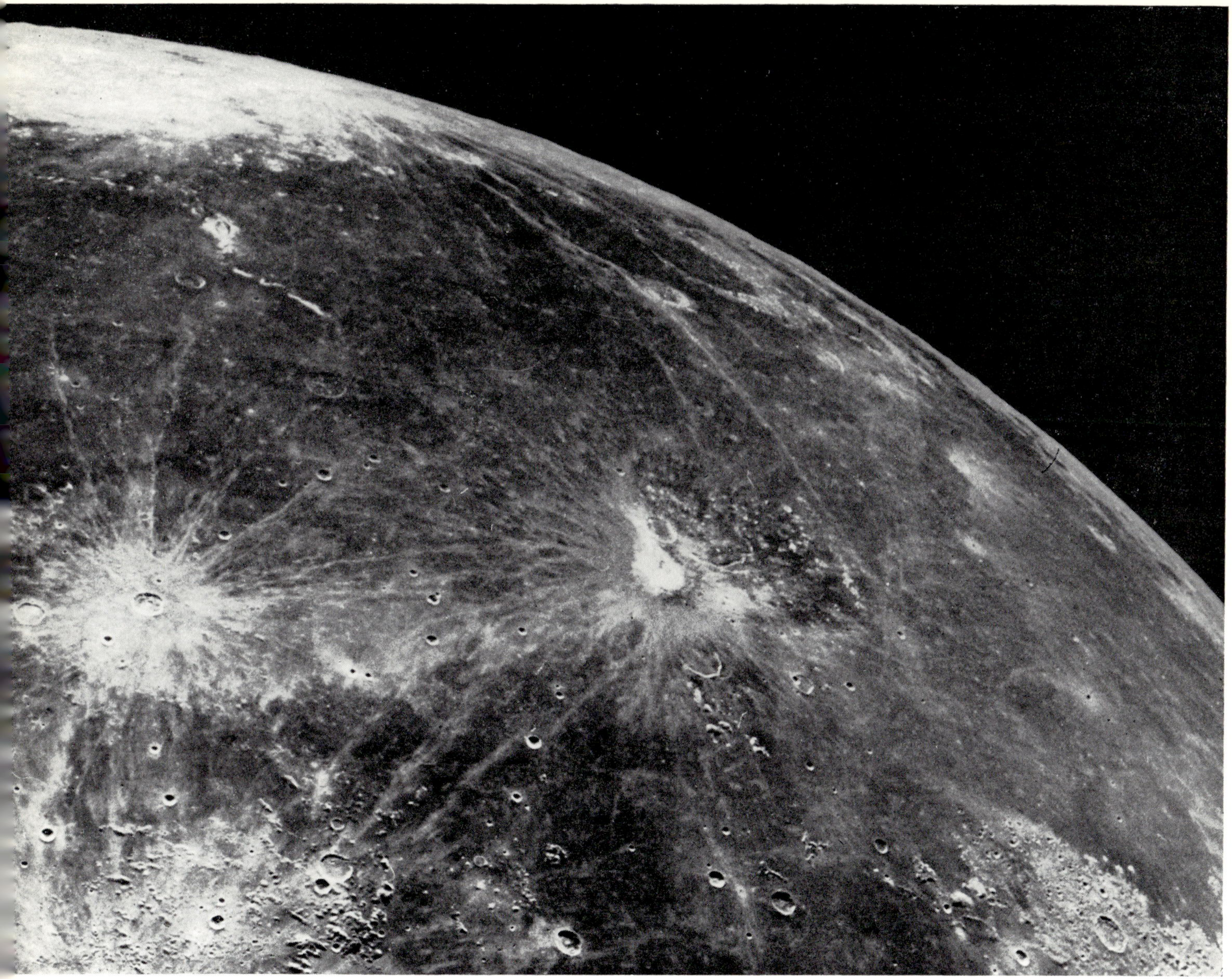

◀ **2 Circles in Circle, 1923, by Vassily Kandinsky.** 'The gases solidified and became balls swirling in mathematical circles.'

3 The Moon. The surfaces of the spheres were unruly and chaotic and gave rise on earth to biological man.

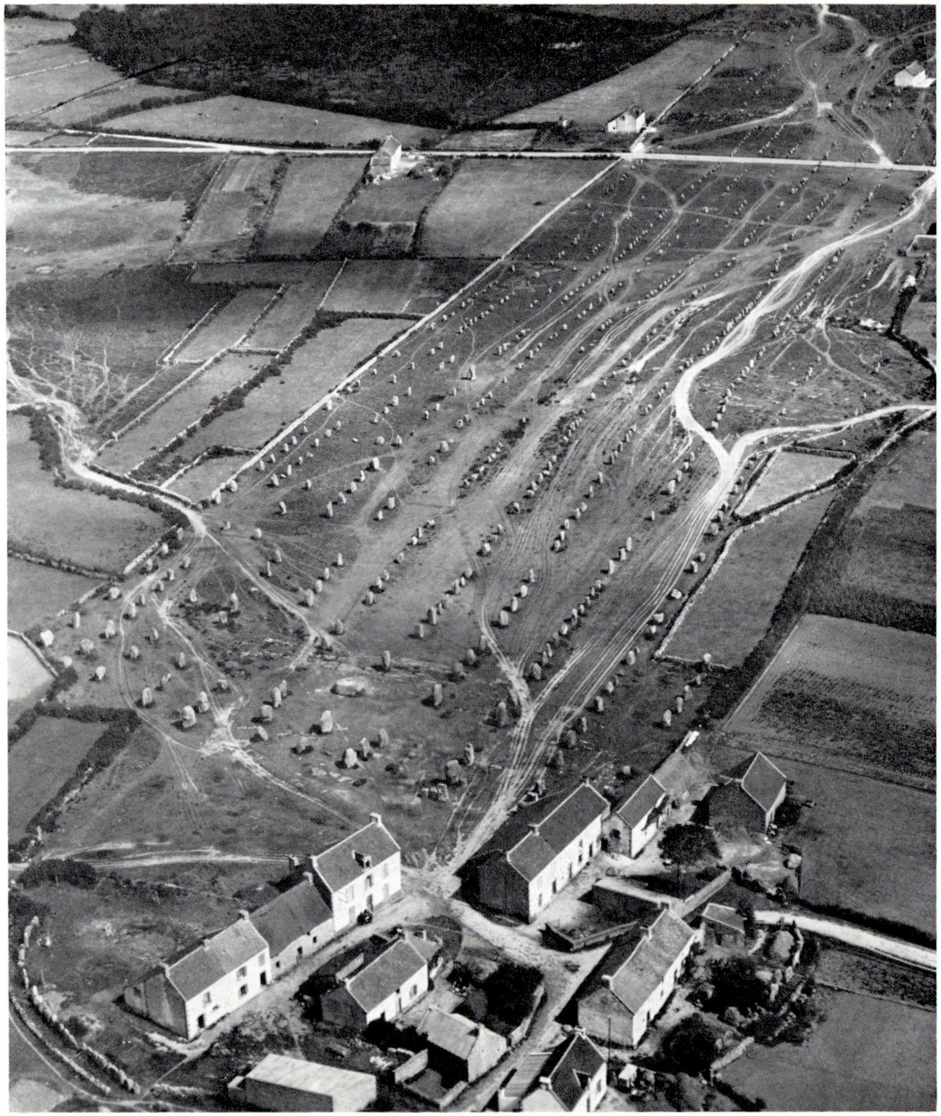

4 **Carnac: Avenue of Menhirs.** Man's first endeavours to establish himself on earth by the creation of law and order were expressed in a geometry that was truly monumental.

5 **Stonehenge.** The straight line and the circle are the rudiments of all geometrical patterns of landscape. ▶

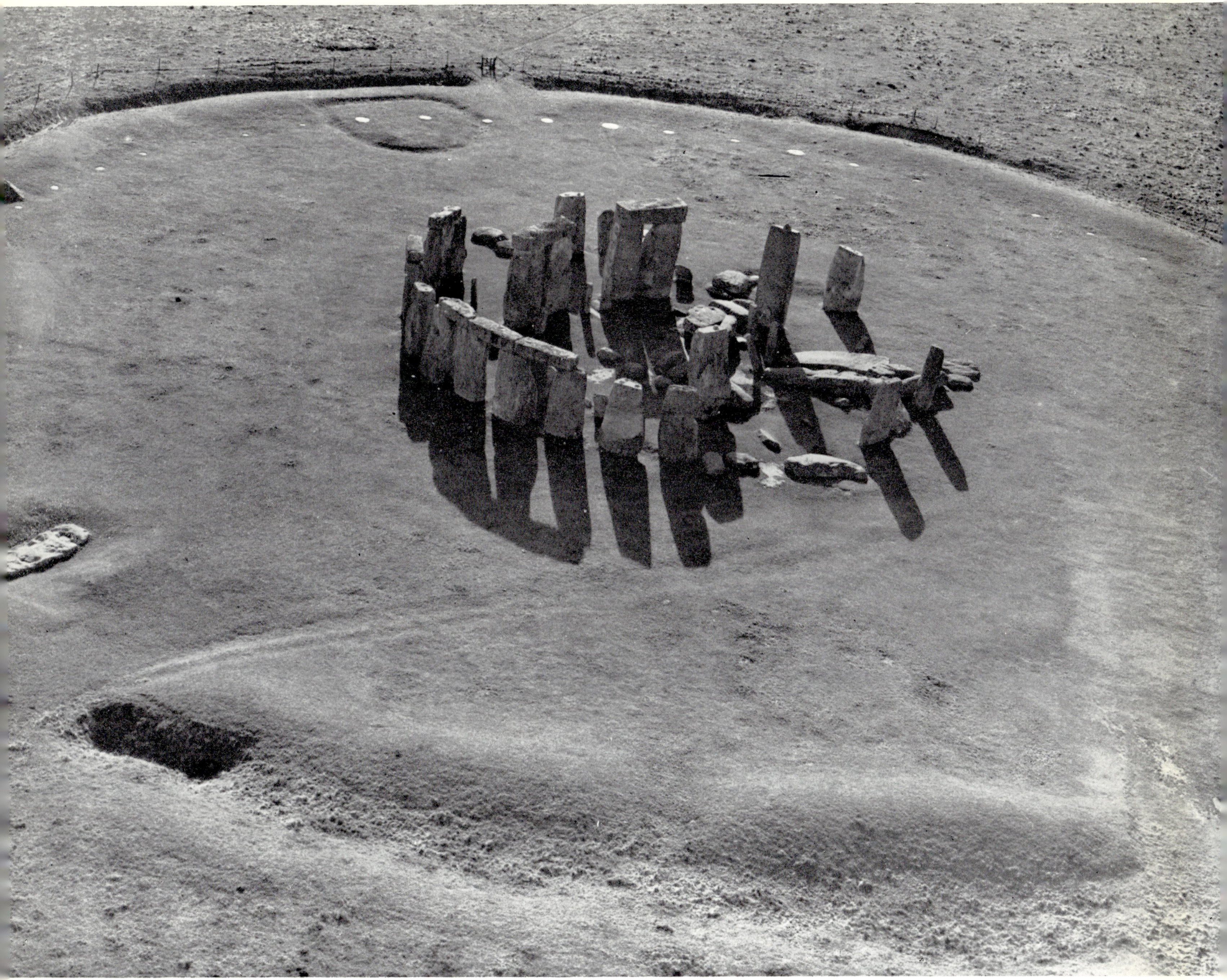

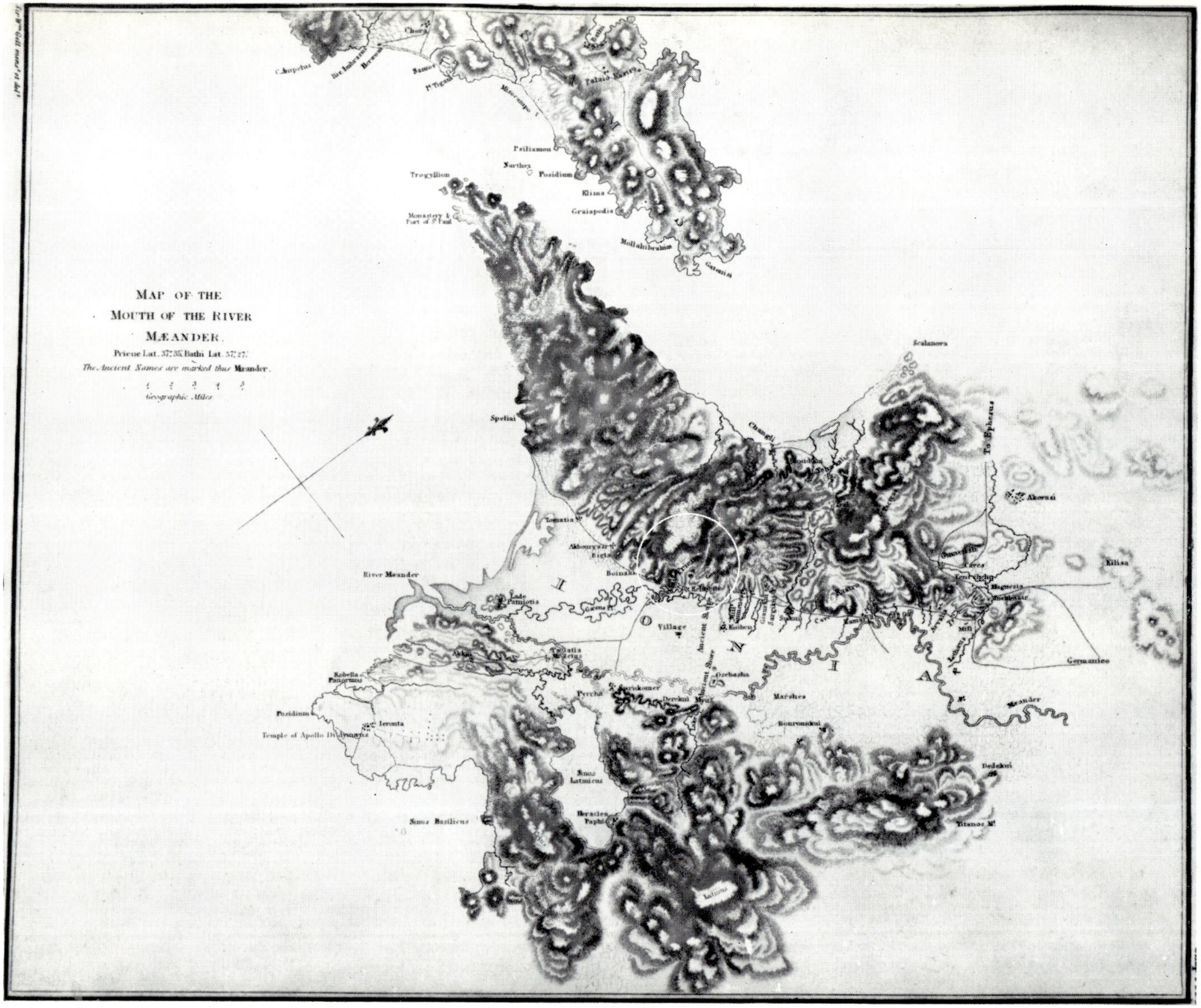

6 **Priene: The Valley of the Meander, Asia Minor** (from a plan made in 1812). Priene lies seven and a half miles due north from Miletus.

Priene was laid out as a model city by Hippodamus of Miletus, in the fourth century B.C., and is the most agreeable example in antiquity of the relation of geometry to natural landscape. Originally both Miletus and Priene were harbours on a broad estuary.

7 Priene: Ruins as existing in 1812. The town is beautifully ordered and set on the slopes of the mountain. The undulations of the small plateau inspired the three-dimensional geometric design, and there is complete harmony between buildings and landscape.

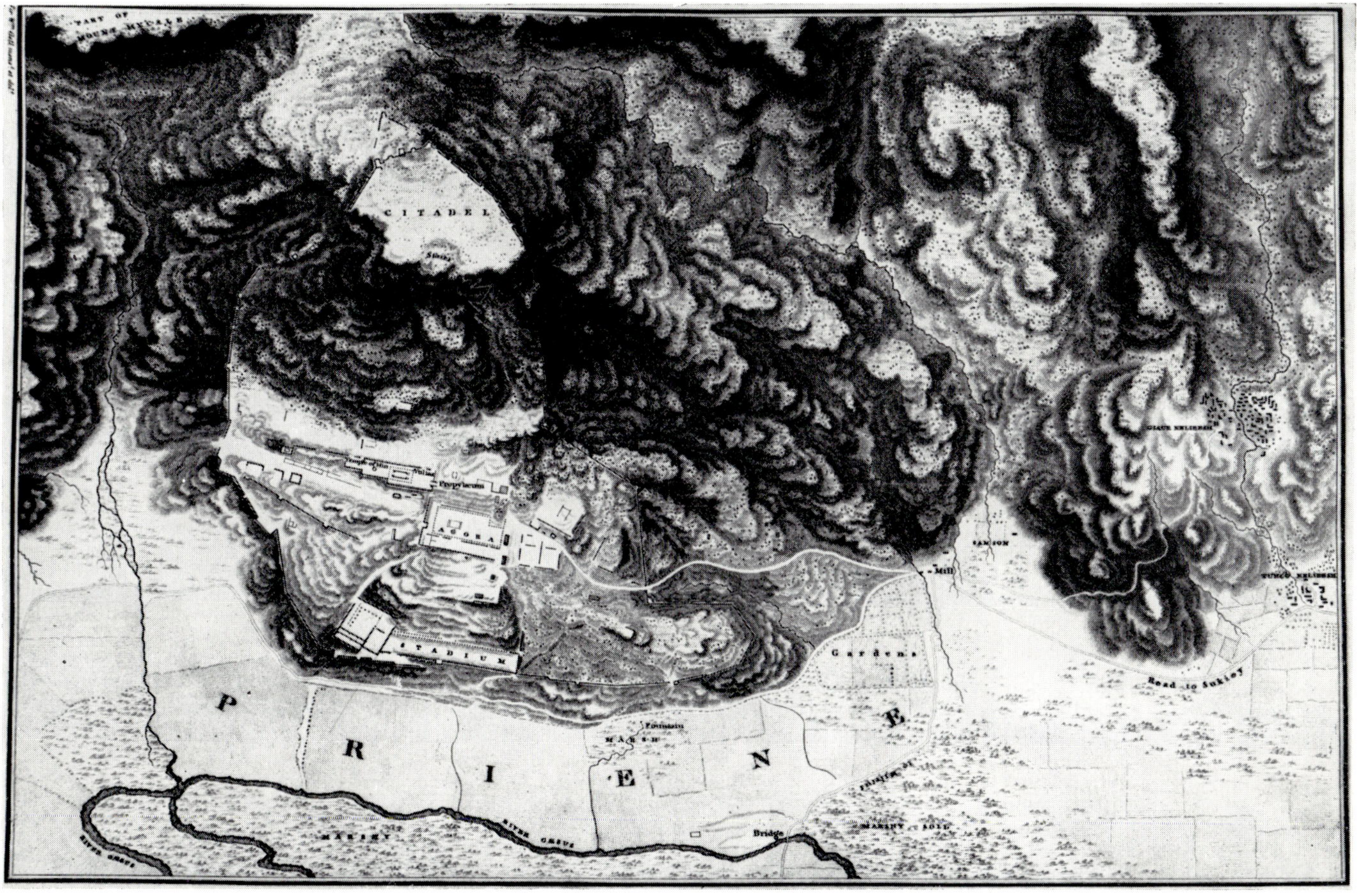

8a **Priene: Detail of capital.** The Greek of the fourth century B.C. was able to comprehend architecture from the smallest detail (so often based on the forms of plants) to the grand designs of the geometrical town. It was this comprehensiveness that enabled him to retain diversity and human scale.

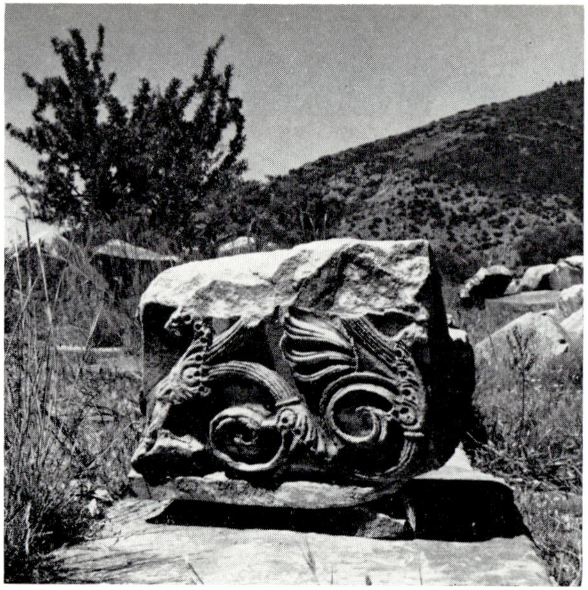

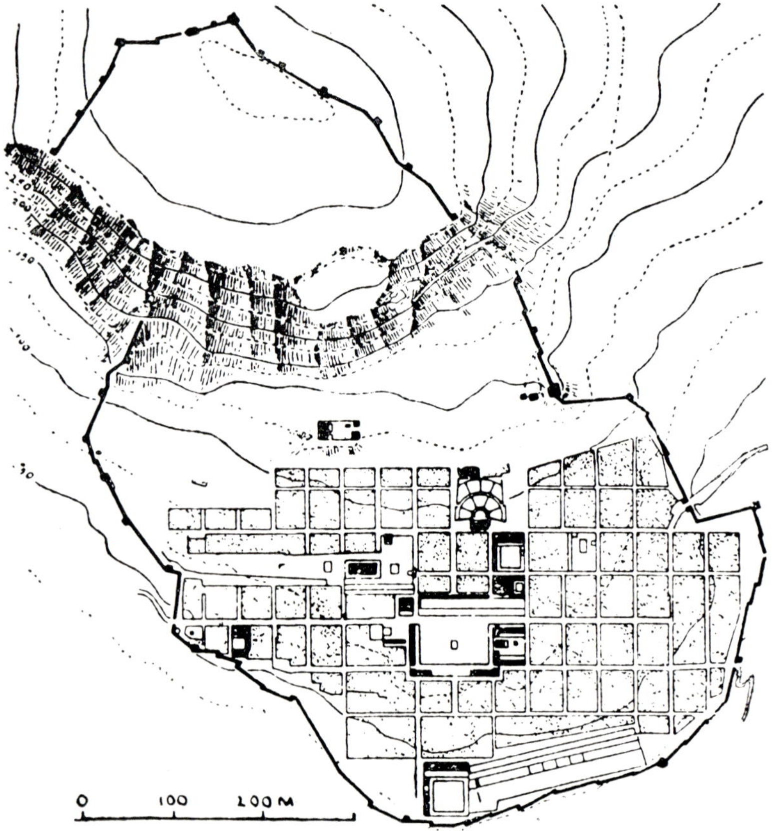

8b **Priene: Reconstruction by Dr. A. von Gerkan.**

9 **Priene: Looking across the Meander valley towards Miletus.** ▶

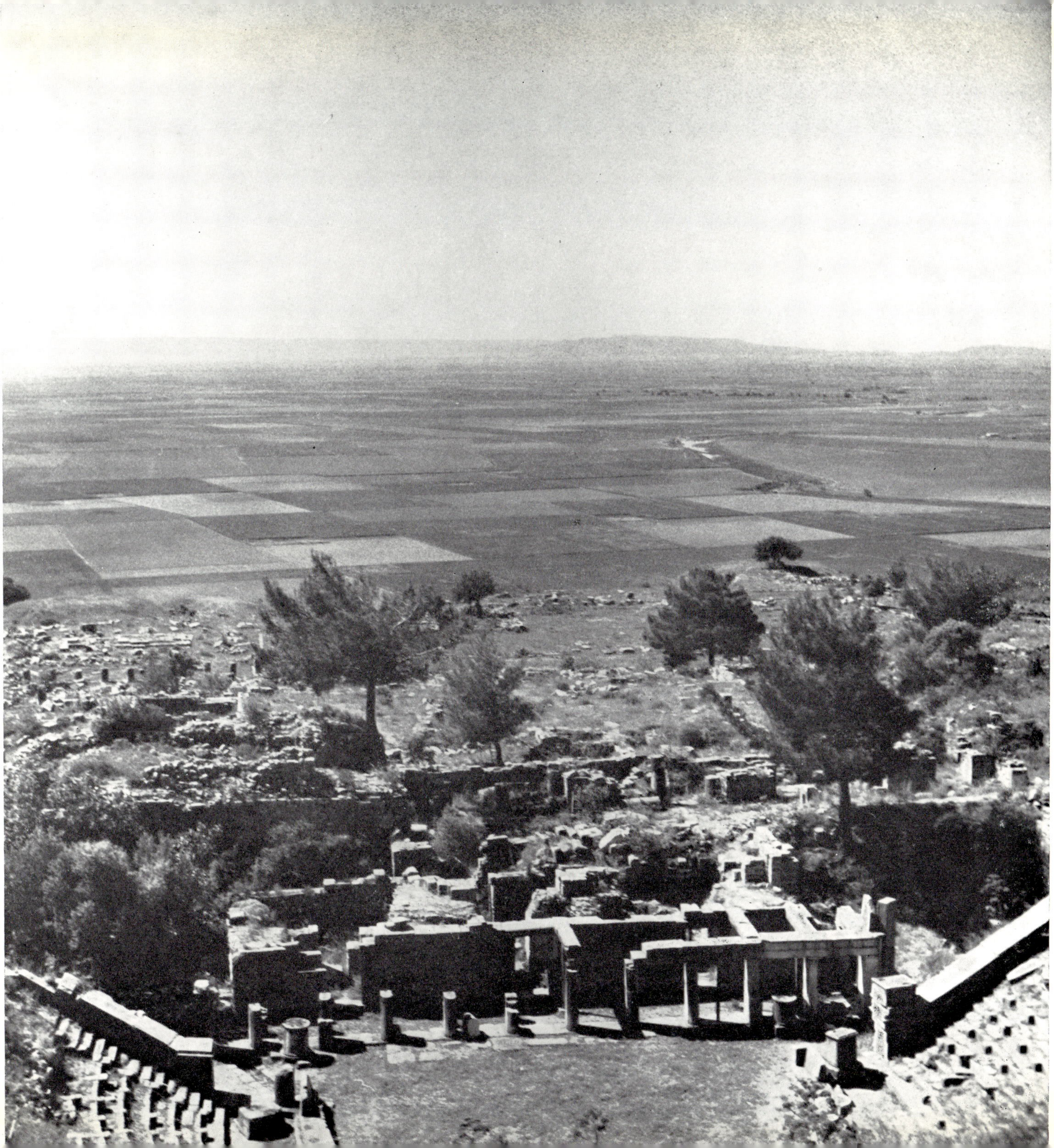

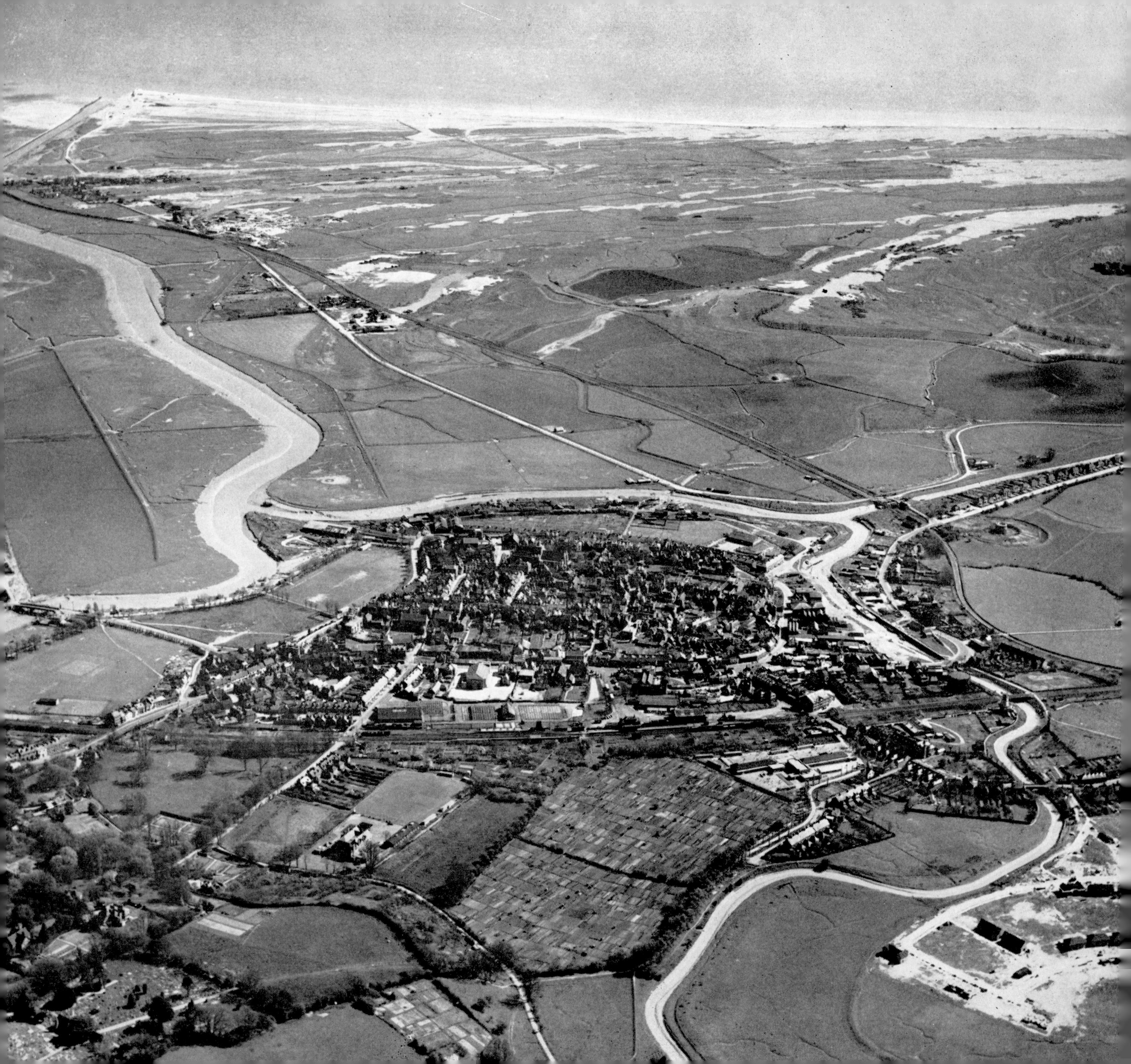

10 **Rye, Sussex.** The medieval town developed through expediency within fortress walls. The charm is overwhelming and nostalgic. The greatest exponent in this century of the art of town planning based on the sentimental was Sir Raymond Unwin, whose influence is still felt today in the making of the new towns.

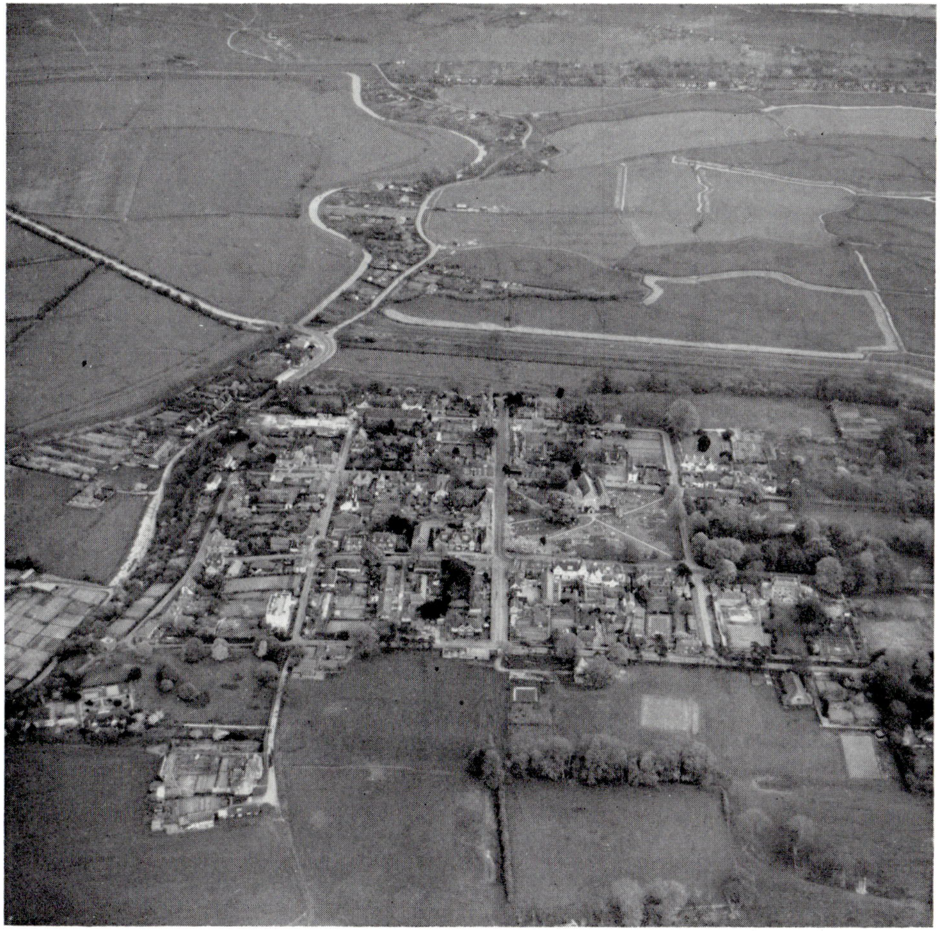

11 **Winchelsea, Sussex.** Winchelsea lies a few miles from Rye and was laid out as a complete town by Edward I in 1280. It well illustrates the rational way of thought of the medieval planner, when given the opportunity of designing a new town on a clear site.

12 **Vincenzo Scamozzi: The Ideal City.** The pattern of this plan is of peculiar interest as showing an endeavour to reconcile the monotonous scale of the fortifications with the domesticity of the city. Note the variety and proportions of the streets and open spaces.

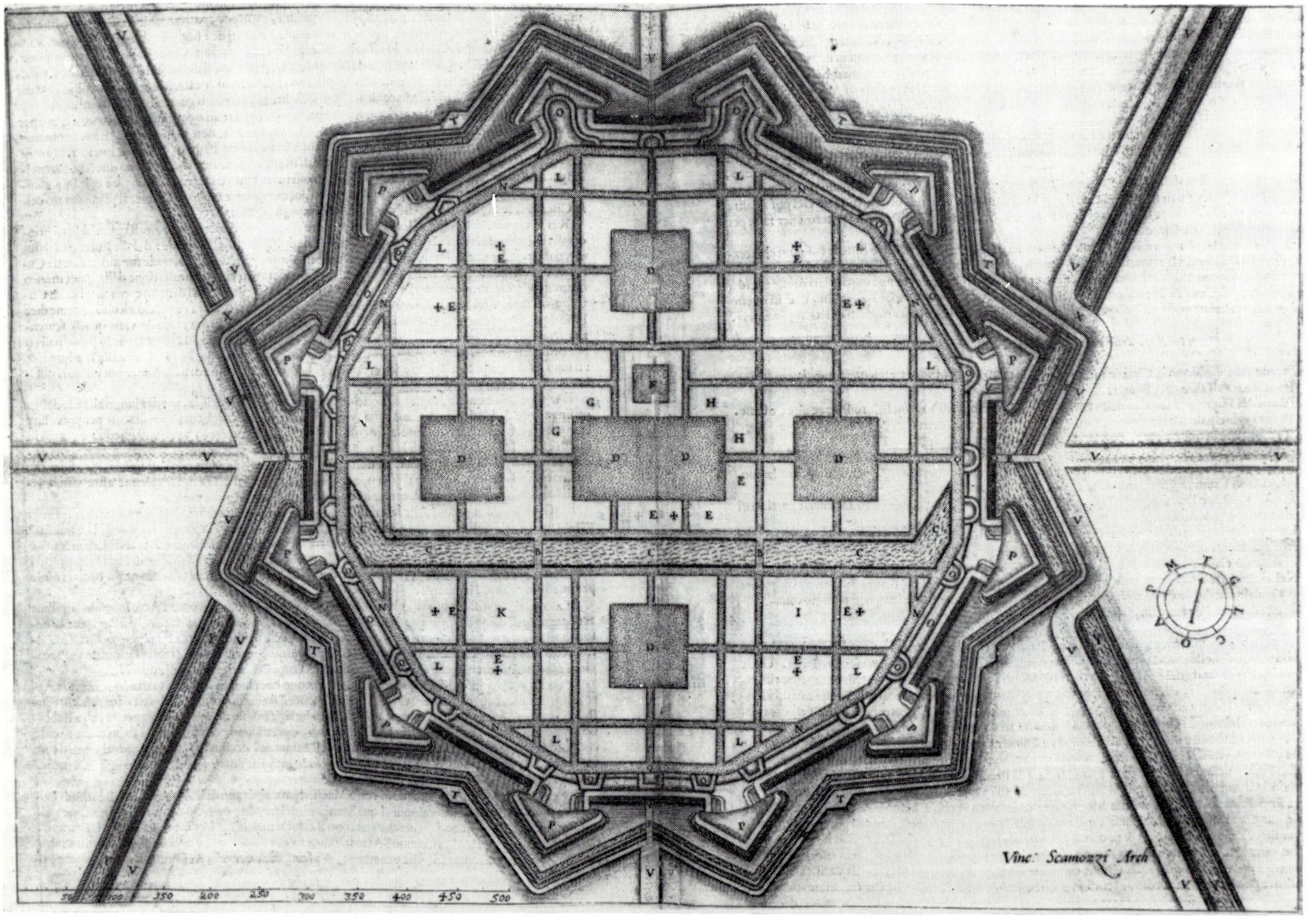

13 **Vincenzo Scamozzi: Palma-Nova.** This illustrates how the architect-planner was unable to realize his conception in practice. The town is overwhelmed by the shape of the fortifications and by the road system. Scamozzi the architect has given way to Scamozzi the engineer. ▶

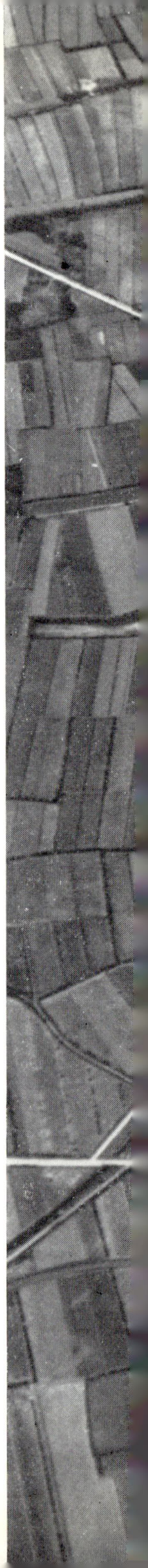

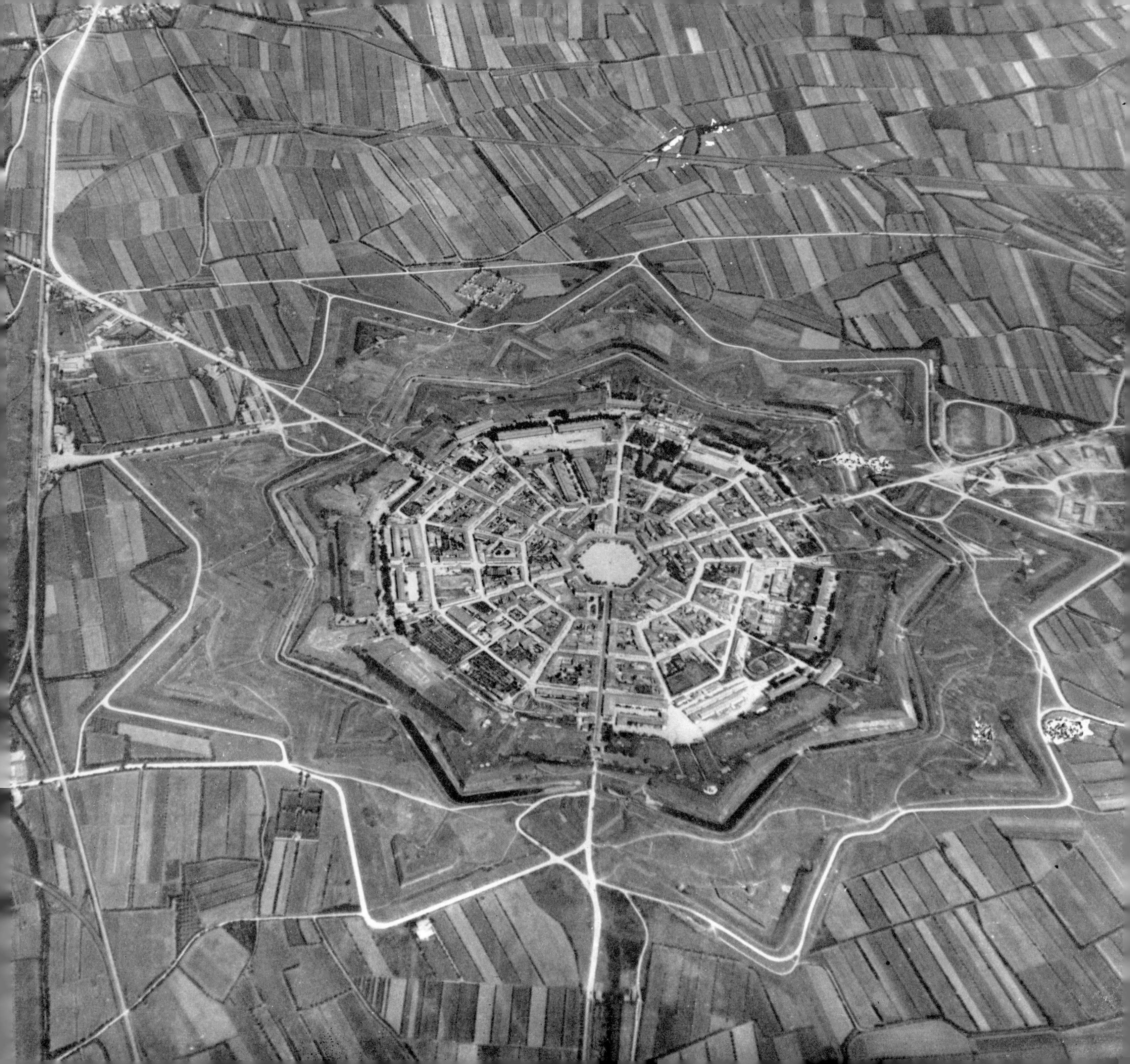

14 **La Roche-sur-Yon.** The fully developed pattern complex arises from two orders: that of the individual who gives the field pattern, and that of the community which gives the urban geometry.

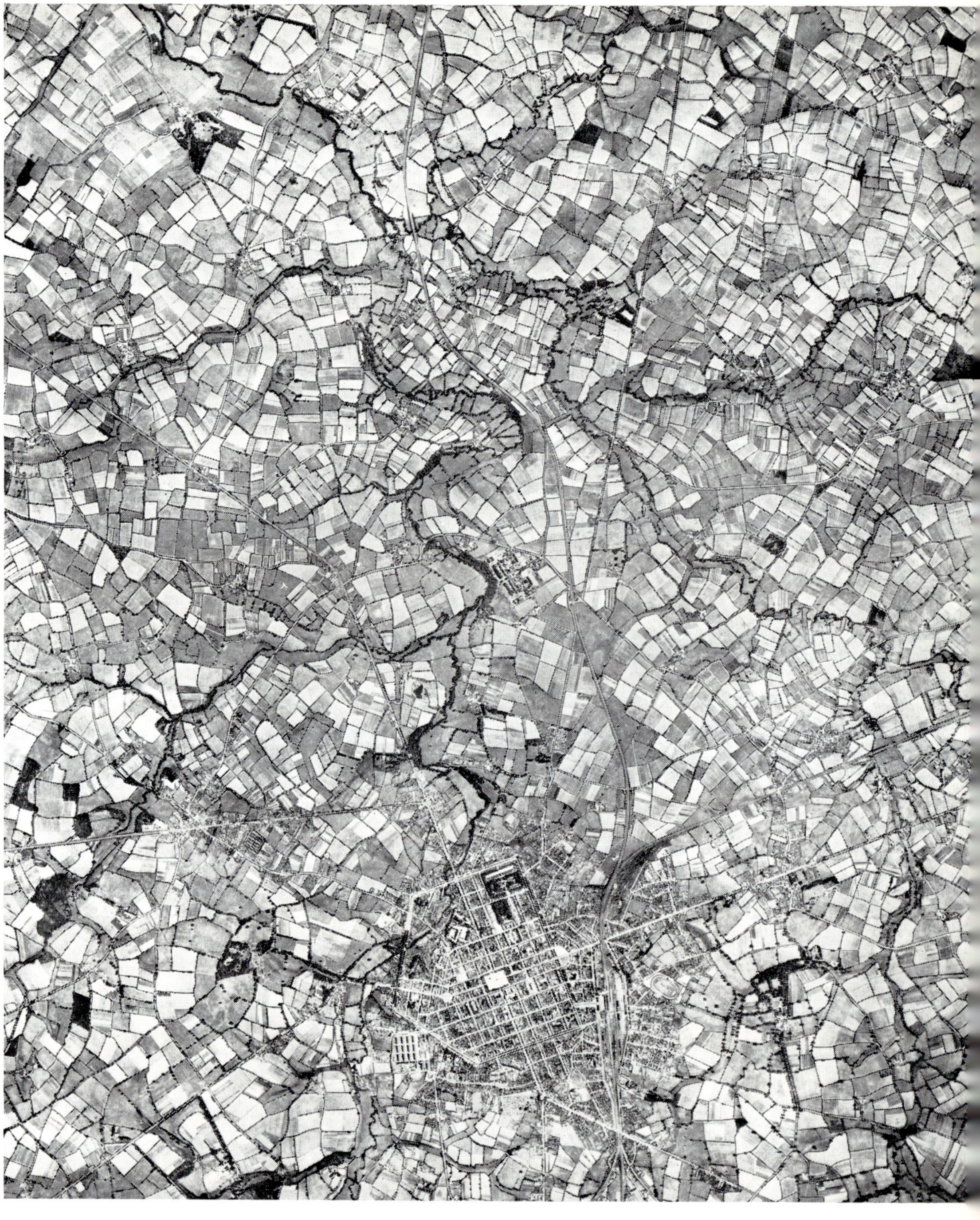

15 **Salt-pans, Batz.** These pans illustrate the contrast of geometry and natural form arising from pure functionalism unrelated to human living conditions.

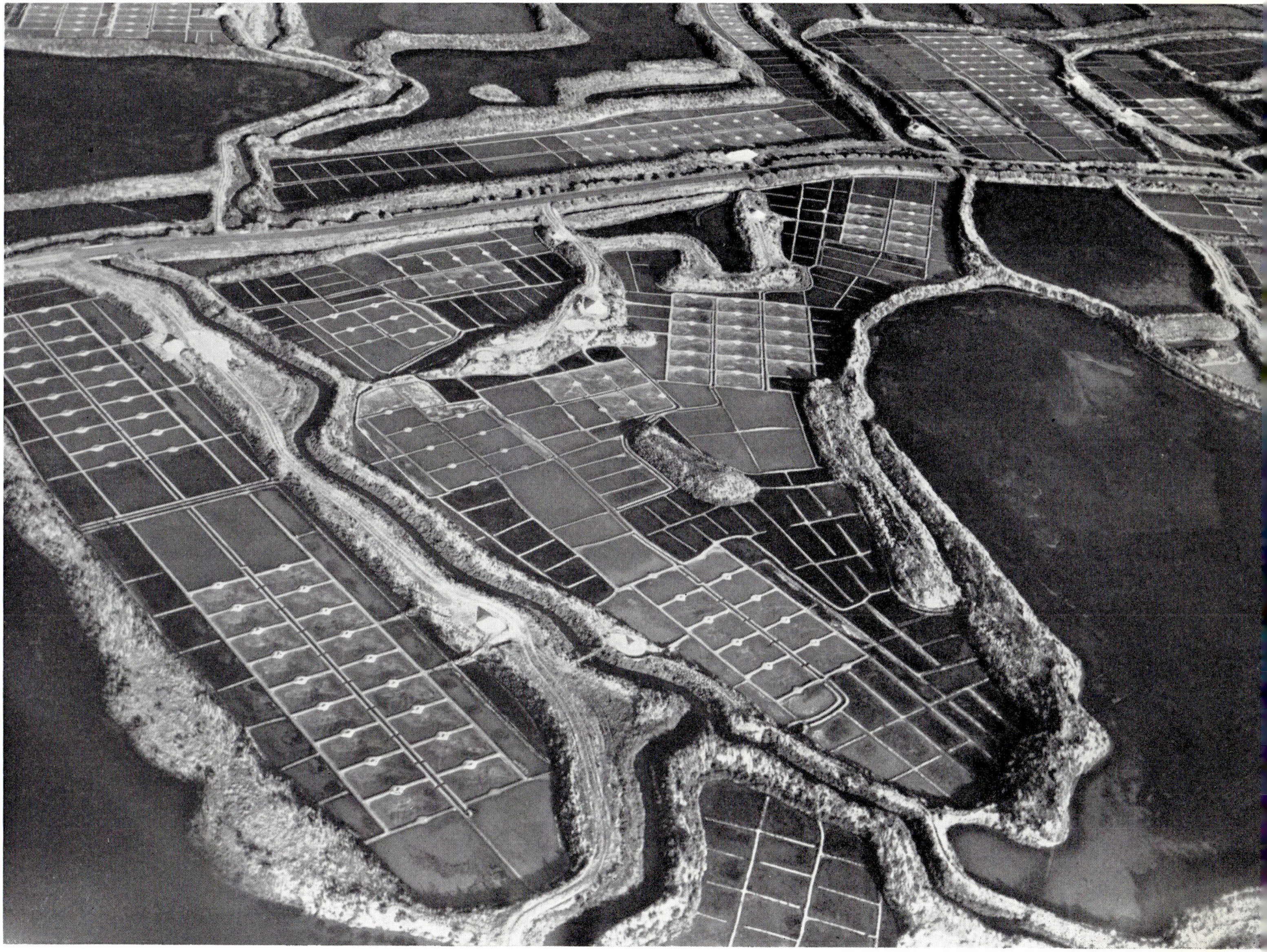

16 **Painting by Piet Mondrian: Composition with blue, 1937.** The artist is preoccupied with a geometry which is closely related to that of town planning. One of his works is in fact called 'New York 1942'. Cf. Plate 12, where Scamozzi has endeavoured to break away from the standard gridiron pattern.

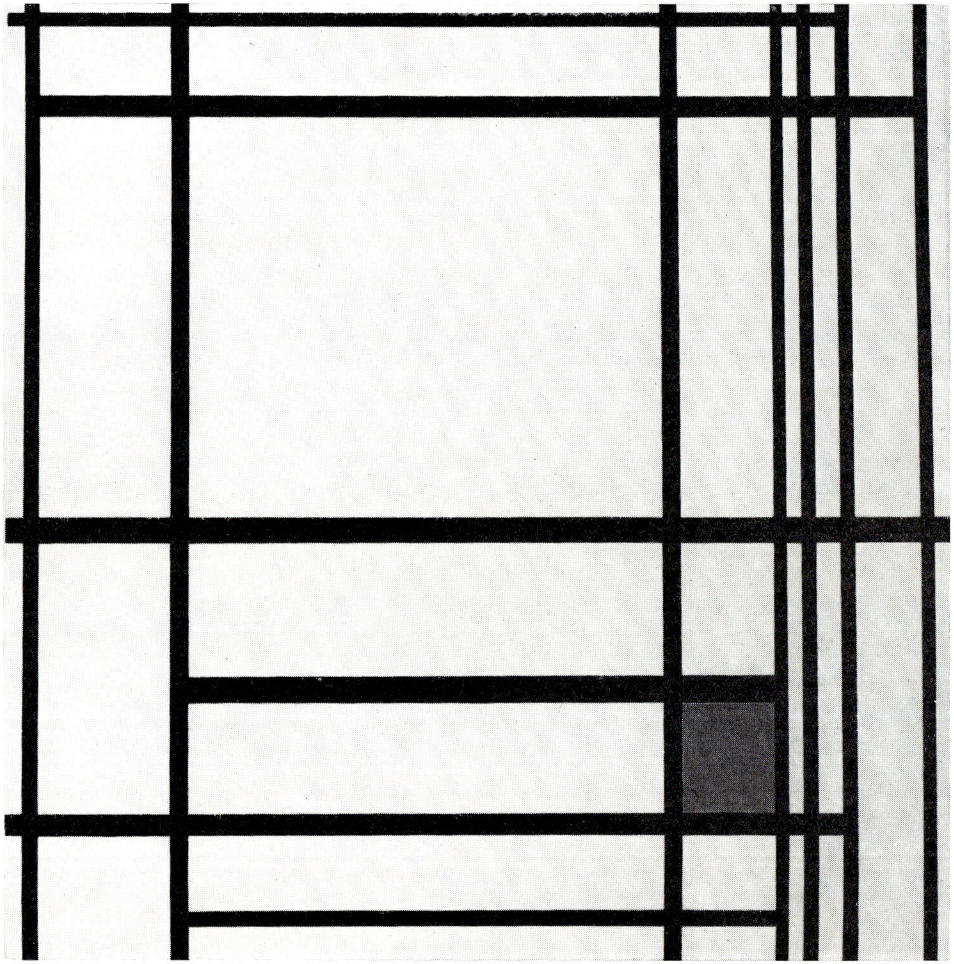

17 **Manhattan.** This extraordinary scene shows what happens when an ordered grid is placed upon the ground and thereafter growth depends upon the law of the jungle. Such growth is as irrational as that of a medieval town, and to many has an equal charm. In both instances natural form has been rigidly excluded, and its place emotionally has been taken by the accidental. ▶

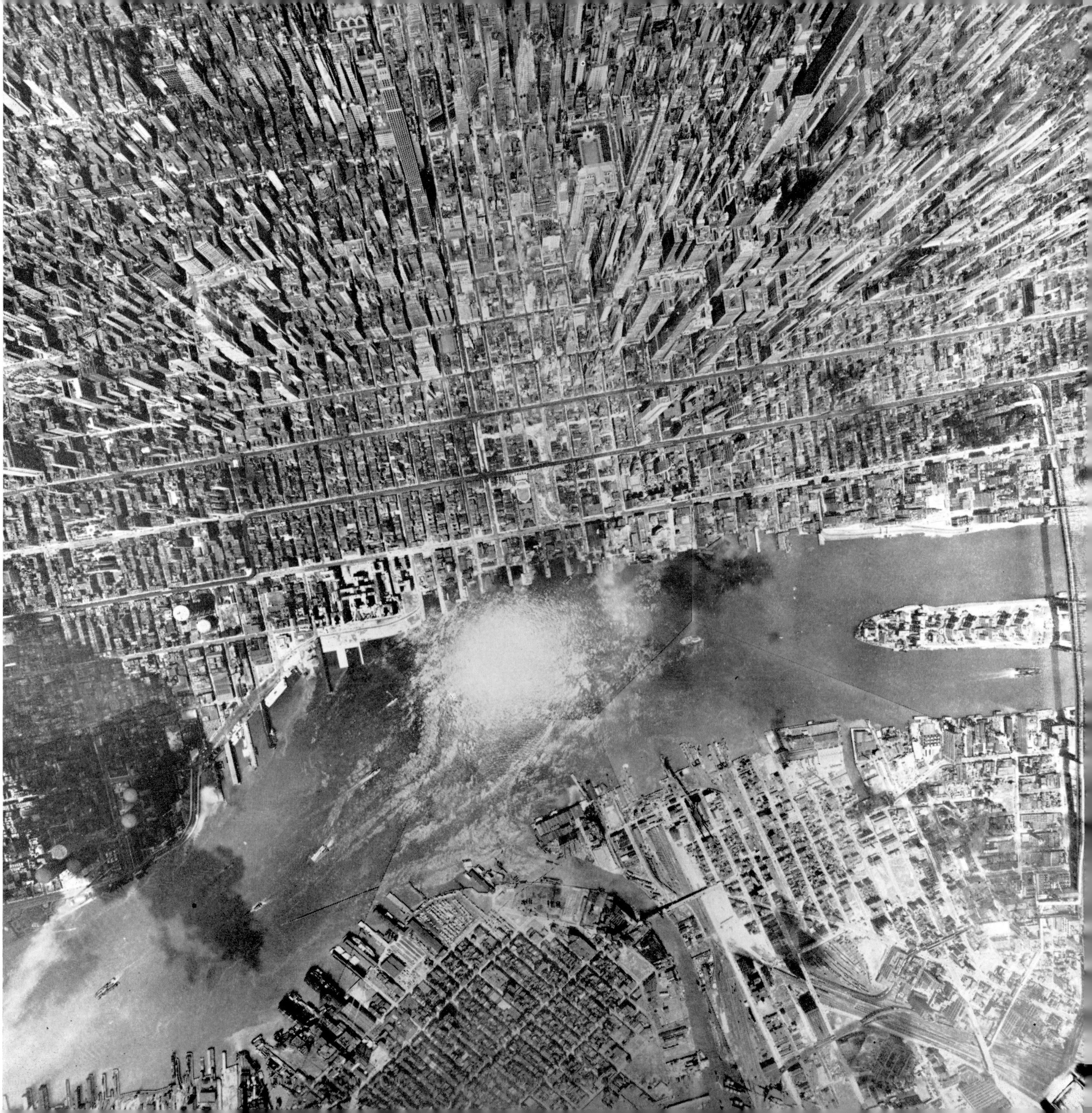

18 **Watford: suburban scene.** The pattern of early twentieth-century urban development based on the semi-detached house.

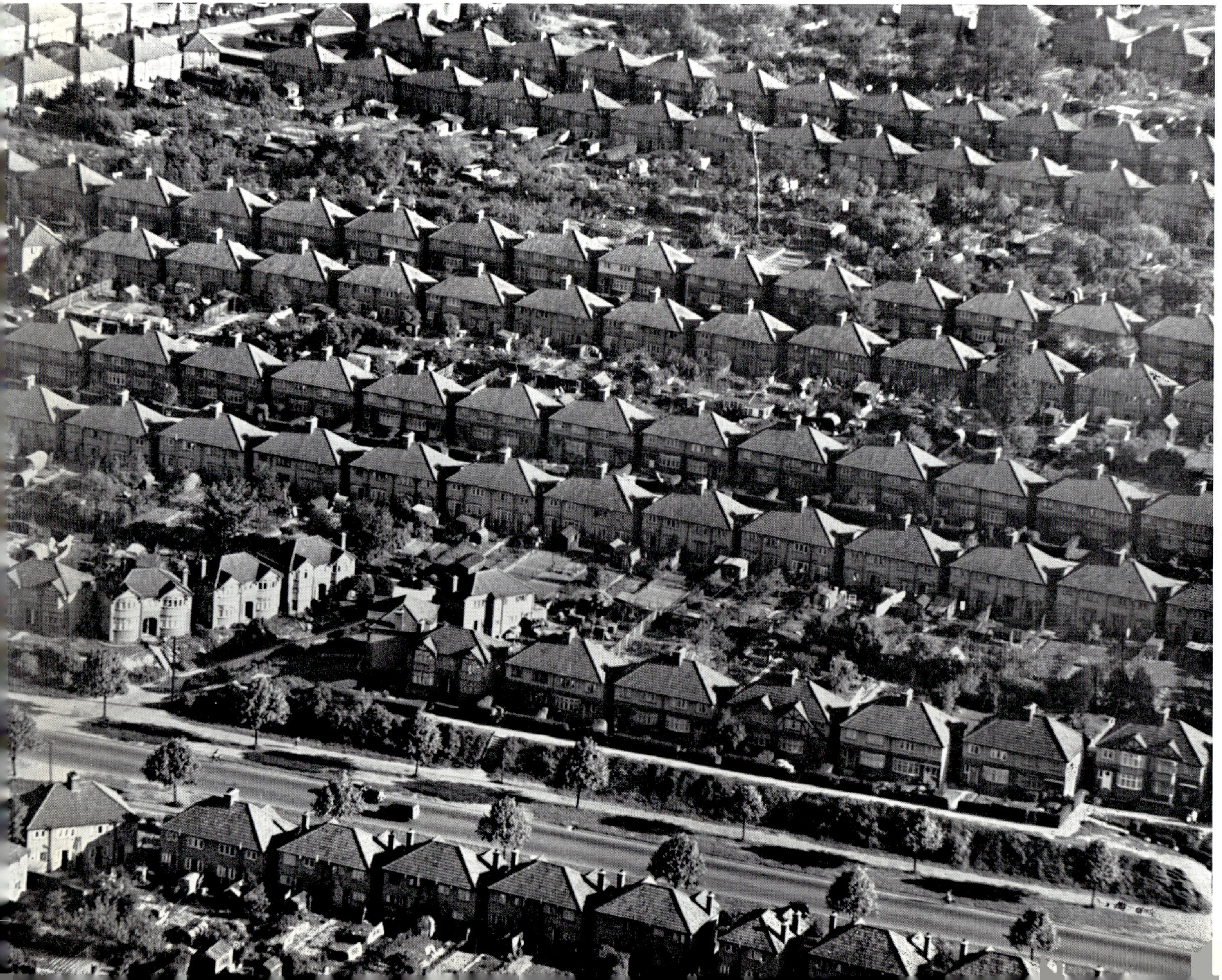

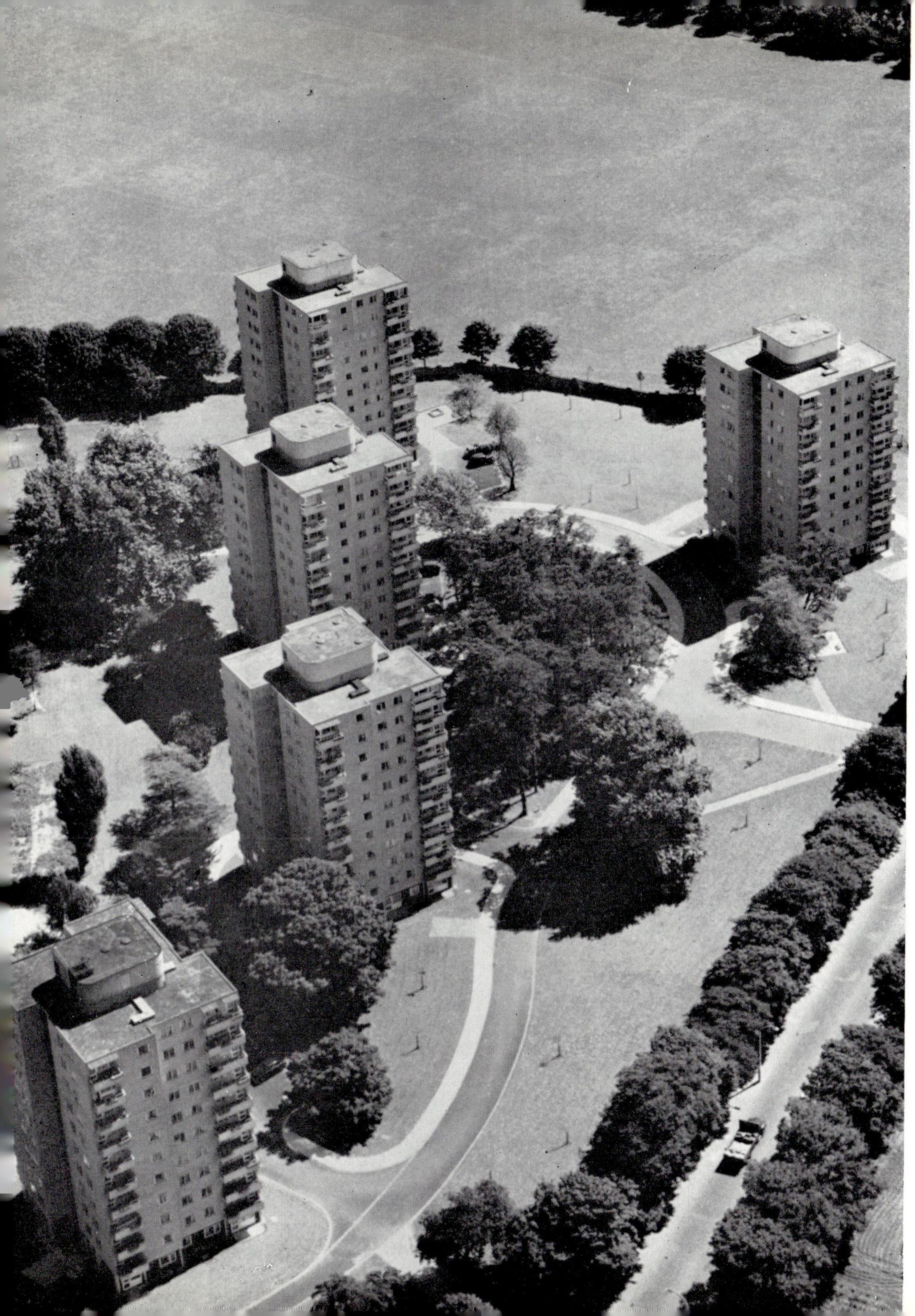

19 **Roehampton: Flats by the London County Council.** Mid-twentieth-century development in extreme contrast to Plate 18.

20 **Project in Toronto, 1954: G. A. Jellicoe.** A design for high-density blocks of flats within an existing grid of roads near the city centre. The ground level was planned to be raised and beneath this, and on a level with the adjoining streets, were the car parks.

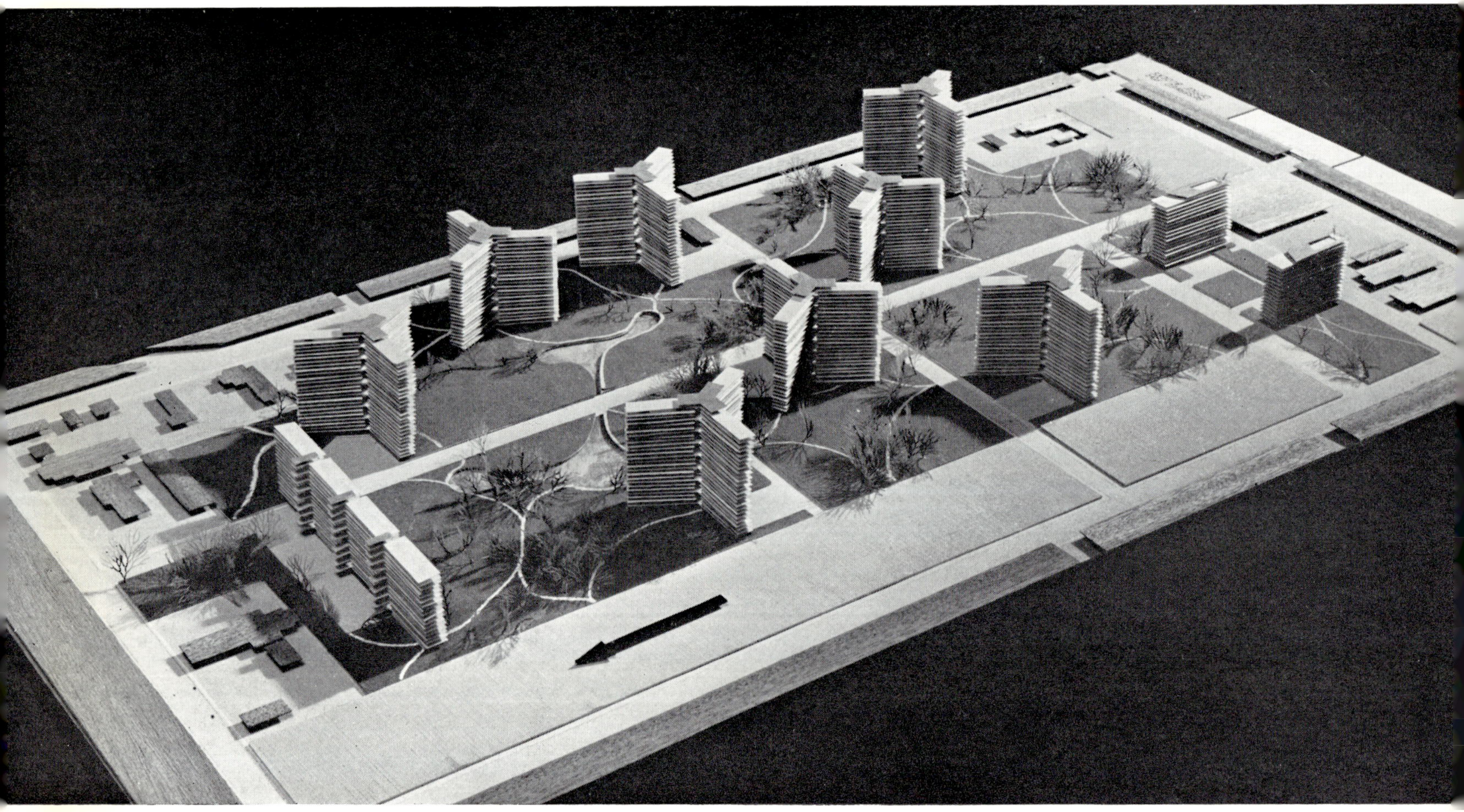

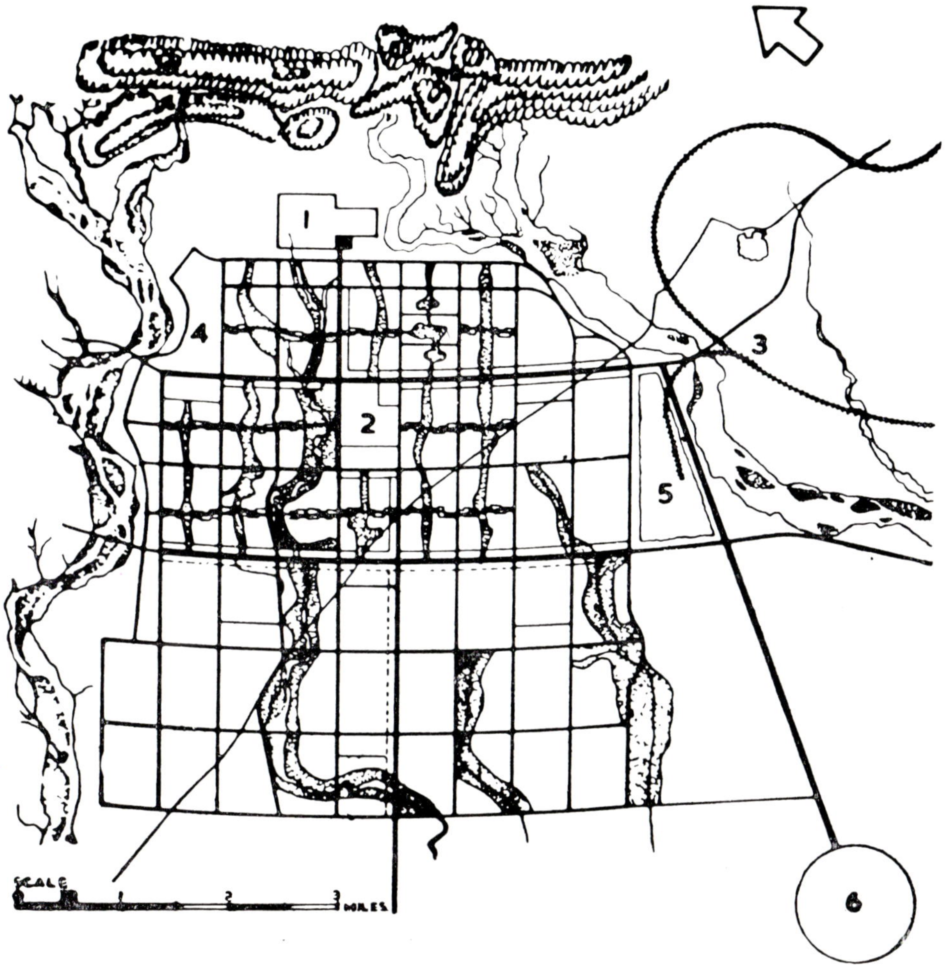

21 **Chandigarh, new capital of the Indian Punjab: plan by Le Corbusier.** 'You have thus a practical city plan of straight main traffic roads in which identification is emphasized by the orientation to the sun and the all-important Himalayas; by the city park opening a quiet way through the road grid towards the Capitol and the mountains; and by the emphasis of the main arteries. A further emphasis is to be given by tree planting selected for shape and colour. This is enough to make a city on a noble geometric scale, underlined by trees. . . .' E. Maxwell Fry, R.I.B.A., 4 January 1955.

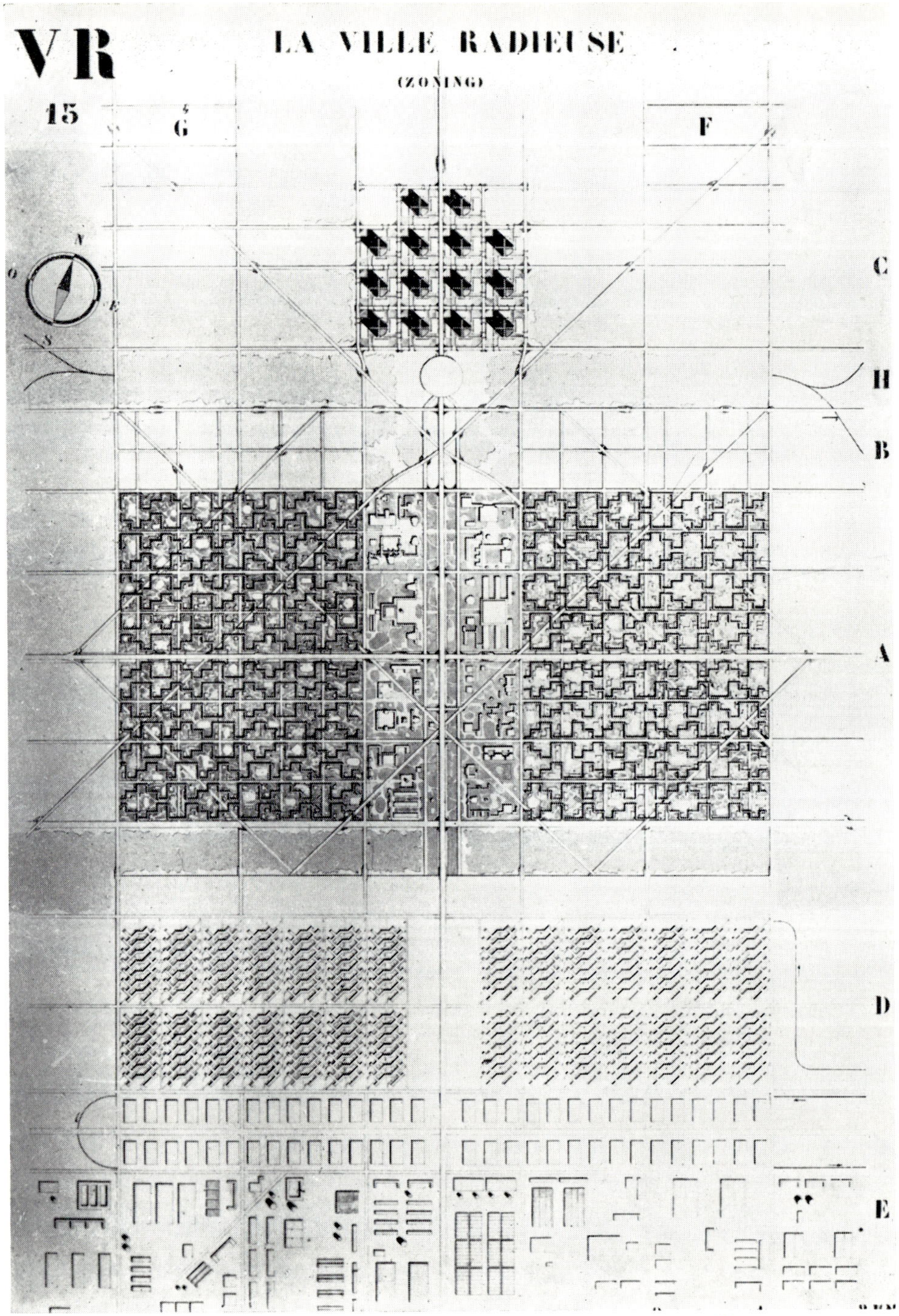

22 **La Ville Radieuse: Le Corbusier.** The ultimate geometry. If such a pattern were taken literally it would mean the decline of individual man and the rise of a competent civilization similar to that of the bee. This should be compared with the designer's later plan for Chandigarh (Plate 21). The pattern of Motopia in reality would also certainly change, perhaps based on an art already explored by artists such as Mondrian (Plate 16).

THE BIOLOGICAL LANDSCAPE

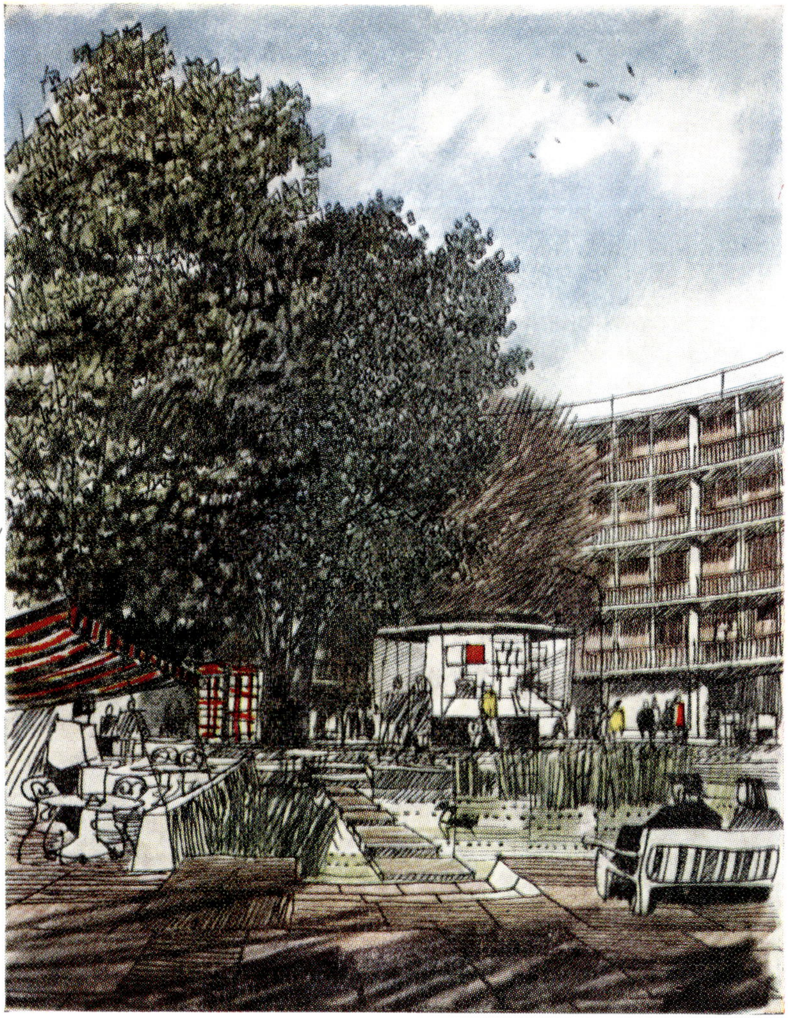

23 **Foliage in a Neighbourhood Circle**

Drawing by Gordon Cullen

When the cells over the envelope of the earth broke (as we are told) biological growth began everywhere, and because of the complex external conditions, developed in diverse manners. That all the animal and vegetable world sprang from the same geometric cell seems a fact accepted by scientists. It also seems clear that a number of animals such as the bee, the ant, and *Homo sapiens* seem to have had, or still have, an overwhelming urge to return to this simple uniformity; but that man alone is able to stand outside himself, meditate upon such a dull destiny, and contest the issue. He sees the mathematical scientists tearing ahead on a brilliant and easy passage, that might quite easily end in destruction equally by war or personal elimination; and because he can still stand outside these things, he is prepared to exert himself in the much more difficult struggle to retain personality. Just as nature when we look out is fantastically complex and varied, and just as every leaf upon examination has individuality, so it might seem that the survival of human individuality may depend upon the survival of human instinct. The urge to go back to the uniformity of our cell (i.e. to mathematics and mass production) is countered by the stimulus we receive from the beauty of the natural world around us. Prehistoric man probably saw nature quite differently, as something of which to stand in wonder and awe. It is still awe-inspiring to reflect that even in the modern world we should all perish within a few days if nature ceased to be fertile.

The Chinese, with their superb geometry set modestly within the natural but designed environment, always felt themselves part of nature; and as with vegetation their race reached a 'climax' and became static. But they have taught us many things, and during the last short period of 250 years Western man has consistently endeavoured to conserve nature within his architectural environment. The housing of the counter industrial revolution at the beginning of the century was wholly due to this, and there is no more significant proof of flowers as a need and not a luxury, for instance, than the mass evasion of the law in obtaining flowers from the Scilly Isles in the war. The history of the biological landscape, therefore, leads from the wildest scenery of the earth, through the rich and varied patterns of nature, until man starts enclosing nature for its own sake within his works. Subsequently he releases her and creates environments (such as the English park) apparently without boundaries. It is reasonable to suppose that the ultimate scene over the envelope of the earth may well be a landscape without boundaries, except for the seashores, and upon and within which are contained man's activities of all kinds, monstrous and domestic. We should then have a picture of a balanced world amalgamating the best of the two great civilizations of east and west.

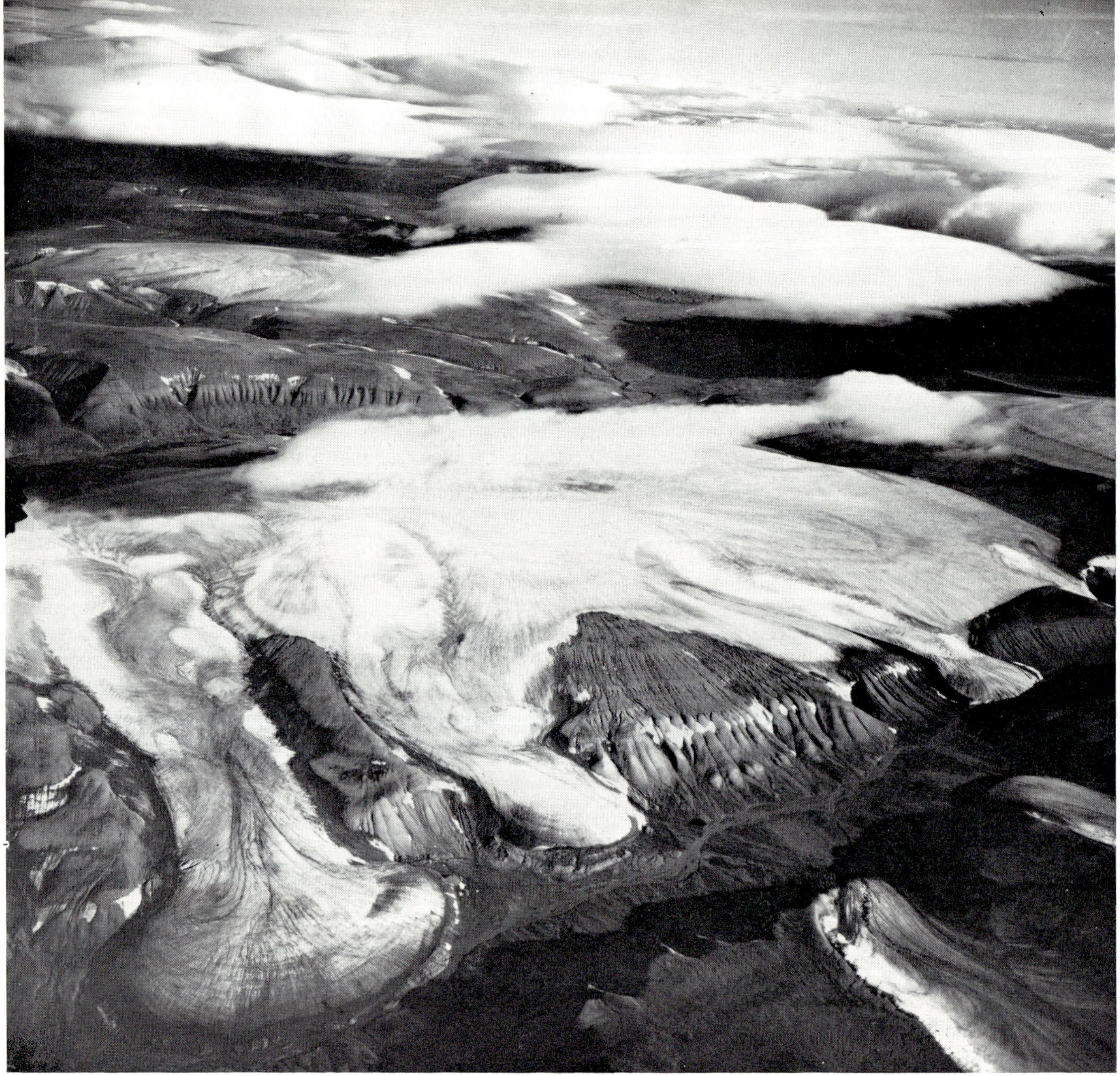

◀ 24 **Edgeoya, Svalbard, Spitzbergen.** First there was ice and rock and total desolation.

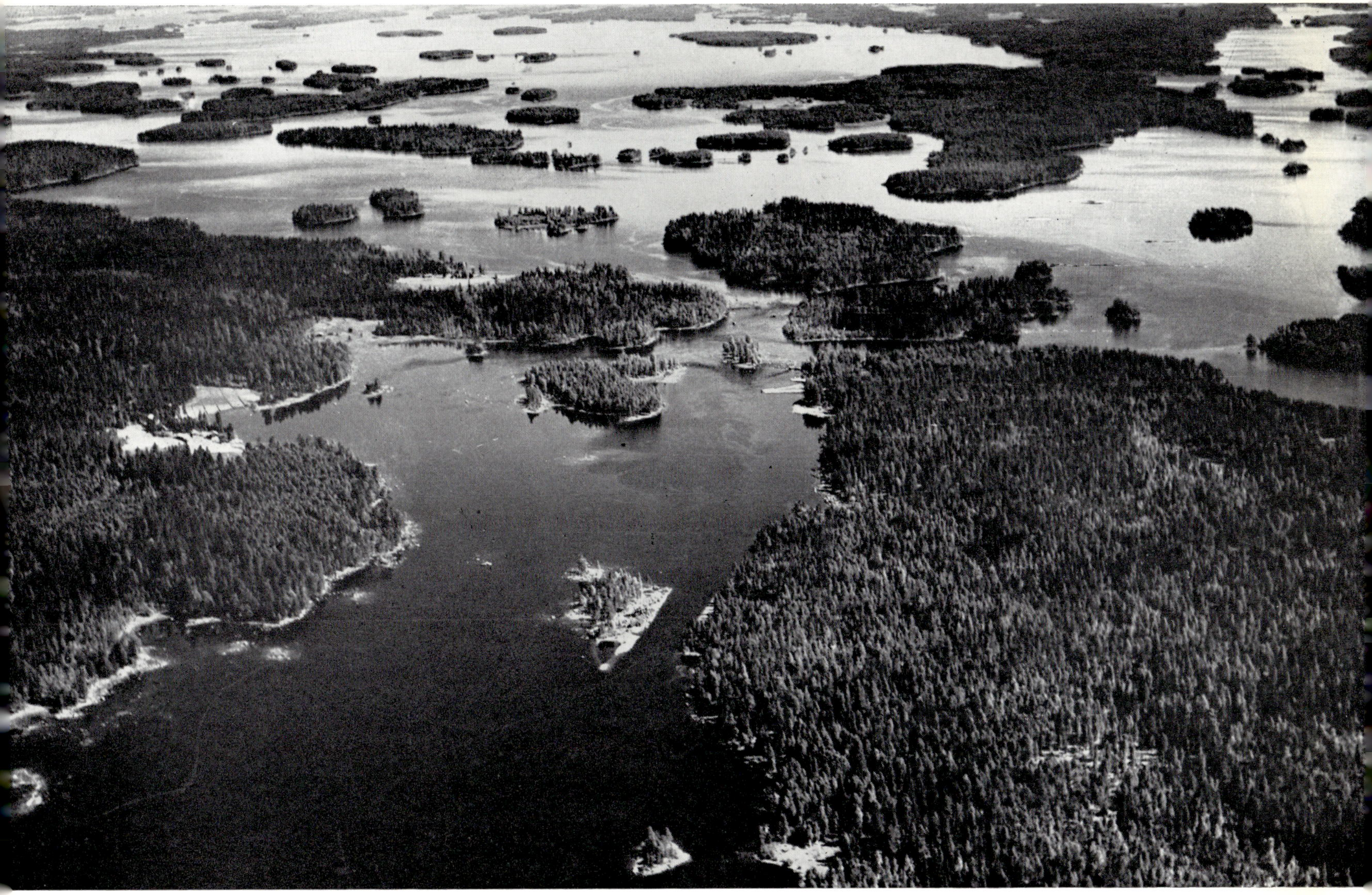

25 **Saimaa, Finland.** Trees and plants appeared before animals and *homo sapiens.*

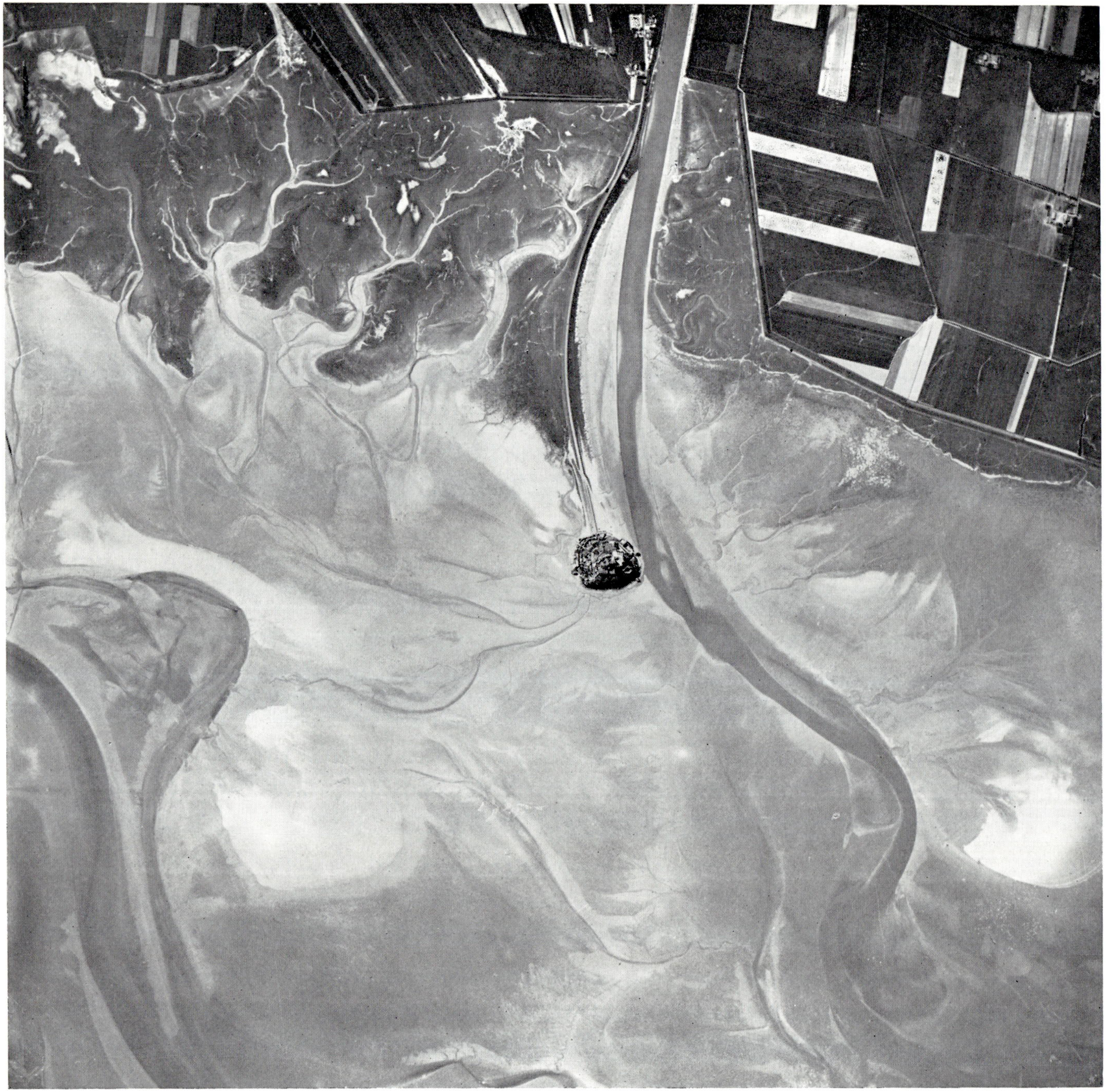

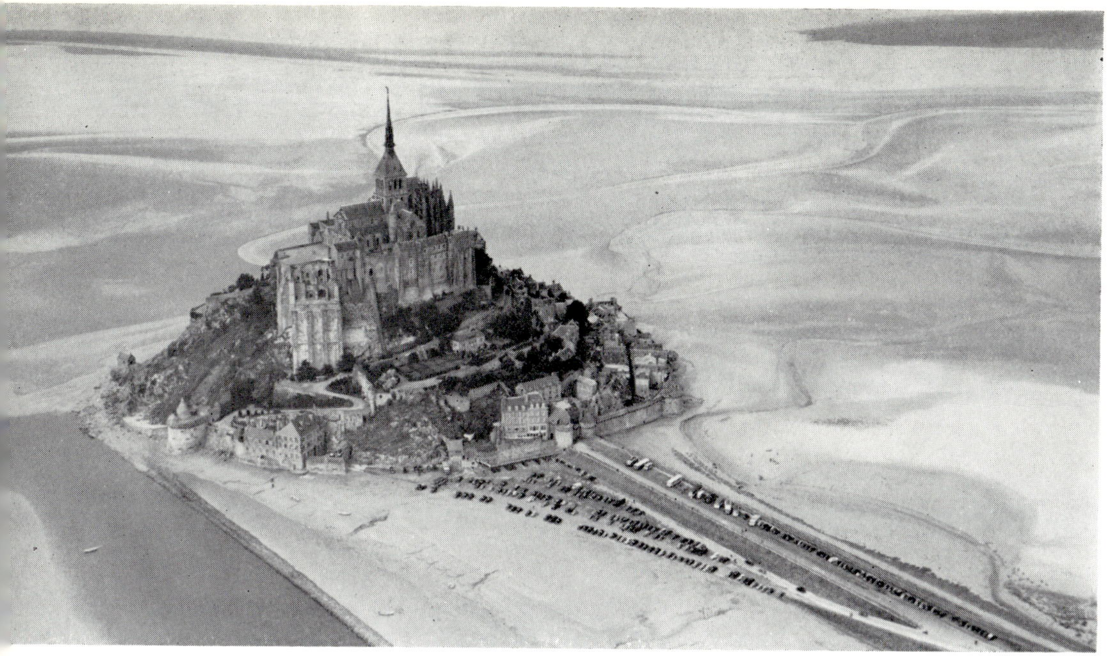

26 (OPPOSITE) **Mont St. Michel: from the air.** We all crawled ashore from the warm waters to make our ordered patterns on the mainland. (We now have become over-rationalized, and sometimes look back nostalgically at our beginnings.)

27a **Mont St. Michel**

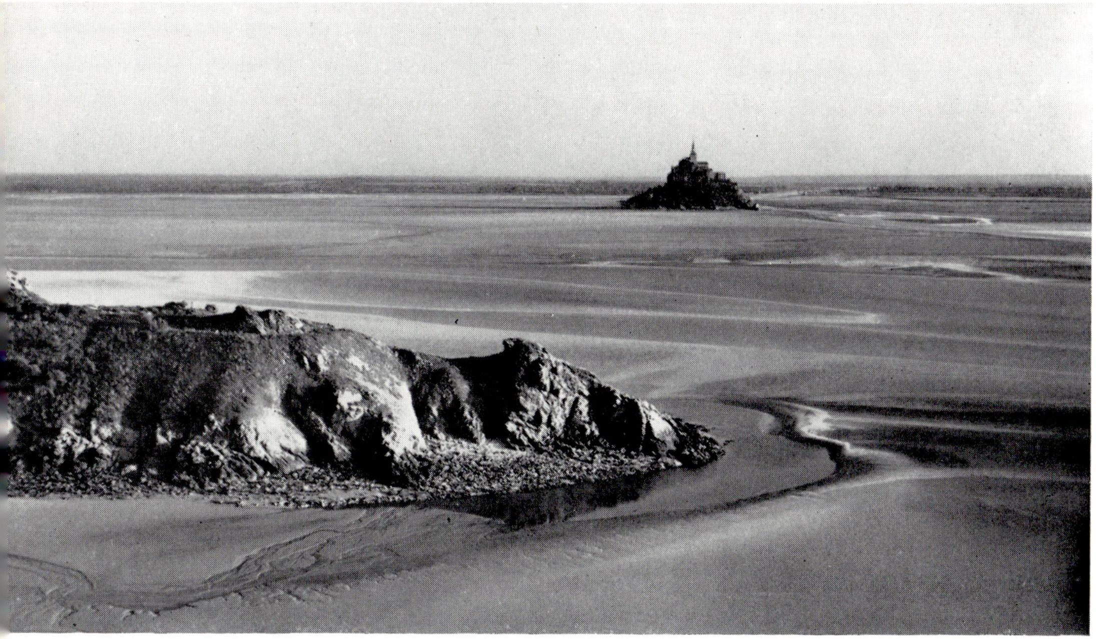

27b **Mont St. Michel**

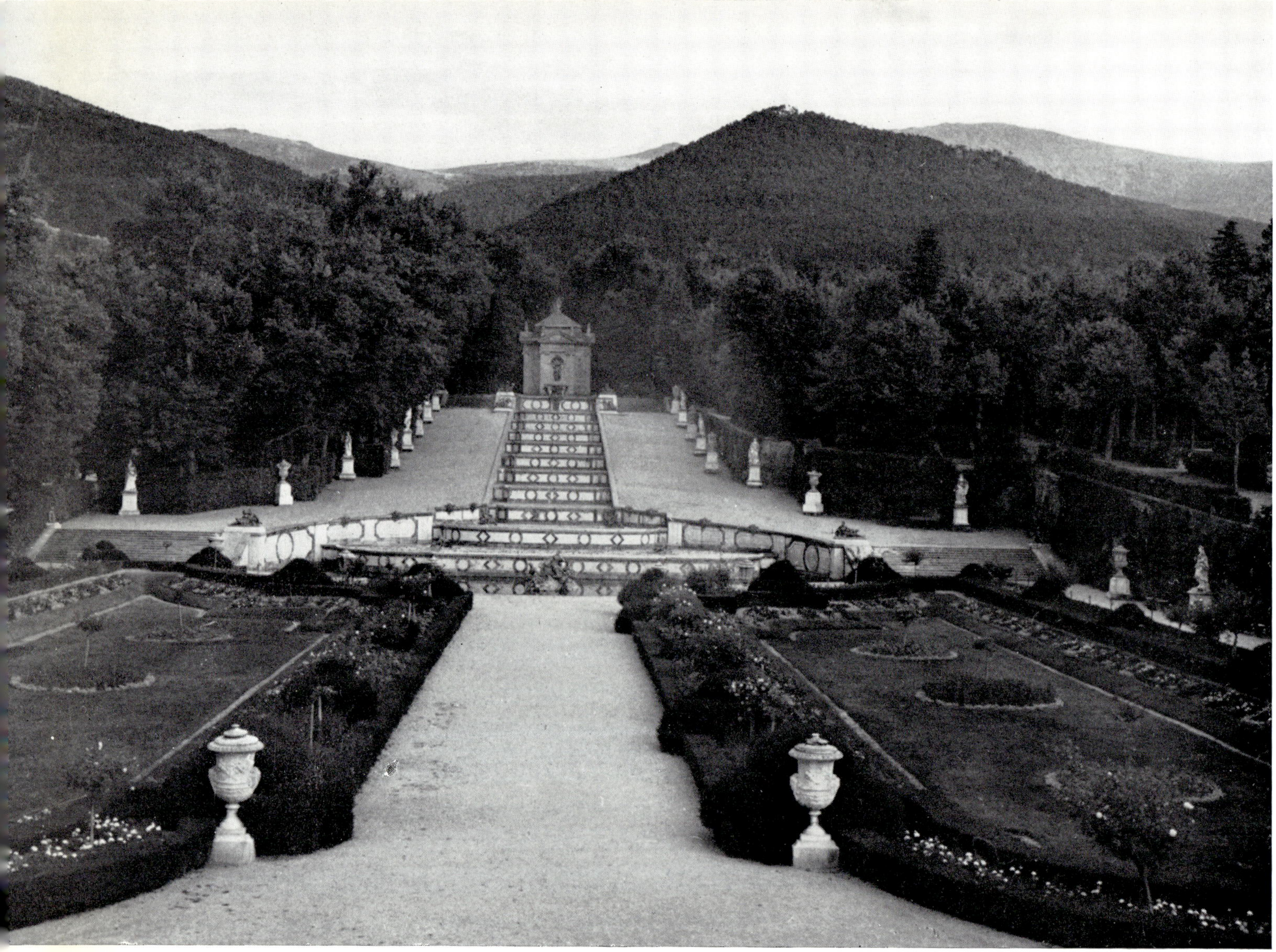

28 **La Granja, Spain.** In the Middle Ages the human spirit had been overwhelmed and confined by the mystery of nature, but in the Renaissance it had acquired knowledge and ventured forth on voyages of discovery. This spirit manifested itself in the manner in which the geometry of the house projected into the surrounding countryside by means of the formal garden.

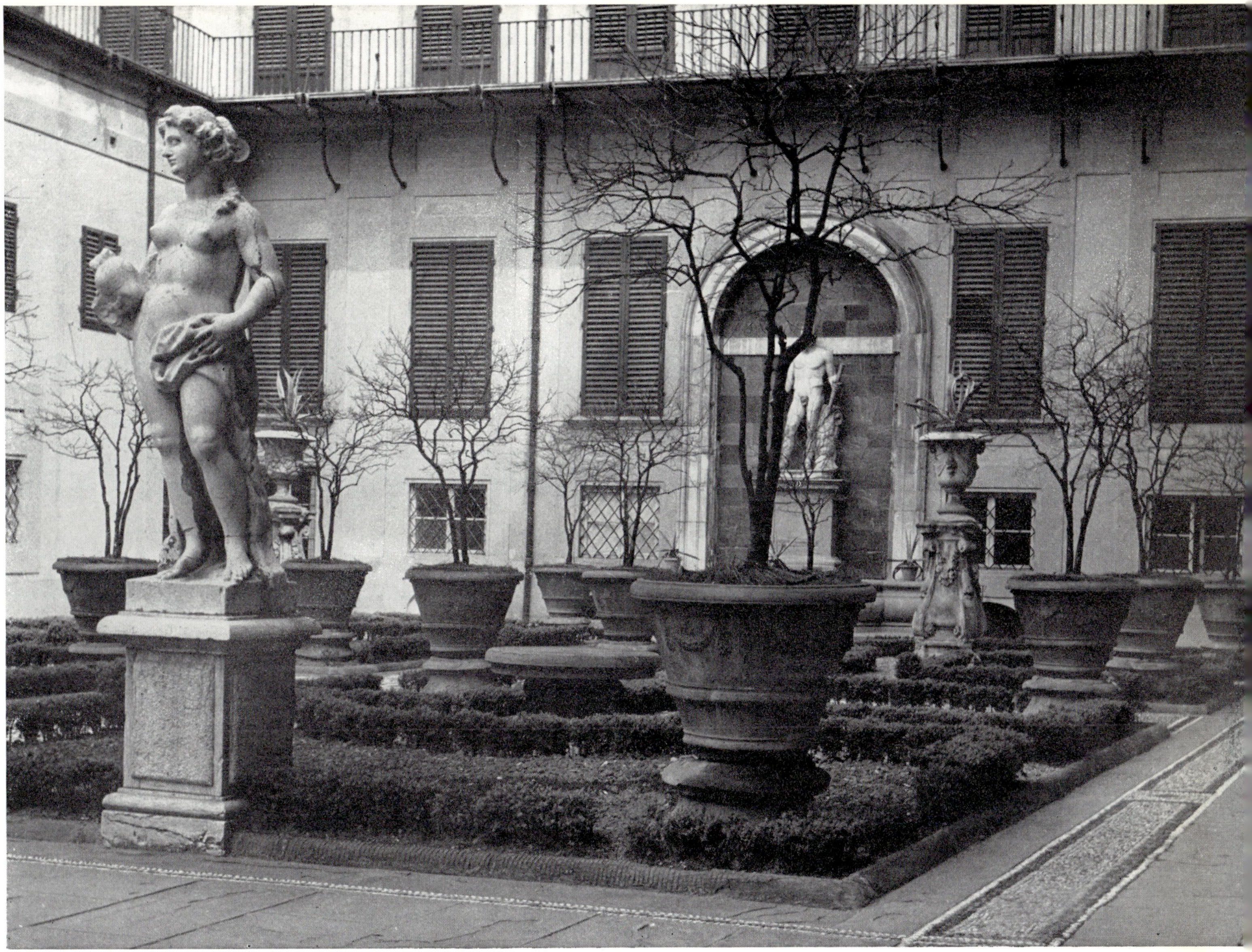

29 **Palazzo Riccardi, Florence.** At all times man has felt the need to cultivate nature within the environment of architecture. The early garden courts of the Italian palaces continue the tradition of castle or monastery garden.

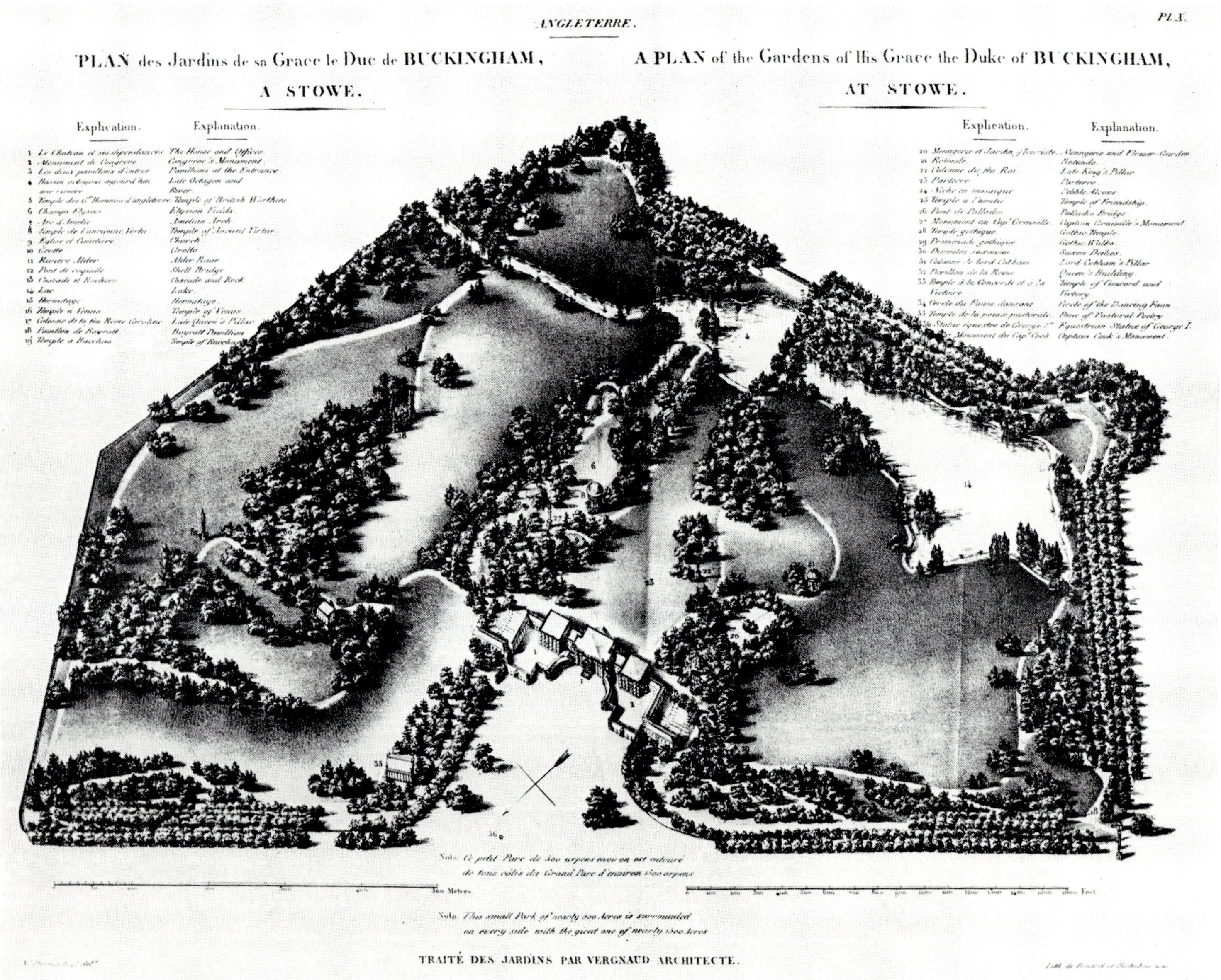
ANGLETERRE.
PL. X.
PLAN des Jardins de sa Grace le Duc de BUCKINGHAM, A STOWE.
A PLAN of the Gardens of His Grace the Duke of BUCKINGHAM, AT STOWE.
Explication.
Explanation.
1 Le Chateau et ses dépendances — The House and Offices.
2 Monument de Congreve — Congreve's Monument.
3 Les deux pavillons d'entrée — Pavillions at the Entrance.
4 Bassin octogone aujourd'hui une rivière — Late Octagon and River.
5 Temple des Gds Hommes d'angleterre — Temple of British Worthies.
6 Champs Elysées — Elysian Fields.
7 Arc d'Amelie — Amelian Arch.
8 Temple de l'ancienne Vertu — Temple of Ancient Virtue.
9 Eglise et Cimetière — Church.
10 Grotte — Grotto.
11 Rivière Alder — Alder River.
12 Pont de coquille — Shell Bridge.
13 Cascade et Rochers — Cascade and Rock.
14 Lac — Lake.
15 Hermitage — Hermitage.
16 Temple à Venus — Temple of Venus.
17 Colonne de la feu Reine Caroline — Late Queen's Pillar.
18 Pavillon de Boycott — Boycott Pavillion.
19 Temple à Bacchus — Temple of Bacchus.
20 Menagerie et Jardin fleuriste — Menagerie and Flower-Garden.
21 Rotonde — Rotonda.
22 Colonne du feu Roi — Late King's Pillar.
23 Parterre — Parterre.
24 Niche en mosaïque — Pebble Alcove.
25 Temple à l'amitié — Temple of Friendship.
26 Pont de Palladio — Palladio Bridge.
27 Monument au Capt. Grenville — Captain Grenville's Monument.
28 Temple gothique — Gothic Temple.
29 Promenade gothique — Gothic Walks.
30 Divinités saxonnes — Saxon Deities.
31 Colonne de lord Cobham — Lord Cobham's Pillar.
32 Pavillon de la Reine — Queen's Building.
33 Temple à la Concorde et à la Victoire — Temple of Concord and Victory.
34 Cercle du Faune dansant — Circle of the Dancing Faun.
35 Temple de la poesie pastorale — Fane of Pastoral Poetry.
36 Statue équestre de George 1er — Equestrian Statue of George I.
37 Monument du Capt. Cook — Captain Cook's Monument.
Nota Ce petit Parc de 300 arpens environ est entouré de tous côtés du Grand Parc d'environ 1500 arpens
500 Mètres.
Feet.
Nota This small Park of nearly 300 Acres is surrounded on every side with the great one of nearly 1500 Acres
TRAITÉ DES JARDINS PAR VERGNAUD ARCHITECTE.

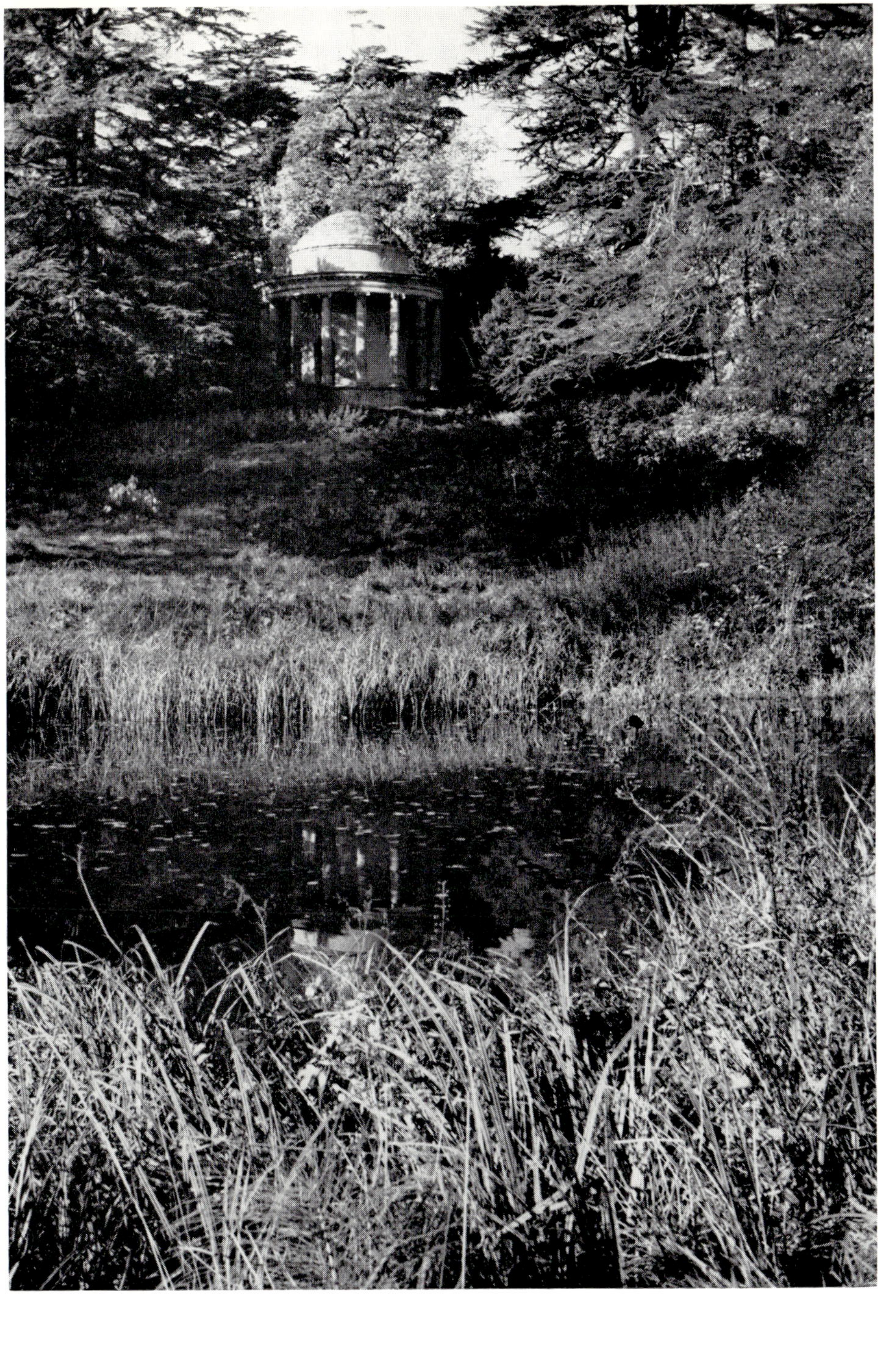

30 (OPPOSITE) **Stowe, Bucks.** In the eighteenth century the English rebelled against the formal geometrical landscape and there originated the English School of Landscape Gardening. From this period dates all biological landscape in Western Civilization, although it was an art long practised in ancient China.

31 **Stowe: The Temple of Ancient Virtue.** Stowe is the most comprehensive example of the English School. The plan shows the great geometric Palladian mansion round which swept the 'ideal' landscape of nature. The Temple of Ancient Virtue (8 on plan) is one of a multitude of incidents without which such a landscape is unfurnished.

32 **Waterlow Park, Highgate, London.** The creation of rural scenes within the urban environment has continued consistently since about 1800. These landscapes appear to be naturalistic, but in reality they are designed with exceptional care and with the eye of the painter. This park is relatively small, but the illusion is one of size.

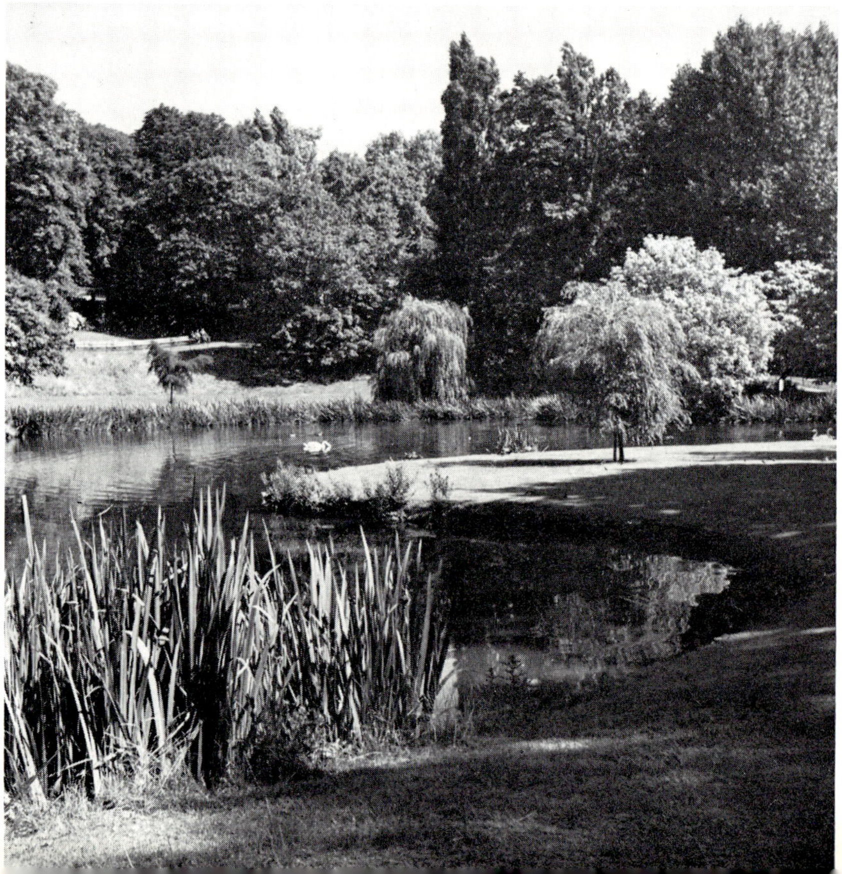

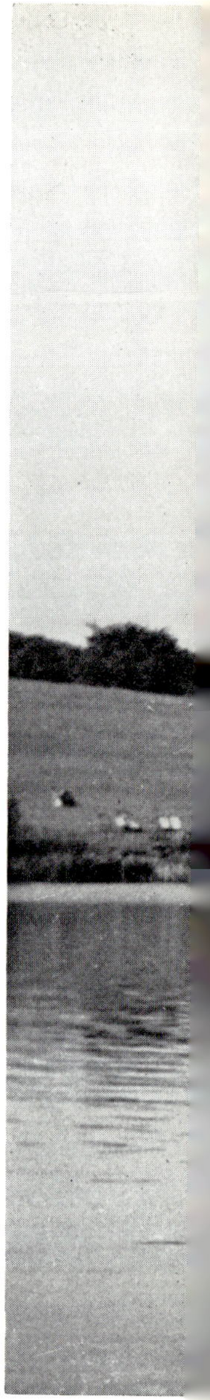

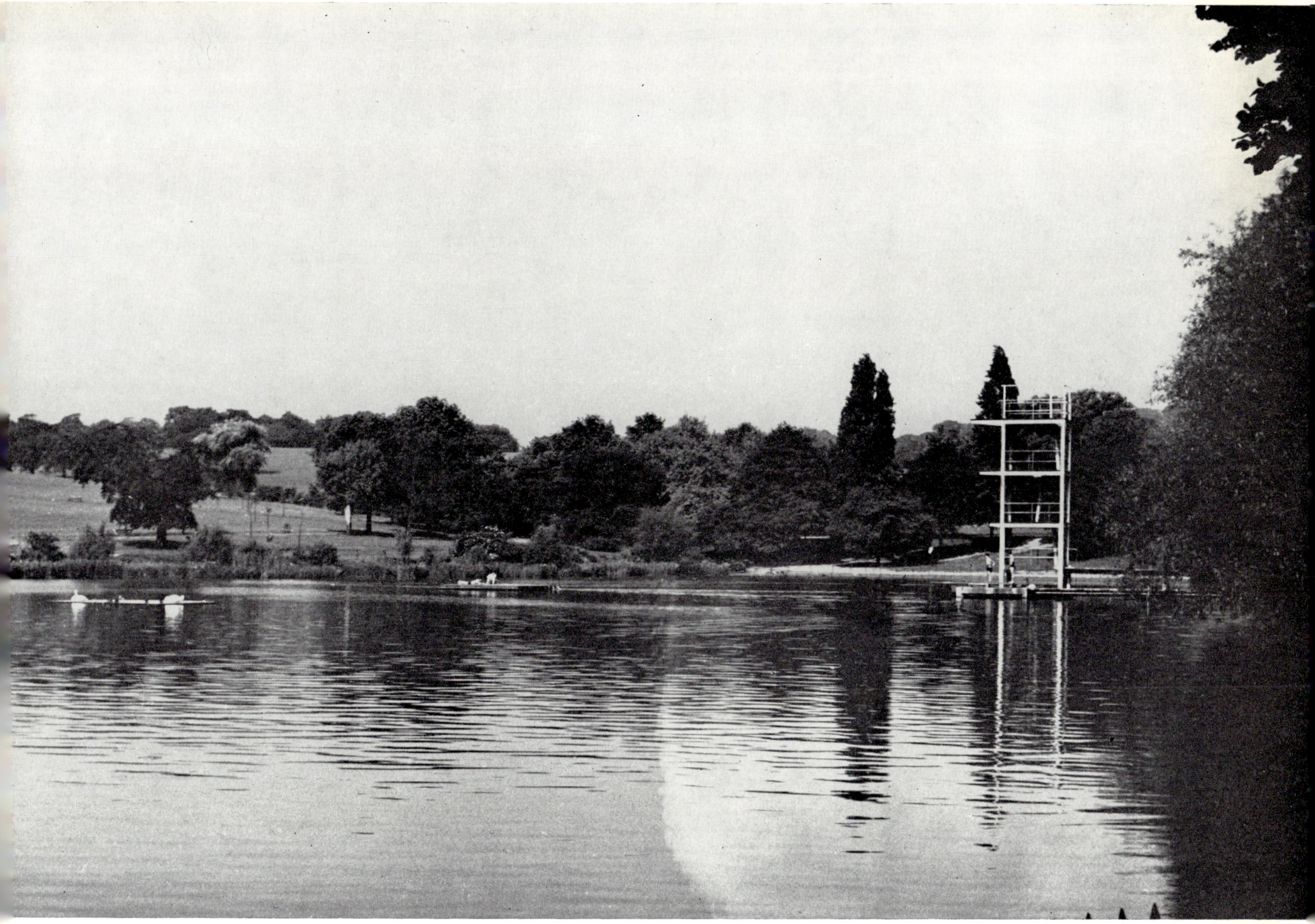

33 **Highgate Ponds, London.** The adjoining Hampstead Heath is large enough for a sense of great space to be generated, not only by the mystery of trees, but by unfinished horizons of grass-clad undulations. The heath is a model of the way in which a populated public open area can retain the element of the wild.

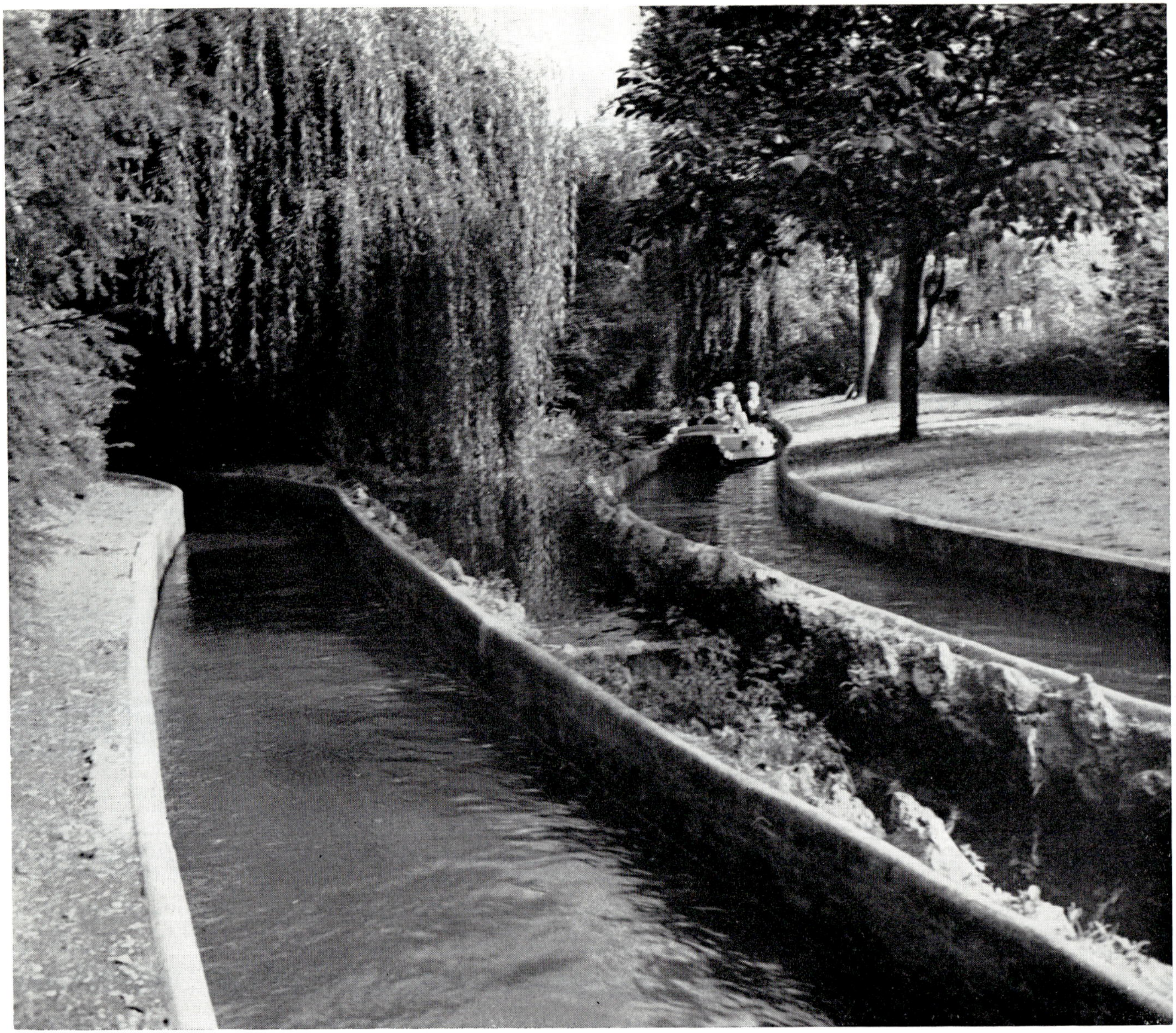

34 **Jardin d'Acclimatation, Paris.** The delights of artificiality I.

35 **Tropical House.** The delights of artificiality II.

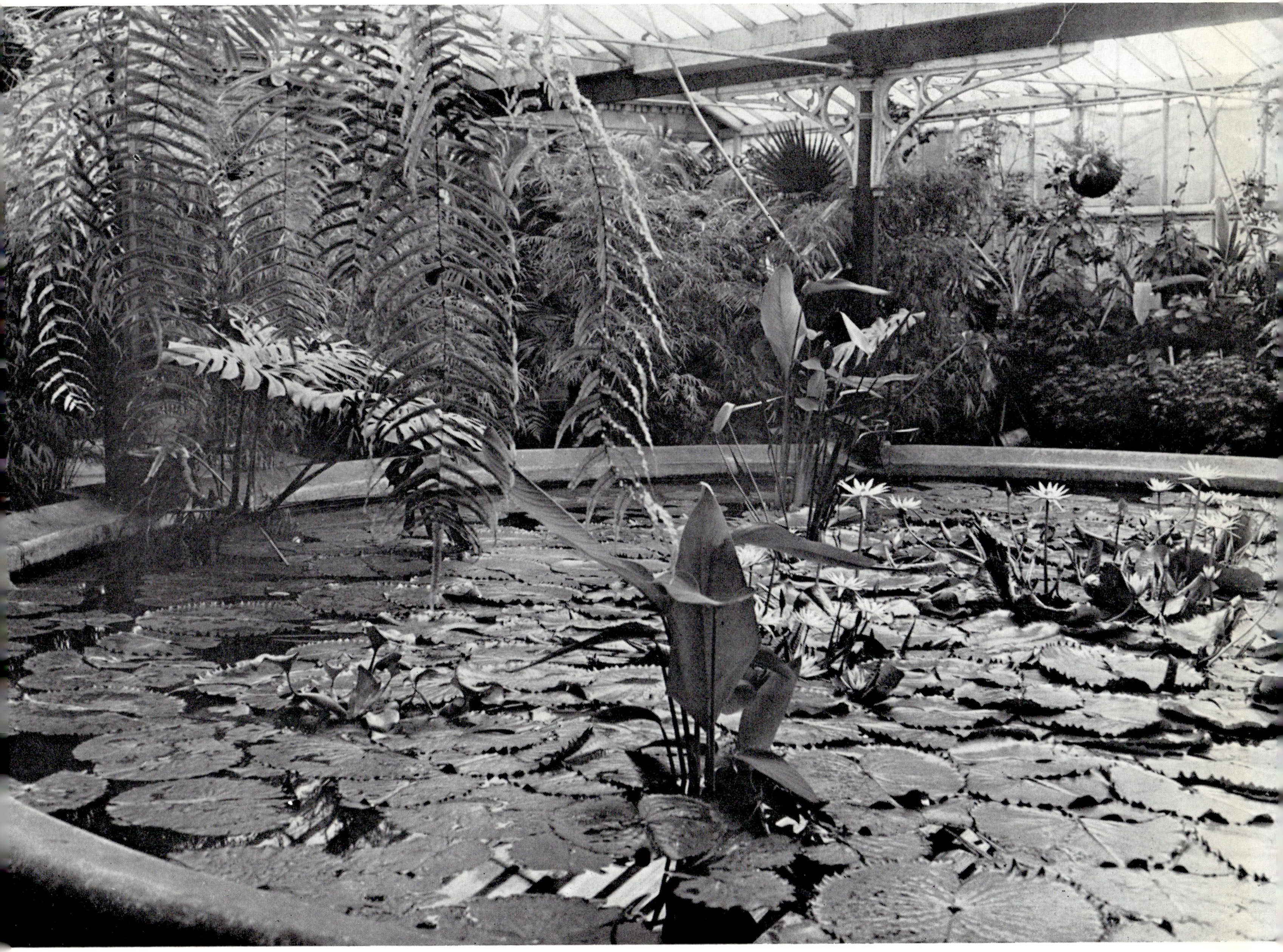

37 **Children: the Secondary school**

36 **Children: the nursery school.** The scene is the churchyard of St. Bartholomew the Great, London, now a public garden.

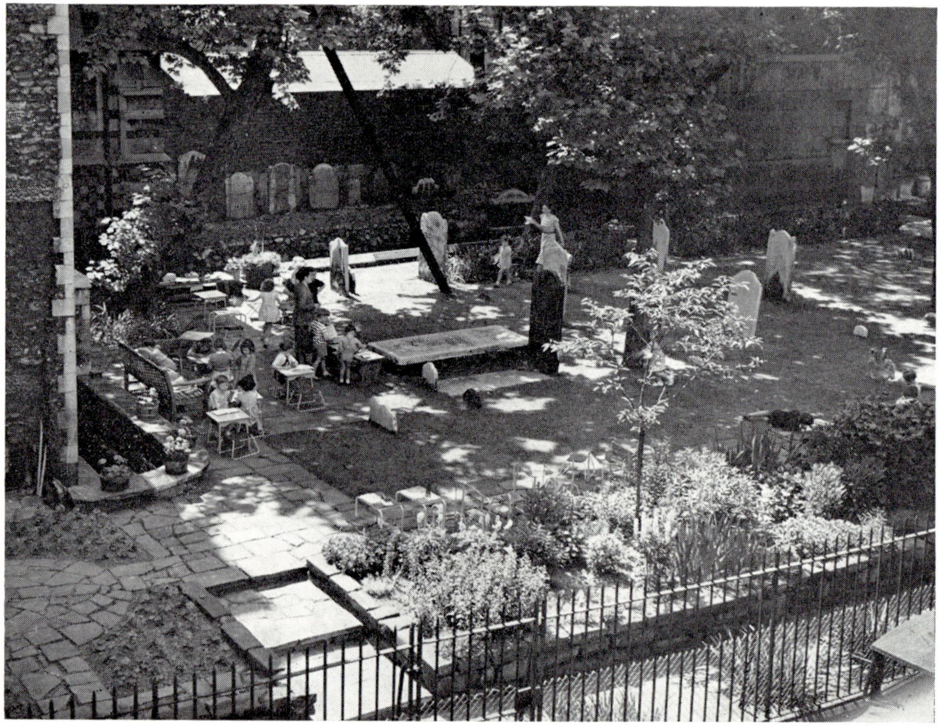

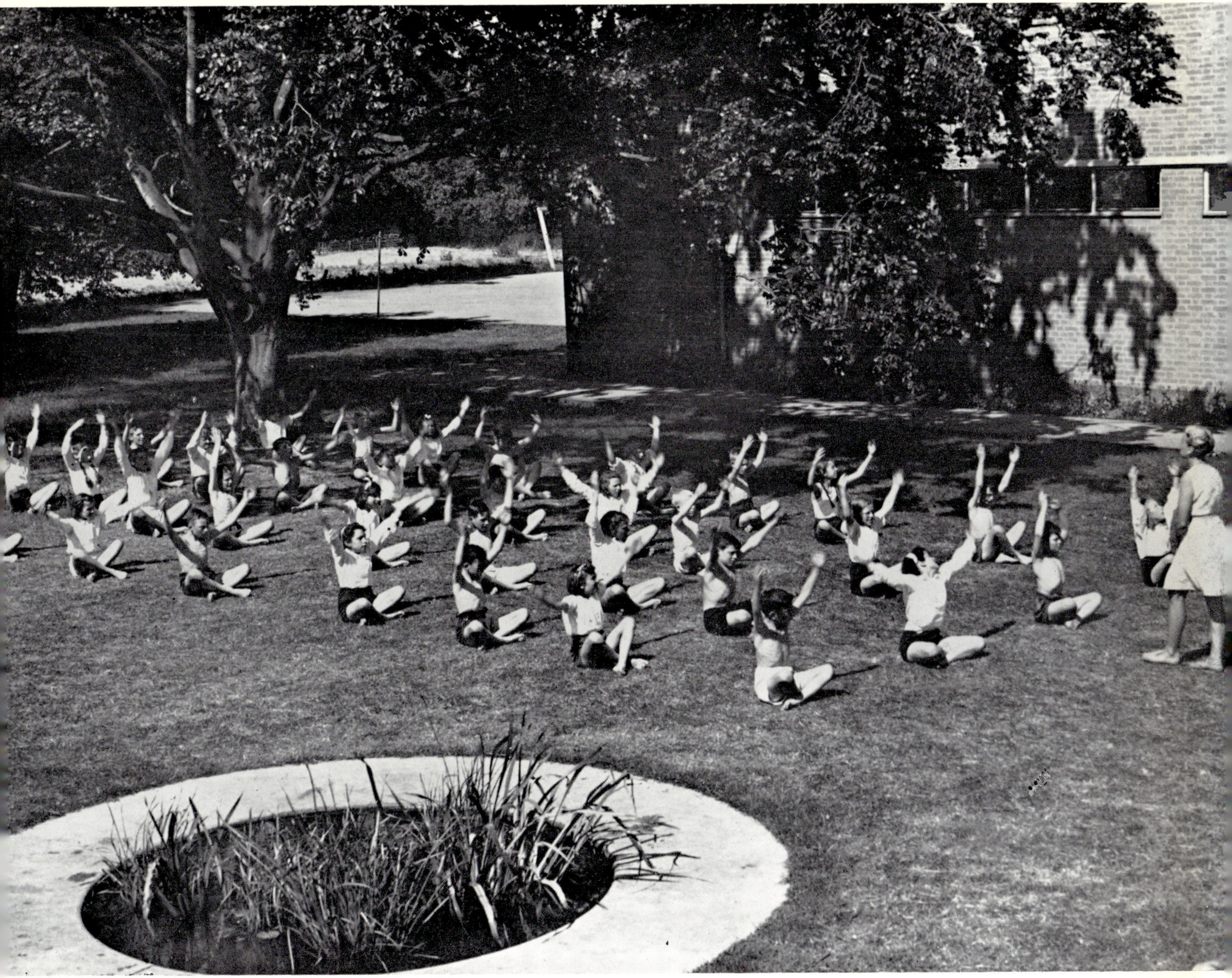

38 **House at Farley Green.** Because of glass, modern methods of heating and of construction, it is possible to transform a living-room from the traditional warm enclosed cell of winter to a garden house in summer.

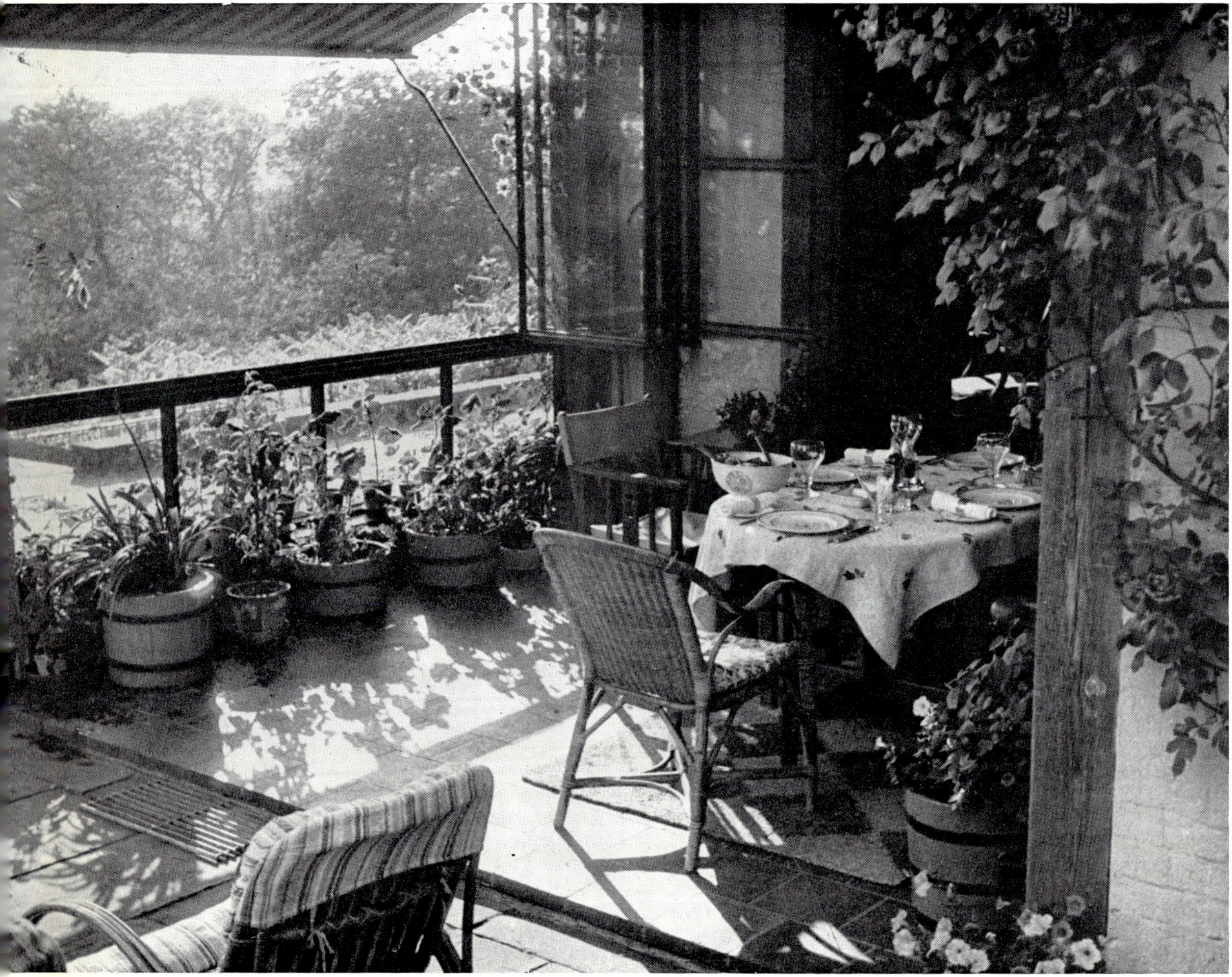

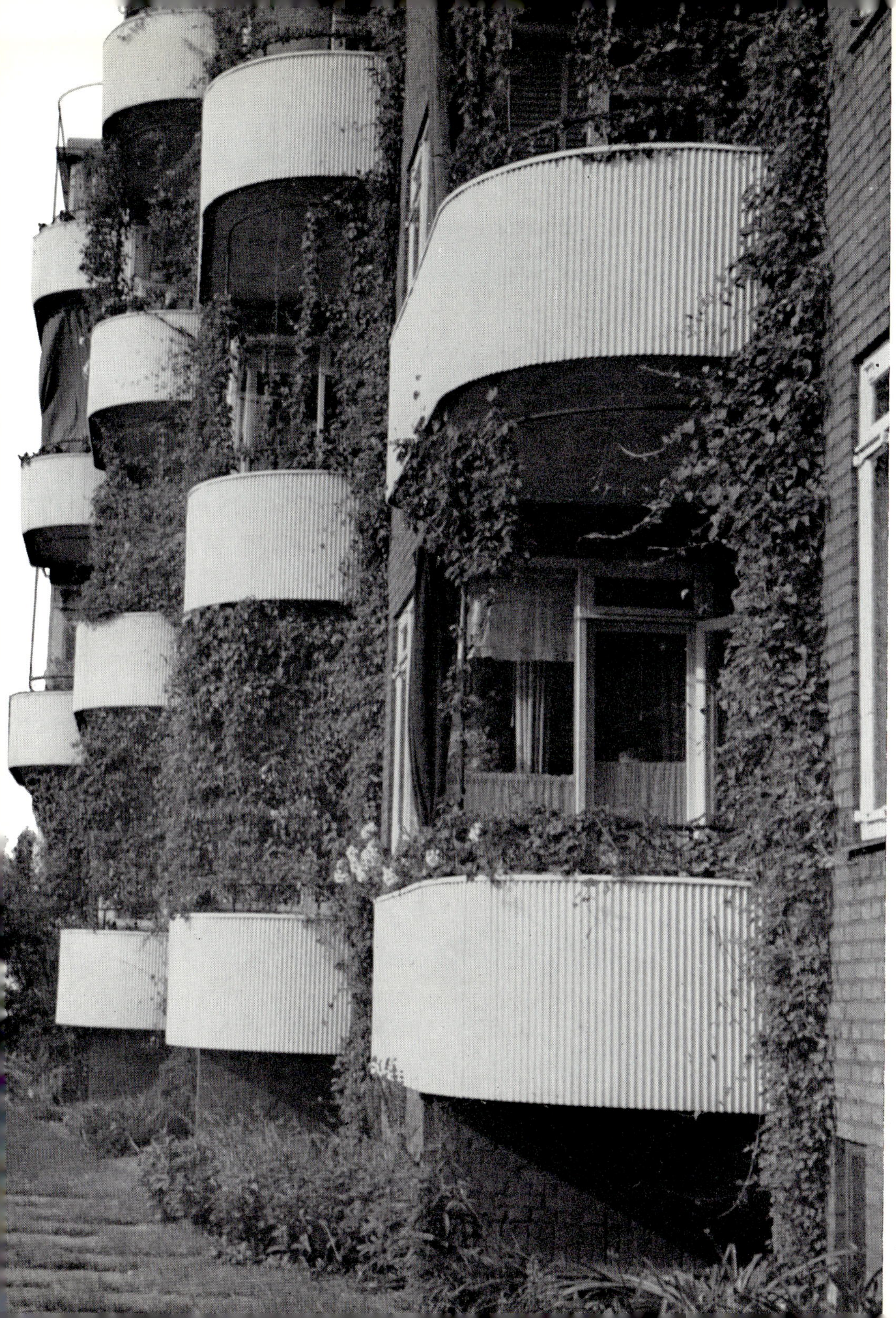

39 **Balcony Flats in Copenhagen.** These entertaining garden balconies have screens or shutters made by *Polygonum baldschuanicum* springing from the ground. They can be open or secretive according to the tenants' desires.

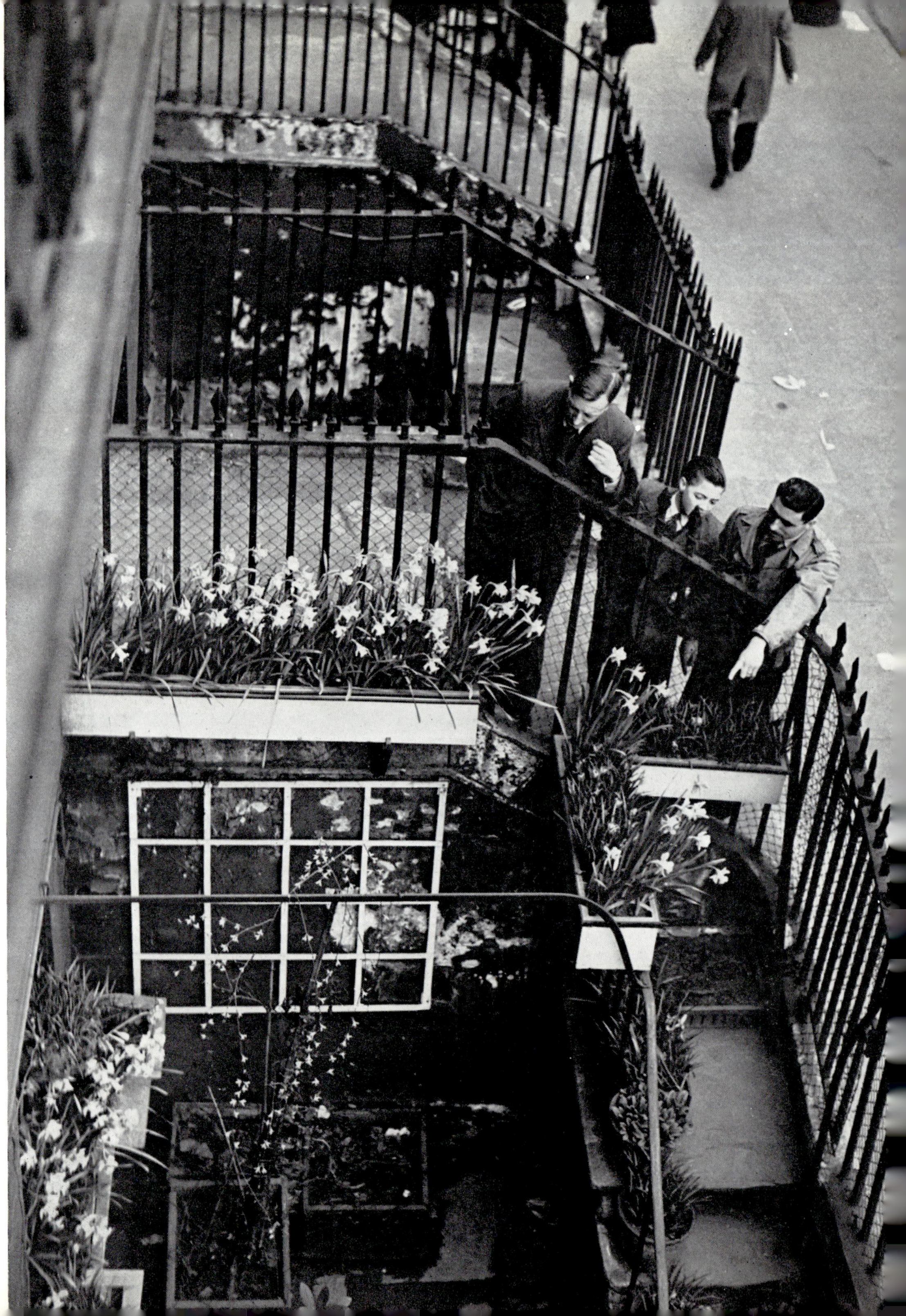

40 Blackfriars Road, London.

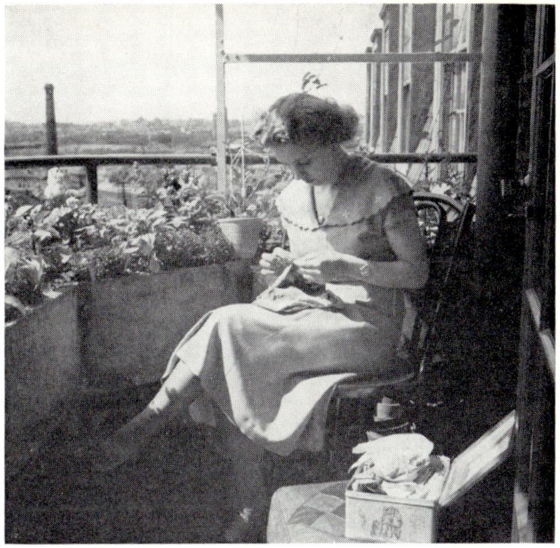

41a **St Pancras, London**

41b **Kingswinford Sunshine Home and Nursery School for the Blind.** Contact is by touch and smell.

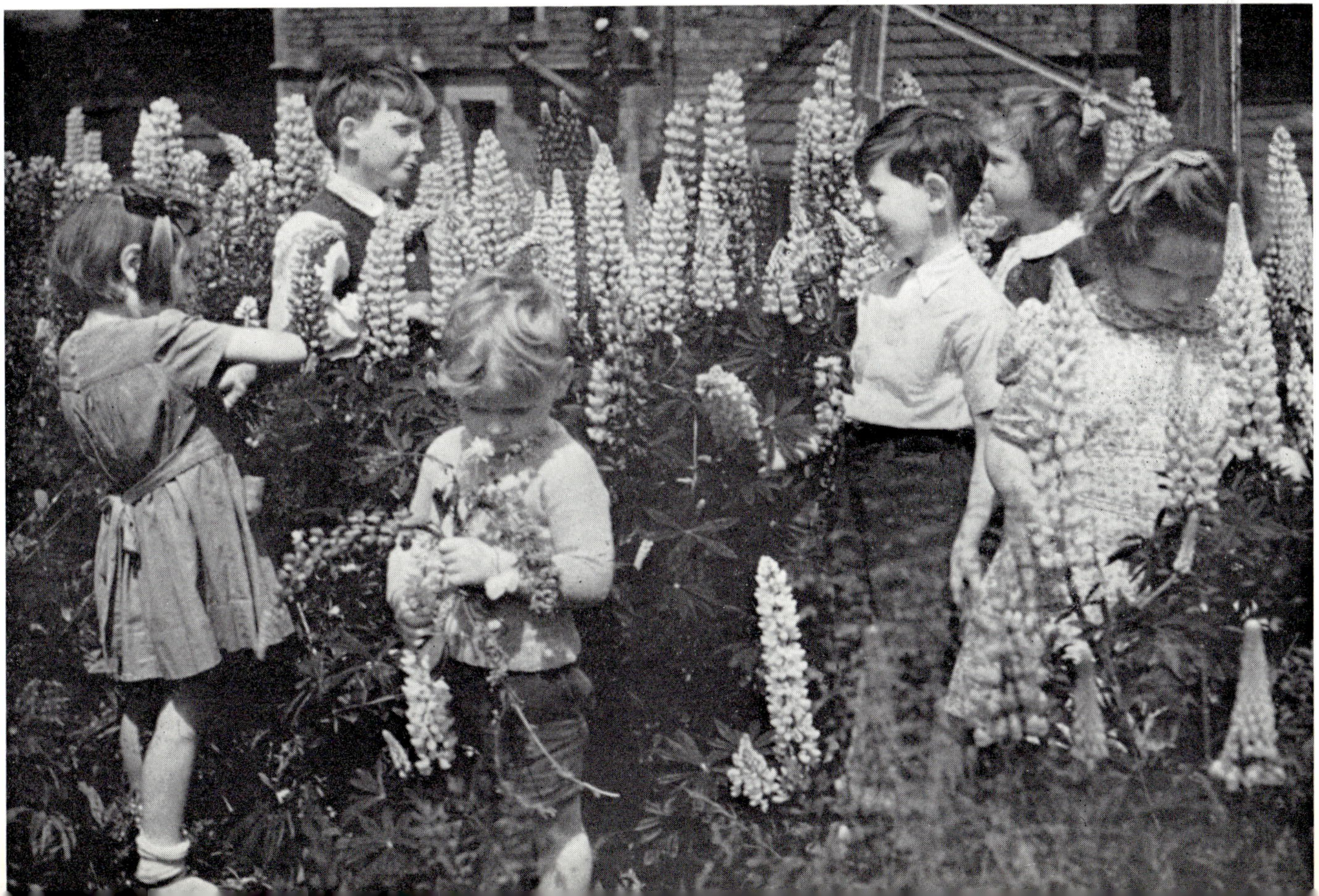

42 A Garden in Highgate, London. This space is only 15 feet wide, but contains such a diversity and wealth of plant life, always in constant change, that it is in a sense a world in itself.

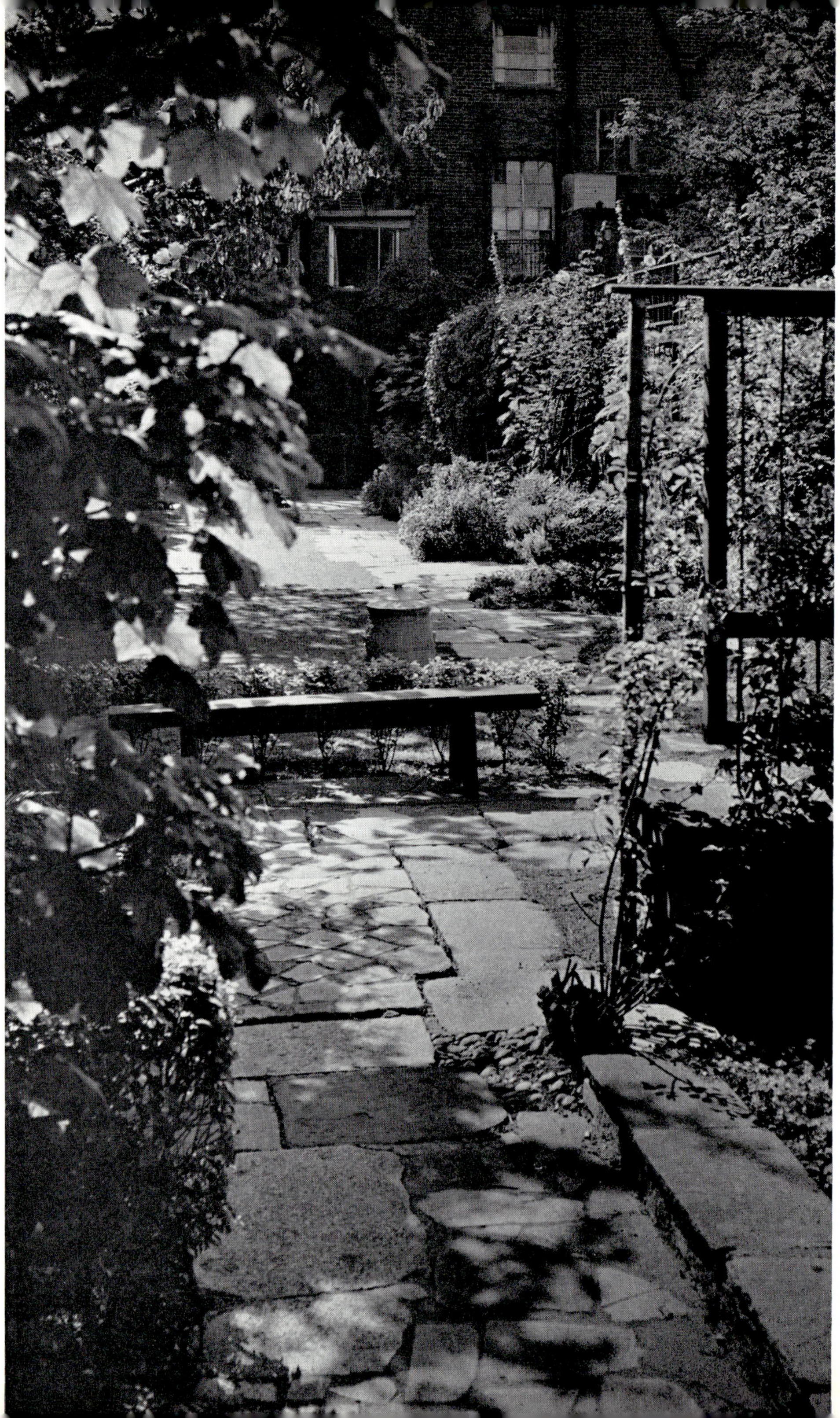

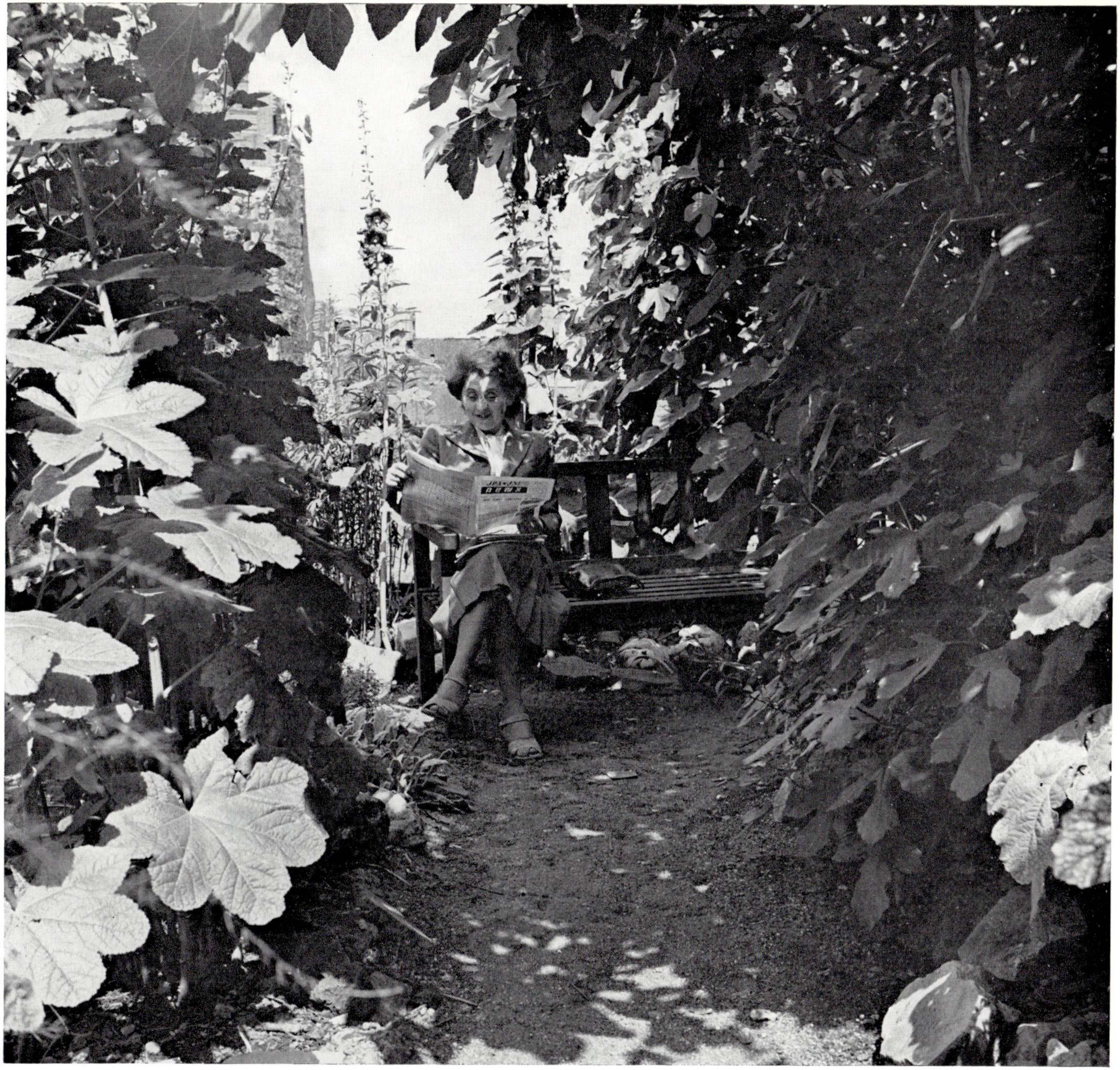

43 A Bombed Site, London

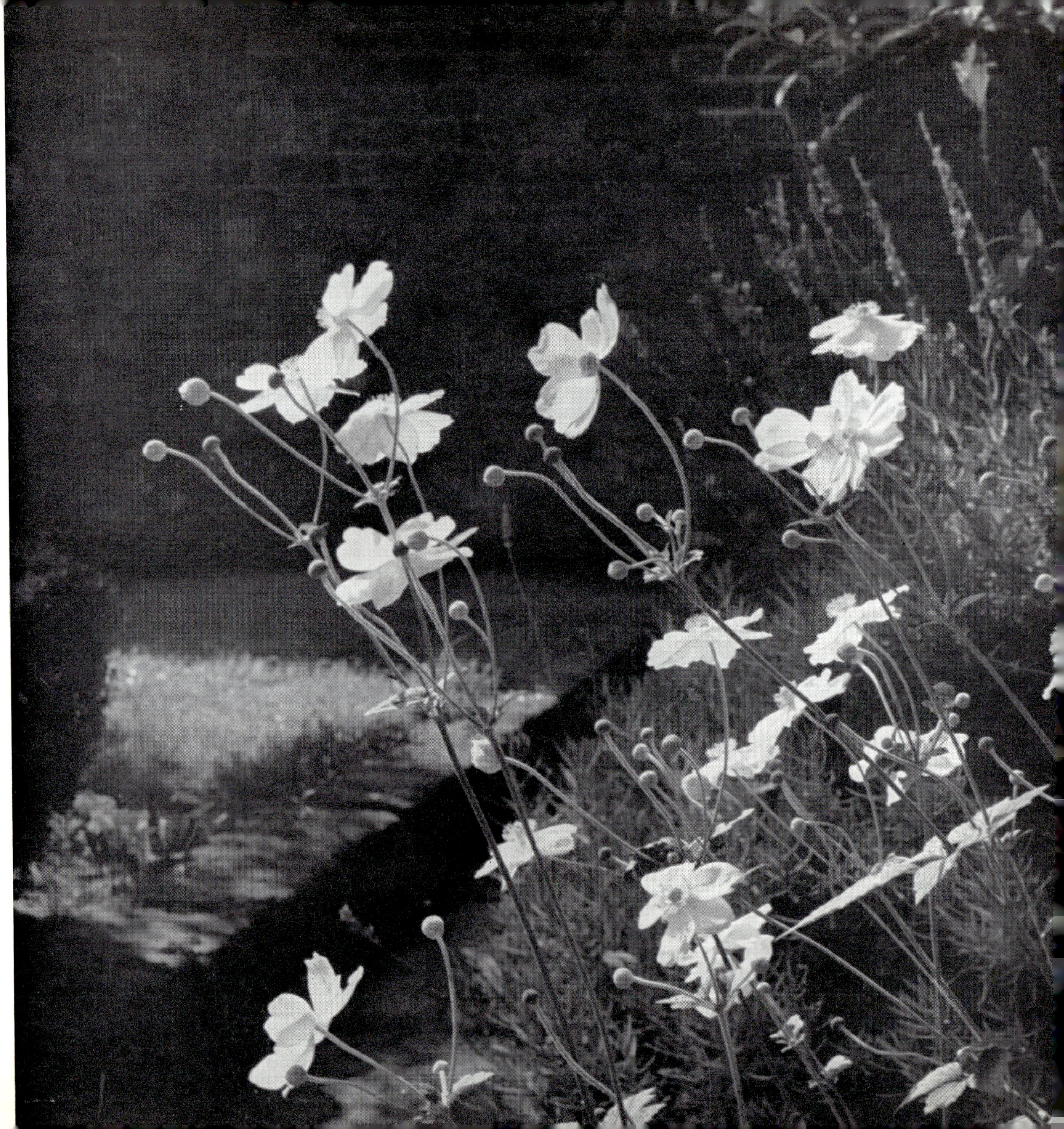

THE TOWN RESIDENCE

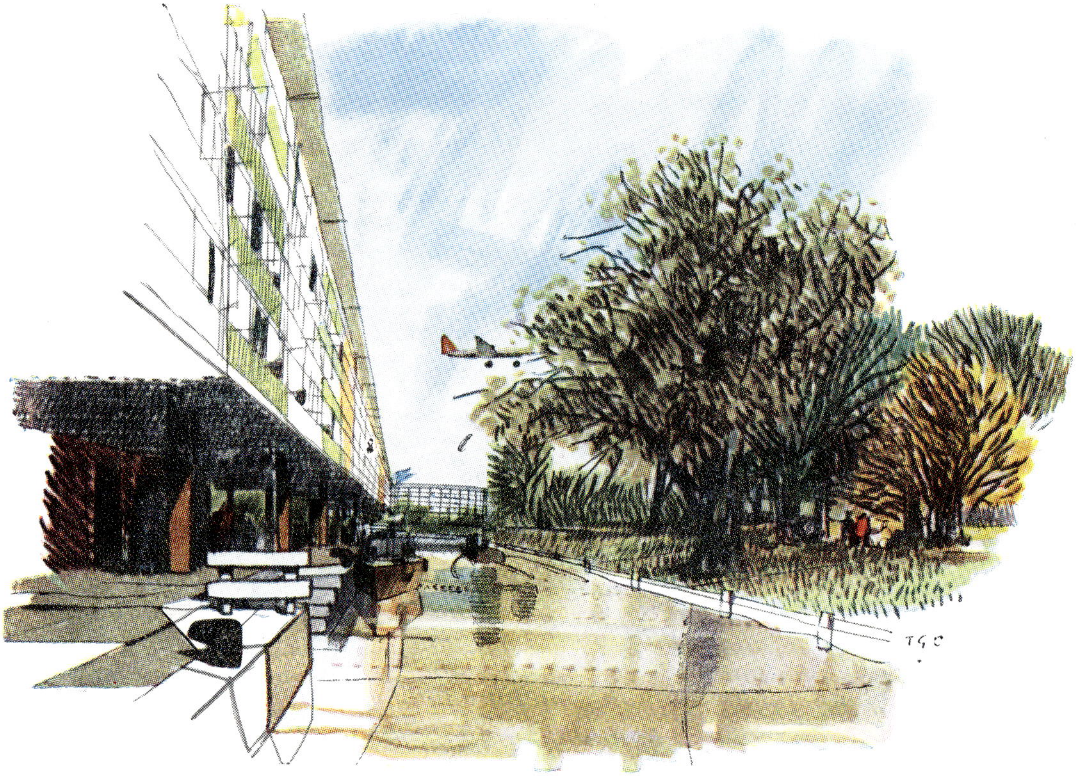

45 Every residence in Motopia has an outlook upon green
Drawing by Gordon Cullen

The town residence of Utopia was based on a comprehensive family unit and was very large and probably overcrowded. The tendency since that time has been to 'fragment' the unit, and this is especially so in the modern world. The newly married couple want a home of their own, and because there is no service as in traditional times, they want it neat and compact and as easy to run as possible. This cell or shell can contain anything from the washing machine to television, and offers the ungregarious a reasonably full life that could be led independently of the world outside.

For warmth, convenience, and economy the historic tendency has been first to huddle houses closely, and then to join them together promiscuously as in medieval London, and eventually, as after the Great Fire, to rationalize this form of structure into the long terraces that culminated in Bloomsbury and Regent's Park. This dignified form of living was eminently suited to our nature and our climate, and fitted the social way of life of the time. The variety of grouping was considerable, but perhaps the widest range within a small area is best illustrated by the contrast of closed and open spaces in the Circus and Royal Crescent in Bath. Unfortunately this system of urban living was so rational and economic that it was used as the basis of industrial housing in the Victorian era. The slums contained all that was economic of the Georgian terrace, with none of the grace. It is no wonder that the twentieth century ushered in a hatred of this home so grossly unfair to the original. After six decades of the semi-detached house in suburbia, and a multitudinous variety of slab and tall blocks of flats in the cities, the terrace form of structure is once more coming into its own. But there are differences from the past that are so great as to throw open wholly new lines of possibility.

Modern systems of heating eliminate chimneys, and the pitched roof has given way to the concrete flat roof. Service rooms such as kitchen and bathroom no longer require external lighting, and consequently allow a deeper building and a narrower frontage. There is no such thing as a front or a back, because all facades are equal in value. Modern methods of mass and machine production call for a great repetition of units, whose rhythm works horizontally rather than vertically. The architects of the Bedford Estate in London raised the whole level of their roads about eight feet above the natural ground-level, standing them upon cellars. Had those same architects been alive today, no doubt they too might have made a further heave and lifted them, as in Motopia, upon the roofs themselves.

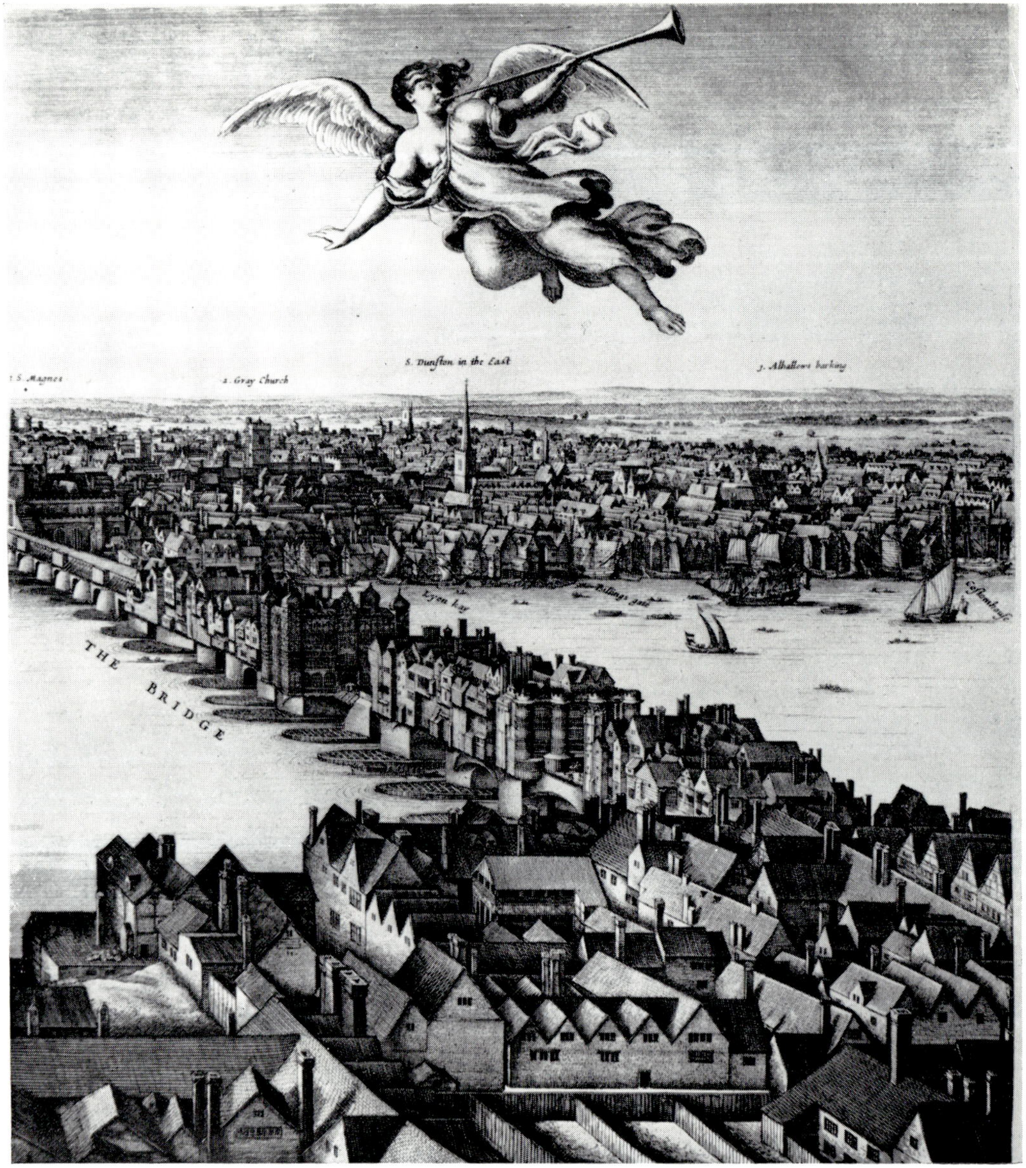

46 **London before the Great Fire.** Nothing in Motopia can compare with the courage of those who built old London Bridge.

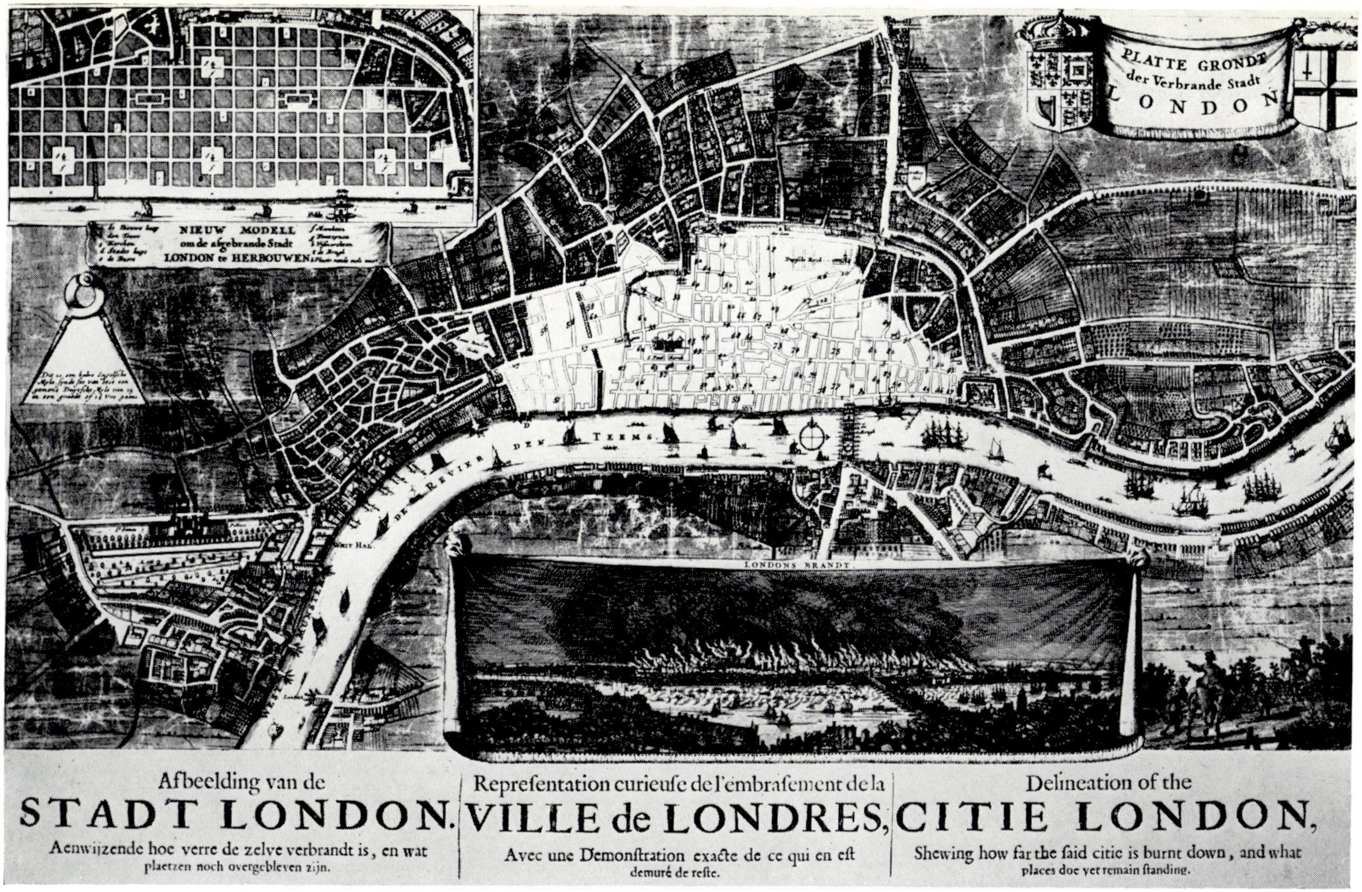

47a **Plan for London, probably by Robert Hooke, after the Great Fire, 1666**. The geometry reminds us of Scamozzi's Ideal City (Pl. 12) and was more rational, if less romantic, than the plans of Wren and John Evelyn, who partly relied on diagonals. It was this rational approach to rebuilding that created the horizontal terrace.

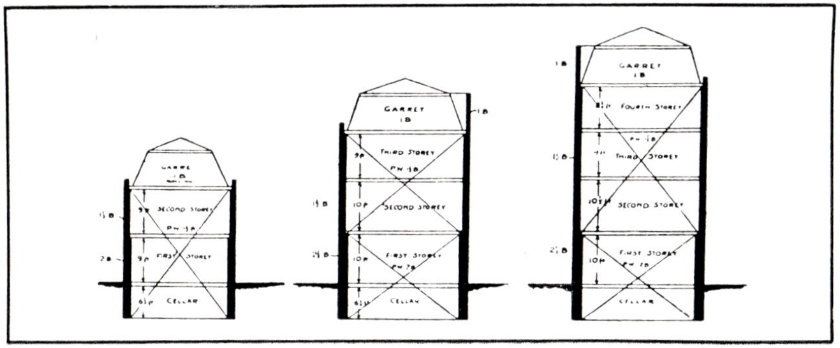

47b **The effects of anti-fire by-laws.** Types of houses of the size allowed after 1666 in side streets and alleys, and in more important streets and main streets.

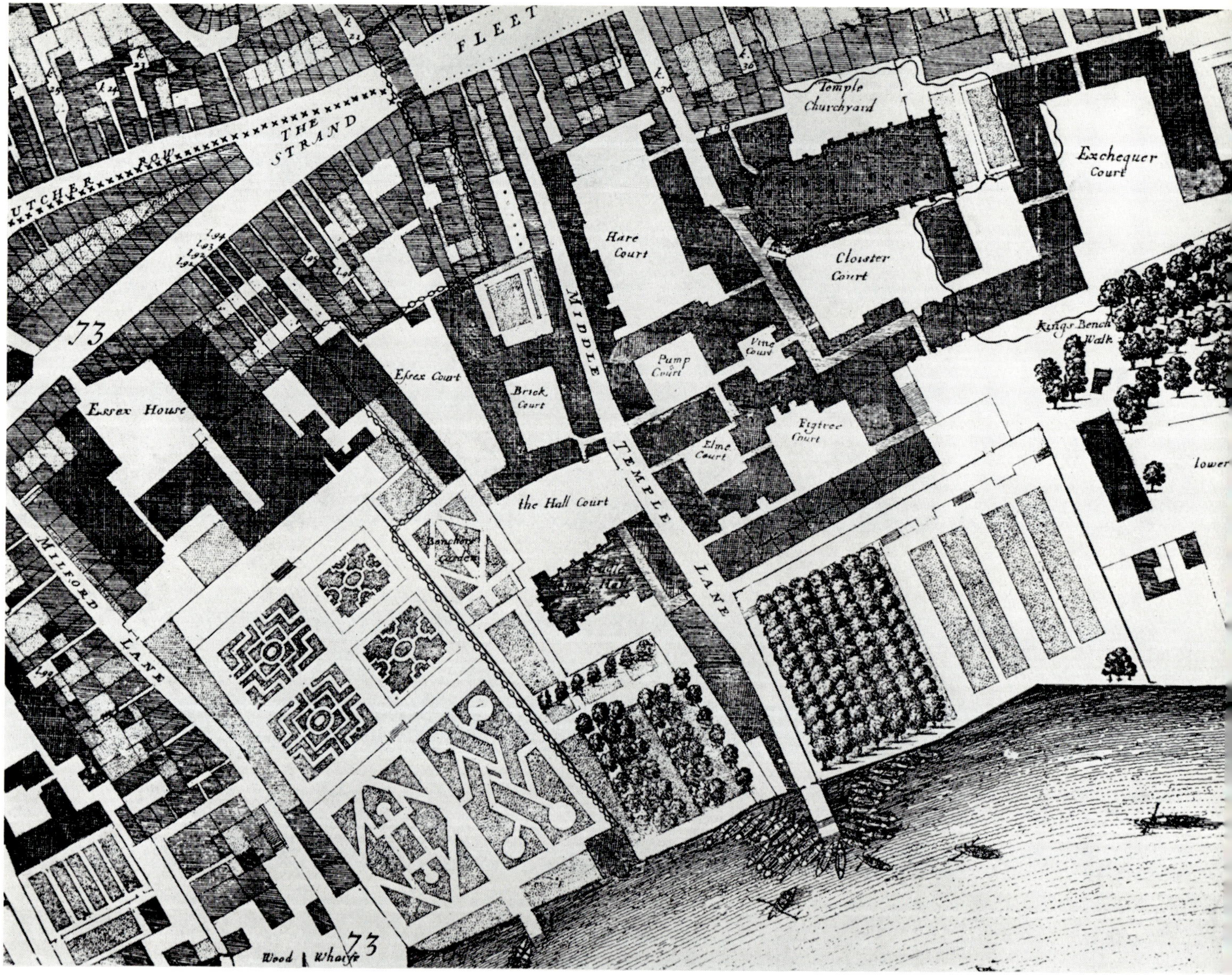

48 **The Temple Courts, from a print of 1677.** A form of dignified enclosure suited to the English character and rising from climatic conditions.

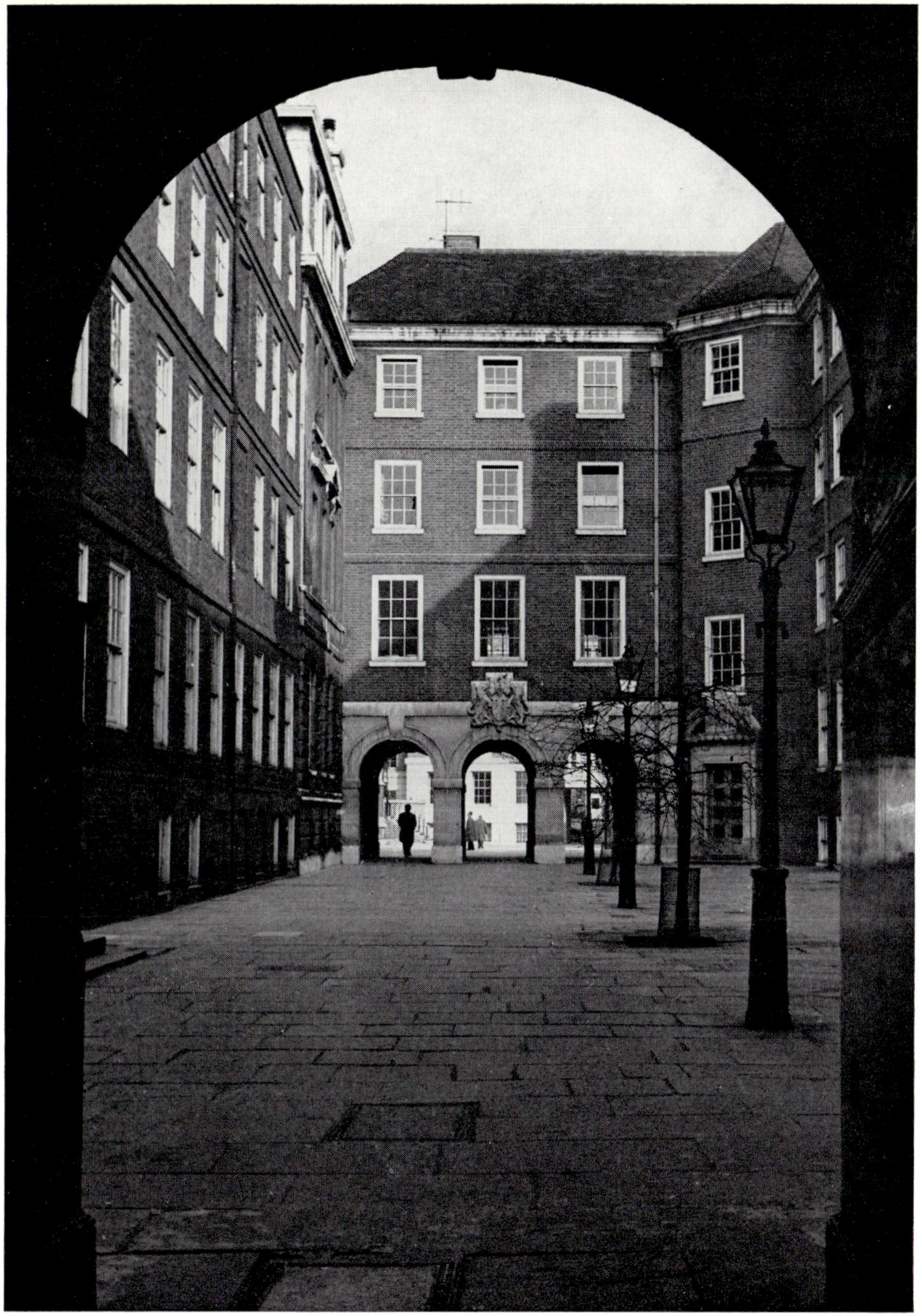

49 Pump Court, Middle Temple.

50 **The Bedford Estate, Bloomsbury.** The layout of the new estates on open land to the north-west of London in the eighteenth century took advantage of all previous experience and projected an urban way of life that for its purpose has never been surpassed. The squares of Bloomsbury are sufficiently large to contain forest trees and create the green view so much desired by the English. It has been said, and it may still be true, that there was no street in London from some part of which a tree could not be seen.

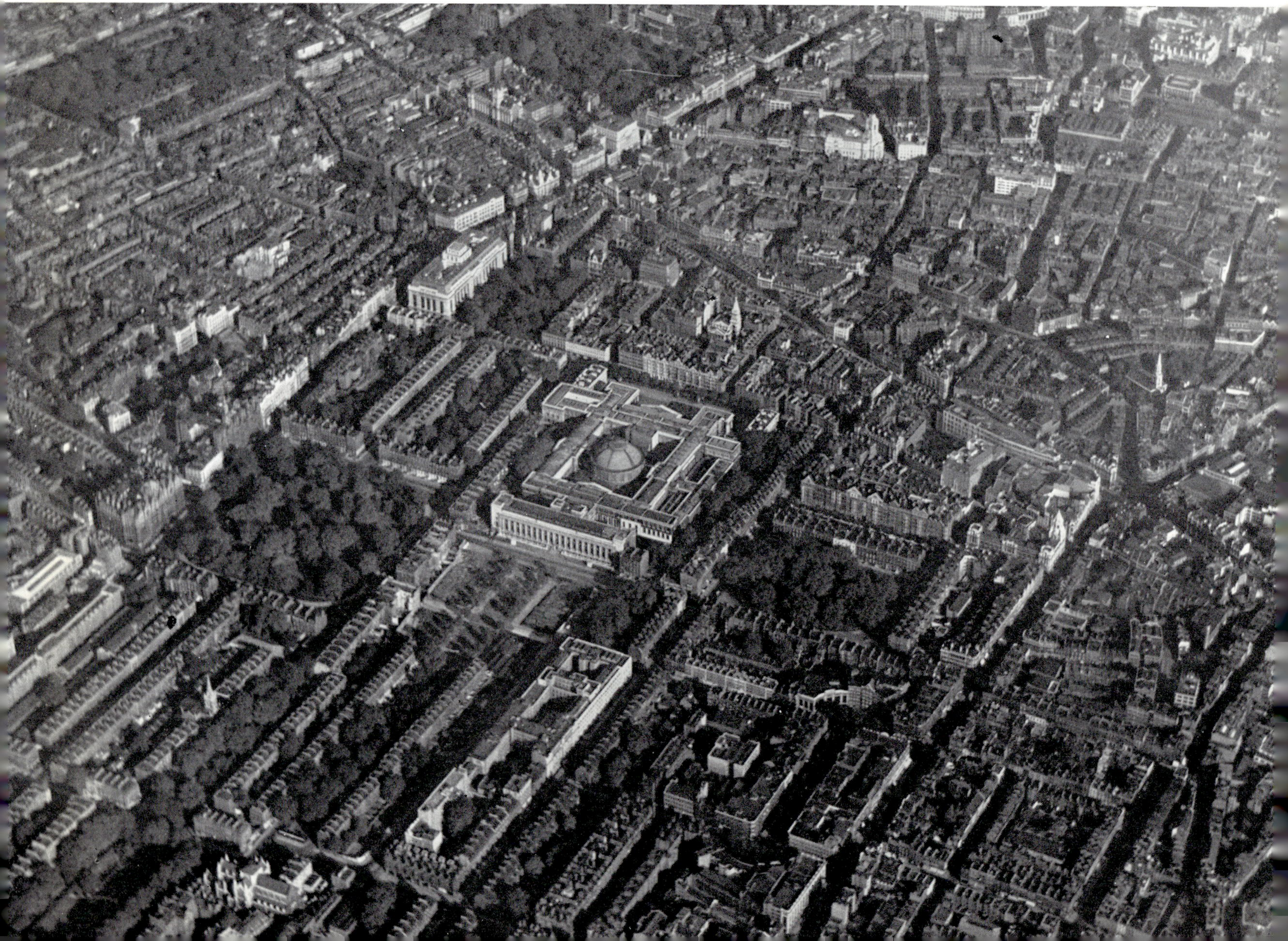

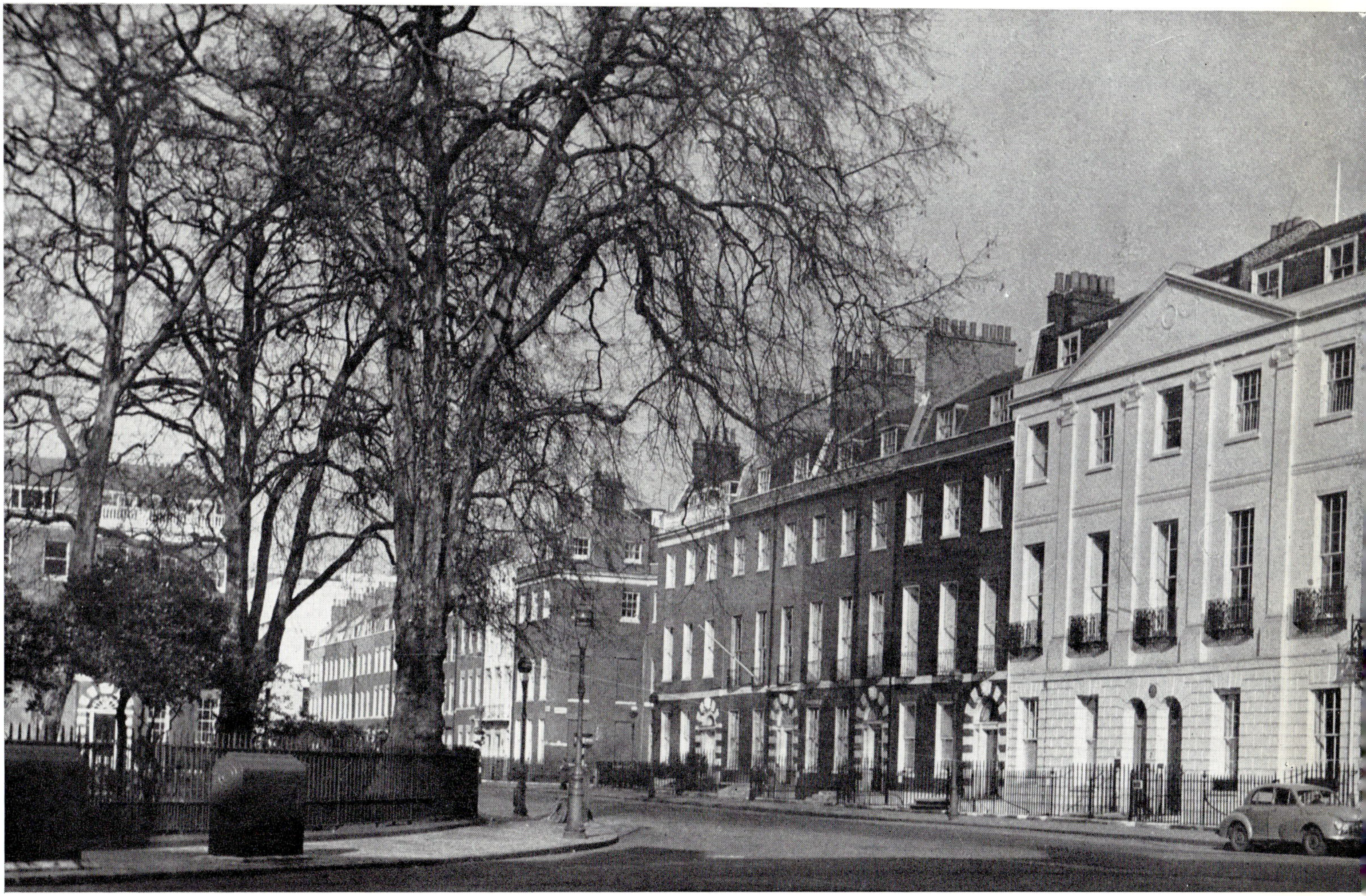

51 **Bedford Square and Gower Street, London.**
It was this view that gave rise to the idea of Motopia.

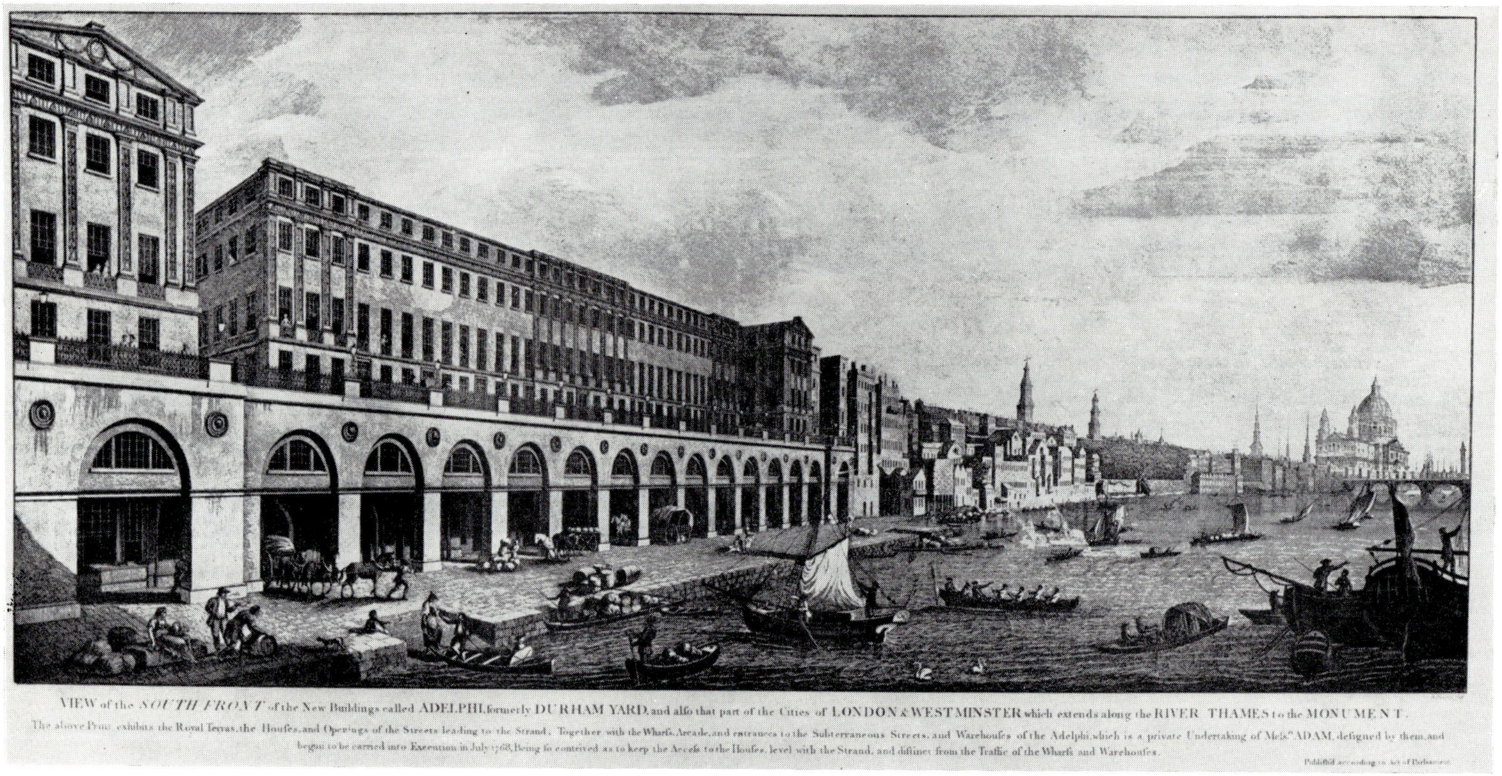

52 **The Adelphi Terrace, by Robert and James Adam (begun 1768).** This courageous speculative development, one of the architectural sights of London, is based on the idea of two-level traffic.

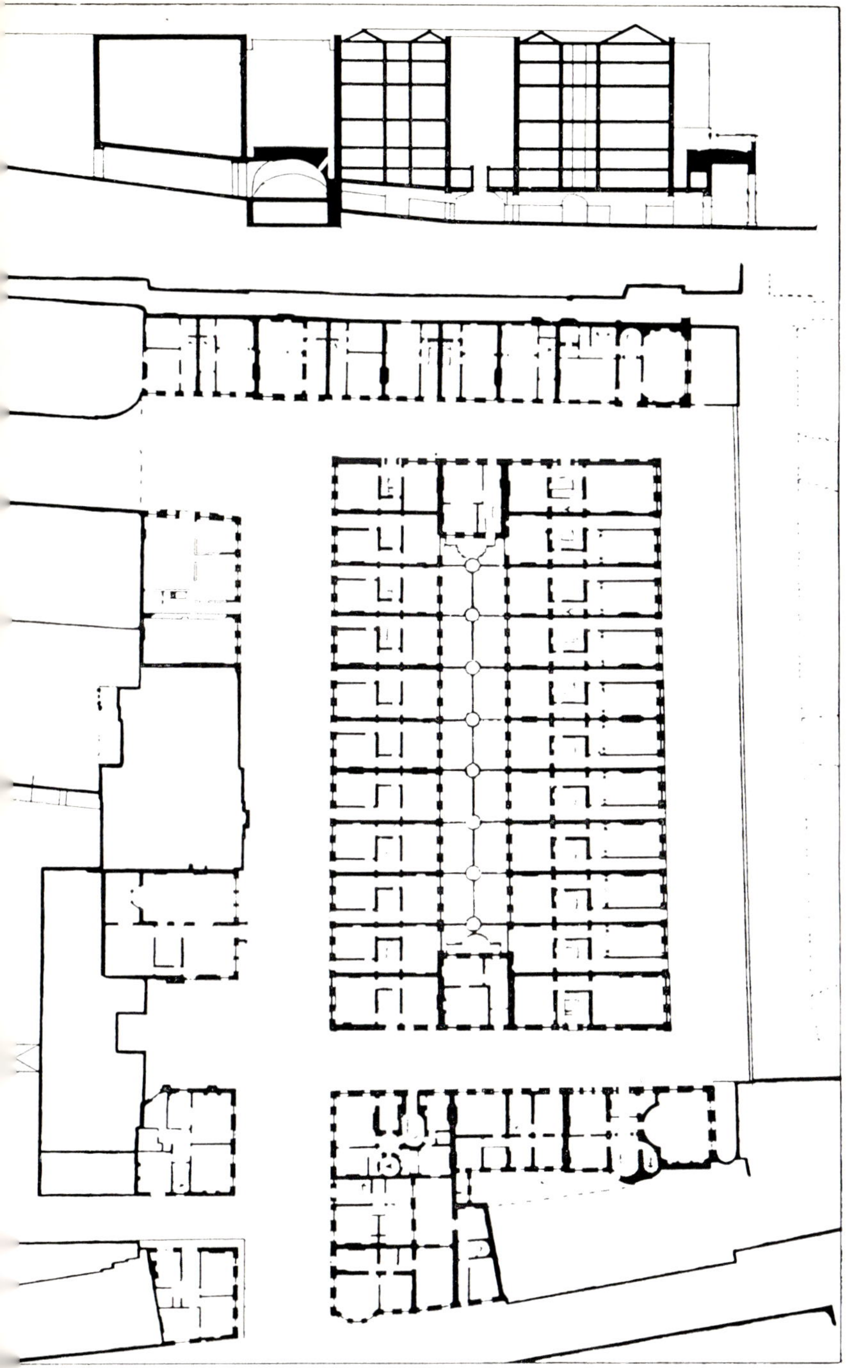

53a **The Adelphi: Plans and Sections** (**S. E. Rasmussen: 'London'**)**.** The section shows the houses built upon a prodigious system of arches, making full use of the fall in the ground from Strand to river. The house plan is typical of the way of life of the period.

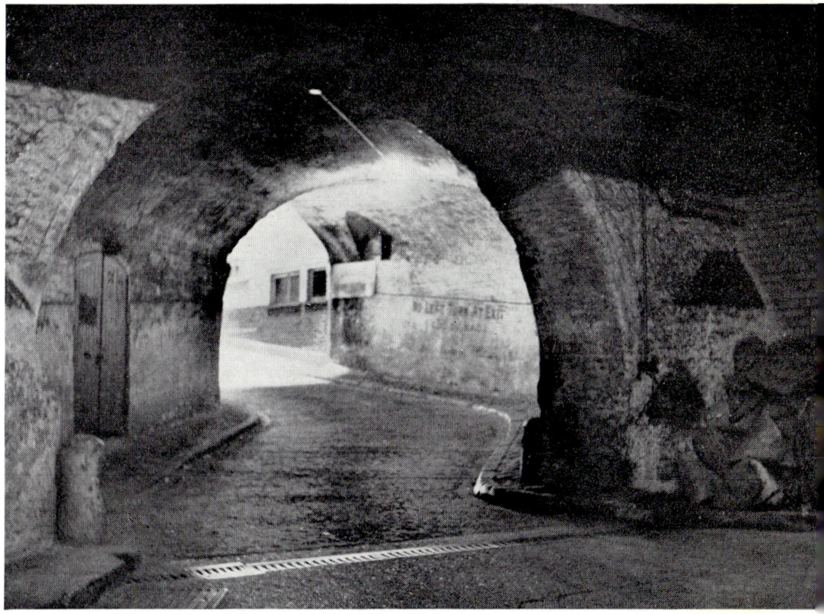

53b **The Adelphi.** The subterranean road.

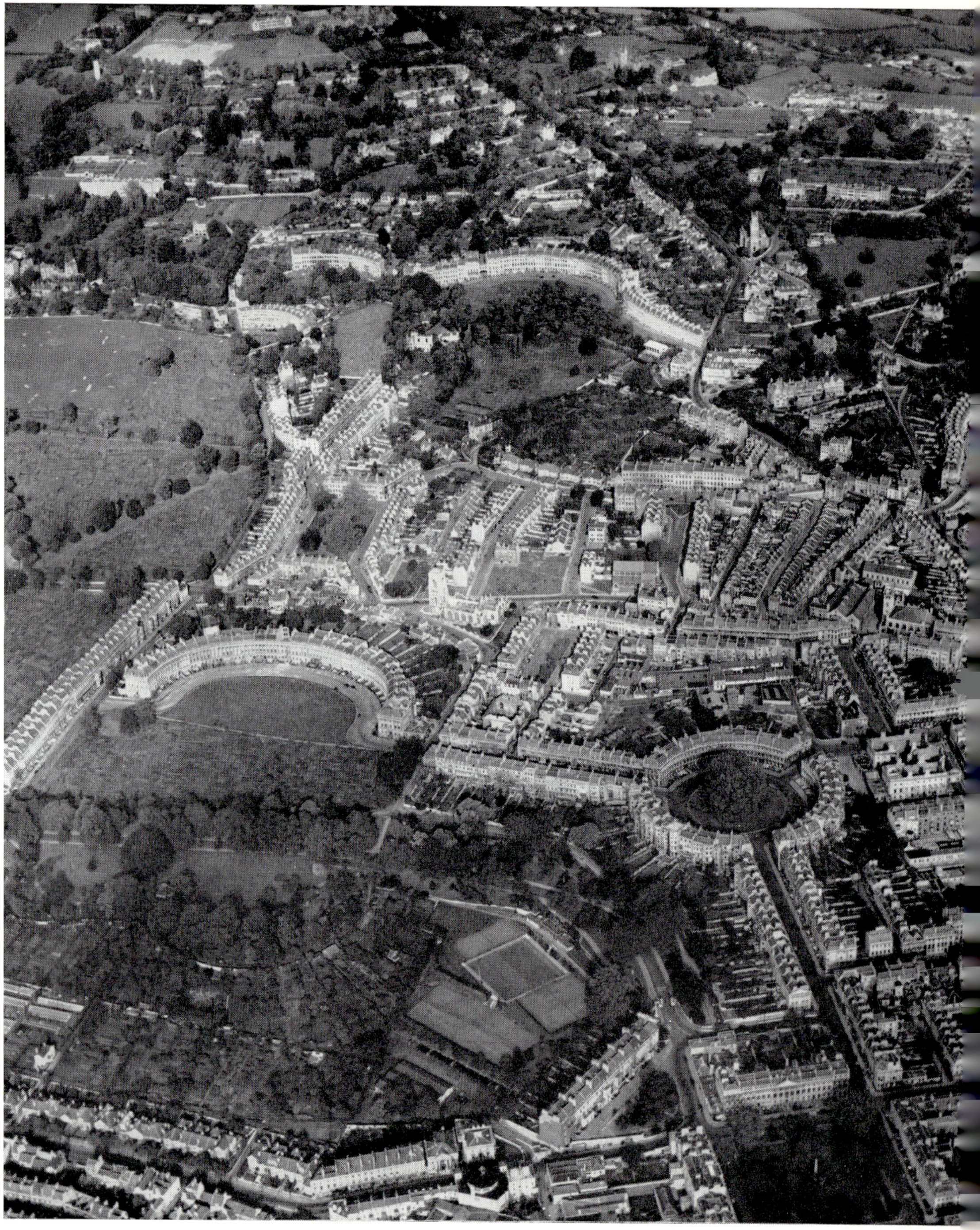

54 **Georgian Bath.** A complex of enclosed and open space in urban design, based on the straight line and the circle. The view is perhaps the most direct and obvious antecedent to Motopia. In the foreground the Circus (1754–58) and Royal Crescent (1767–1774), both by John Wood. In the distance the flowing lines of Lansdowne Crescent (1789–93) by J. Palmer.

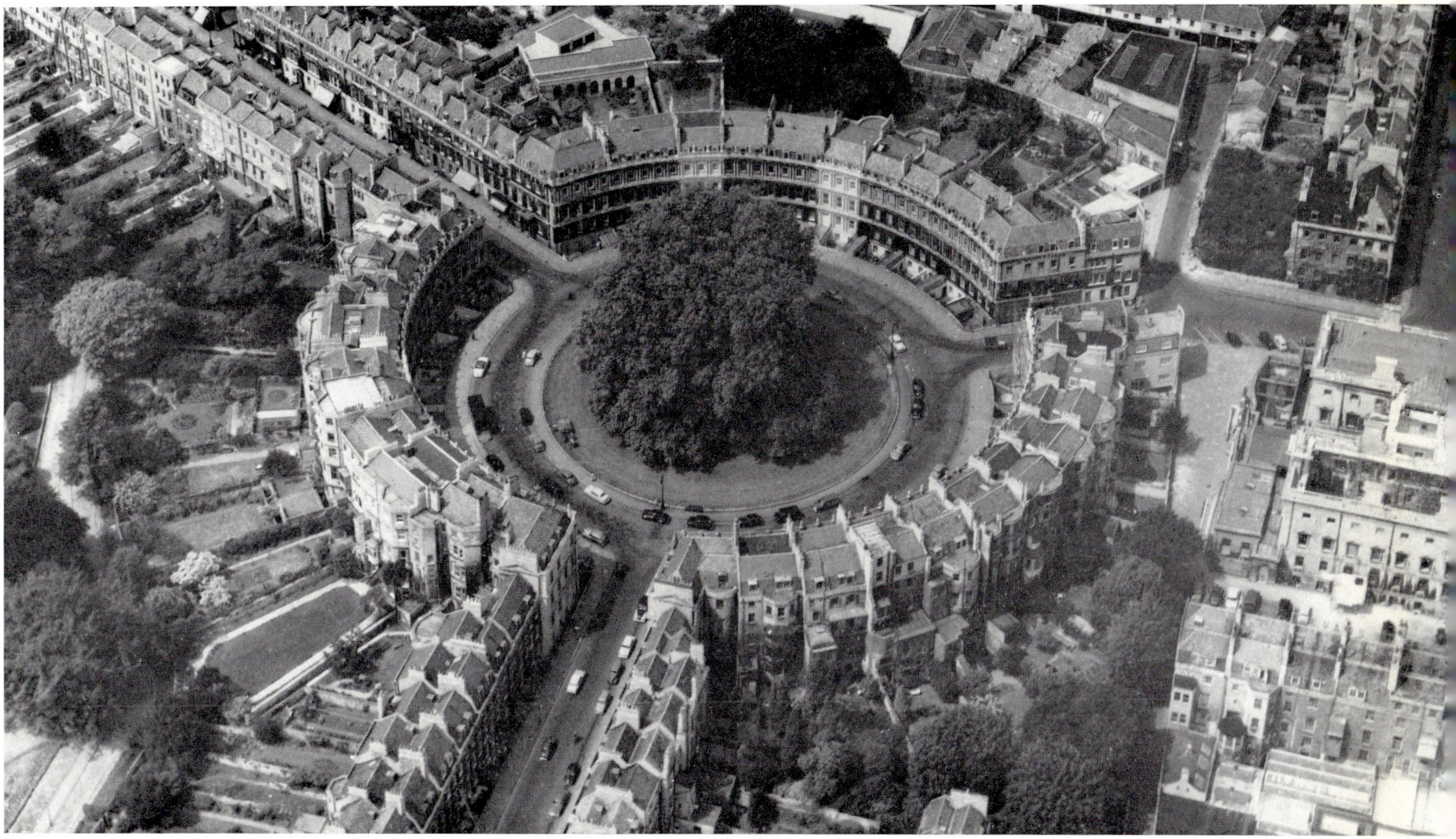

55 **The Circus, Bath.** The size of a circle in Motopia approximates to the road and pavement.

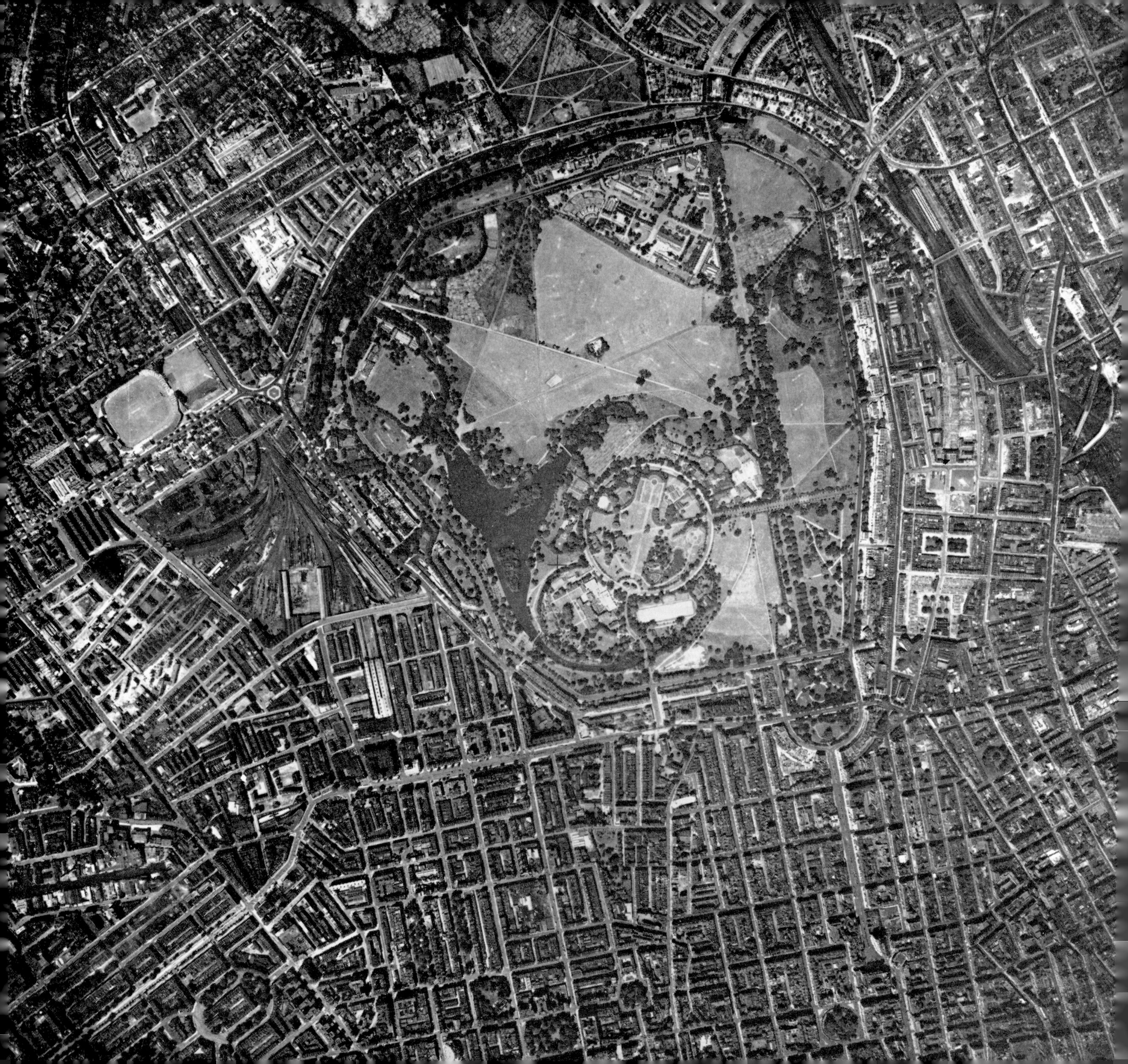

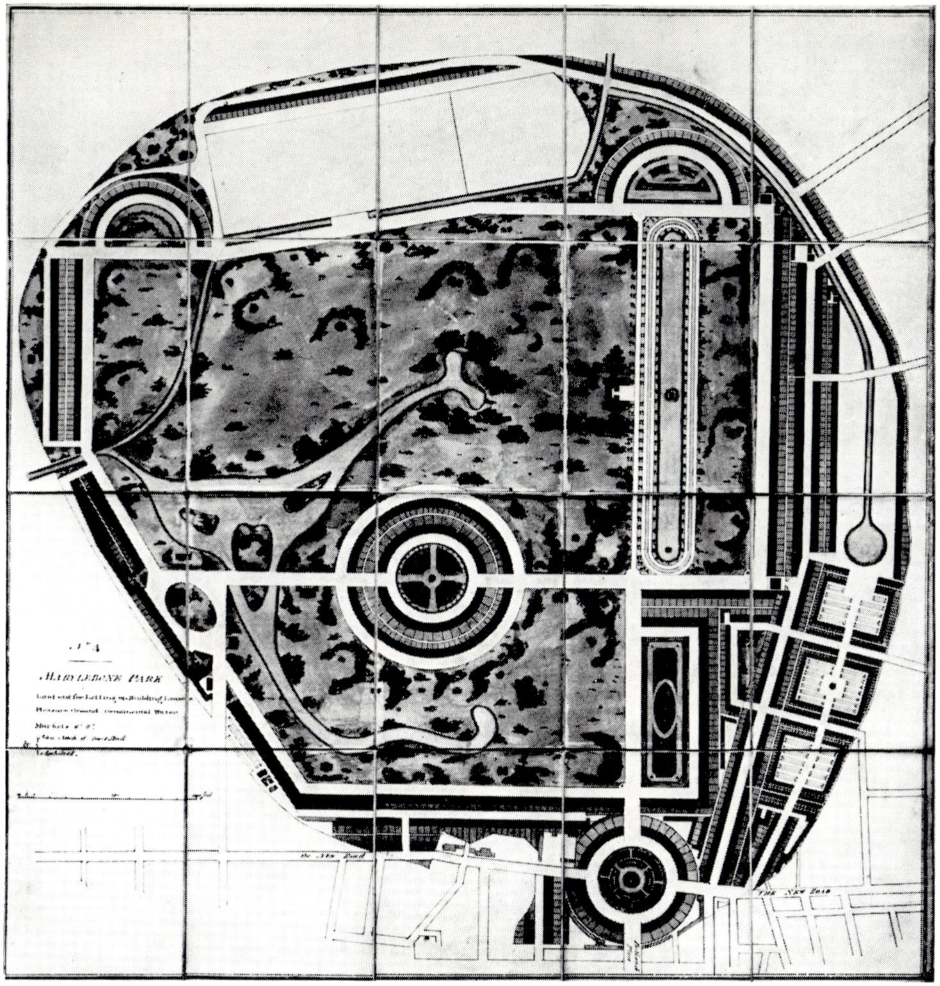

57a **Original plan for Regent's Park, 1812, by John Nash.** The circle and the straight line are interlocked with the artificially made 'natural' landscape. (The rectangles made by the map fold lines are approximately twice one rectangle of Motopia.)

57b **Regent's Park.** The idealized landscape is set within the framework of the surrounding terraces, which may be distantly seen. The buildings within the landscape are themselves very special and related in scale to the individual tree.

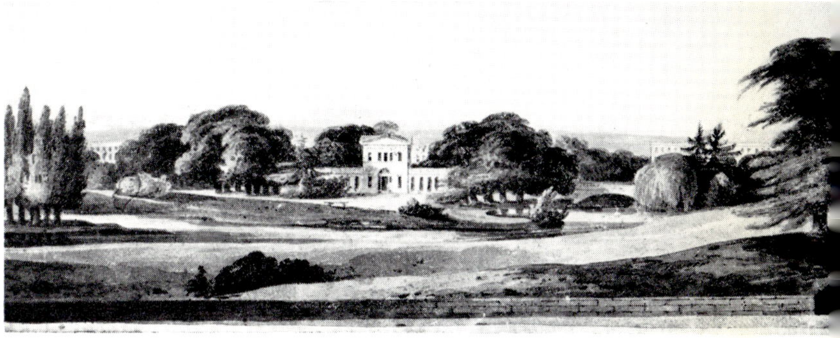

56 **Aerial View of Regent's Park and environment.** The great scheme, in the early nineteenth century, of Regent Street and Regent's Park, by John Nash, was an endeavour to bring the ◀ English landscape park into the urban scene. The contrast with the adjoining eighteenth-century gridiron pattern is very marked, and the intermediate stage of experiment was clearly the terraces of Bath (Pl. 54).

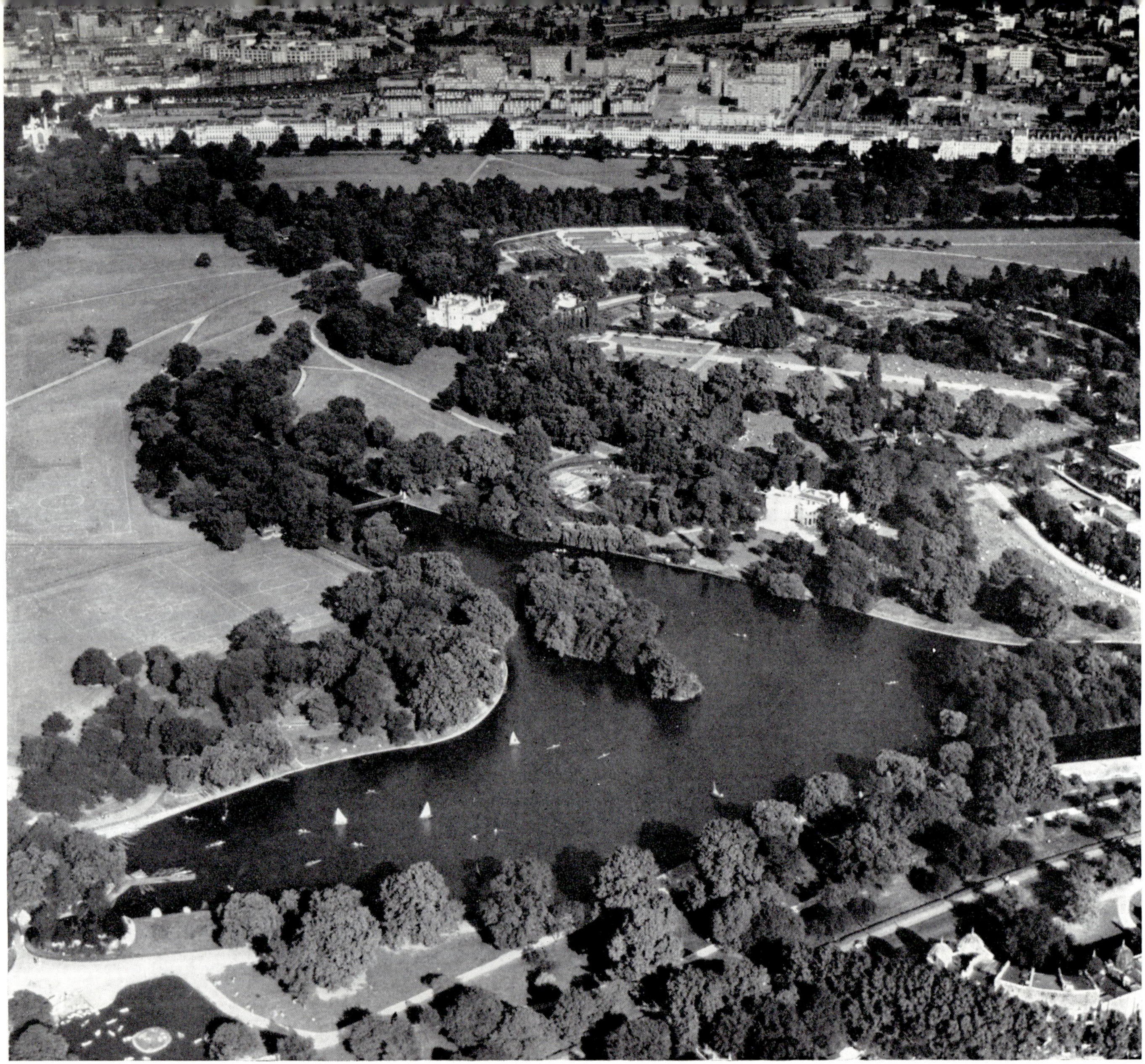

58 **Regent's Park: air view.** The scale of the park is so great that in summer the surrounding frame is often invisible. The intention is to give illusion of space.

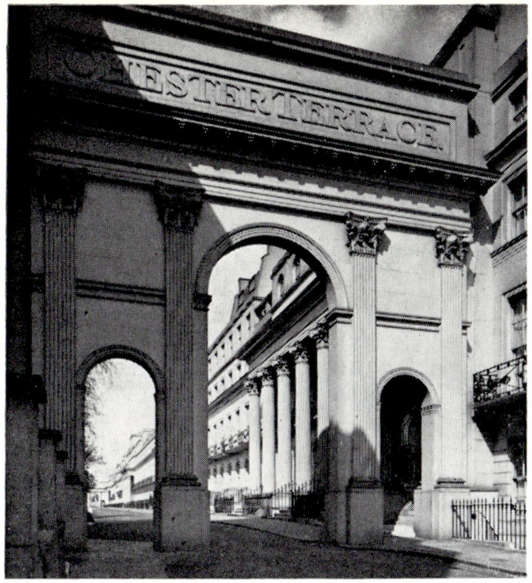

59b **Chester Terrace, Regent's Park.** Great care has been taken to model the facades in three dimensions, in order to avoid monotony.

59a **Chester Terrace, Regent's Park.** The terraces are related in height to groups or lines of trees and are very formal.

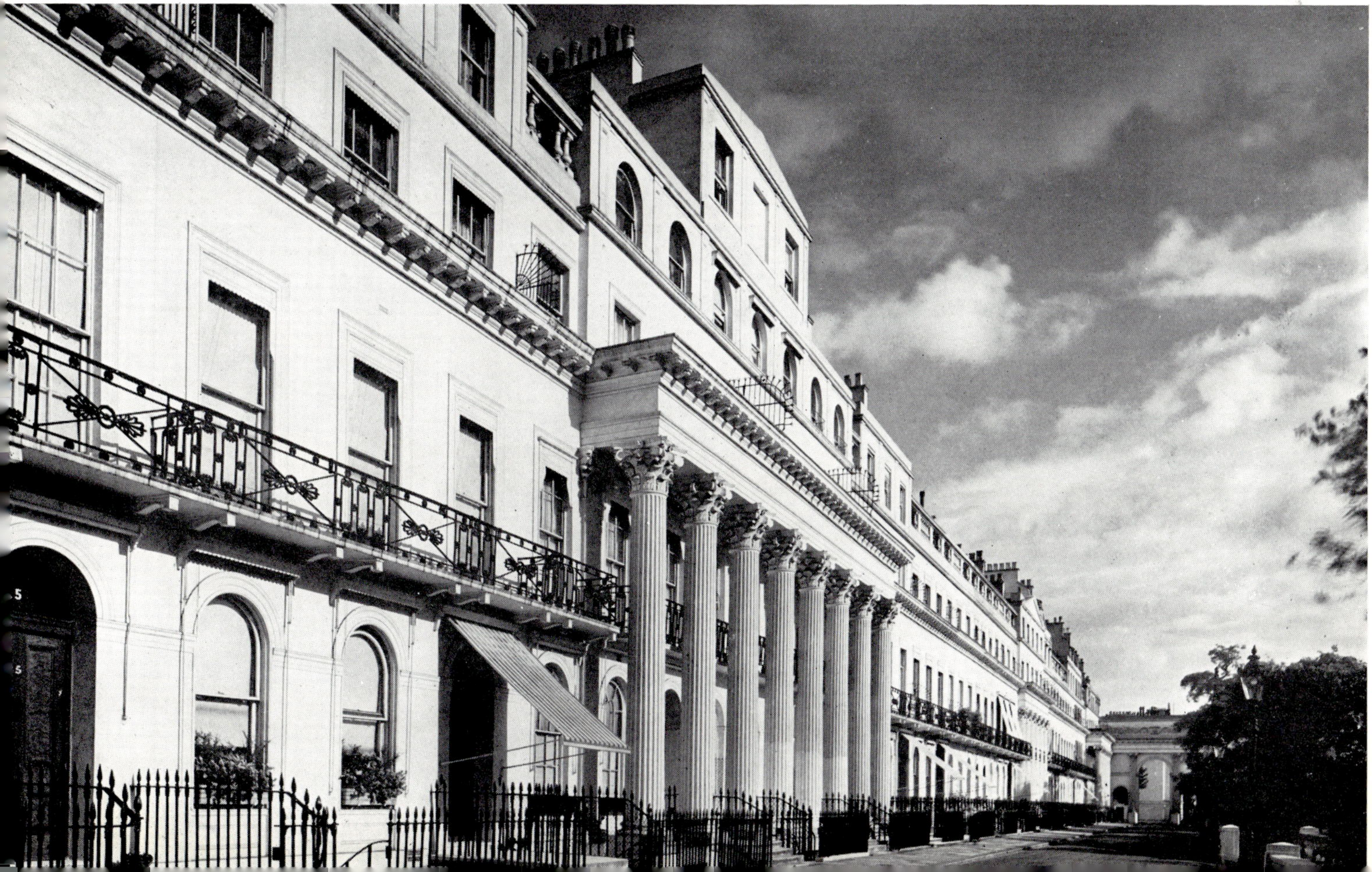

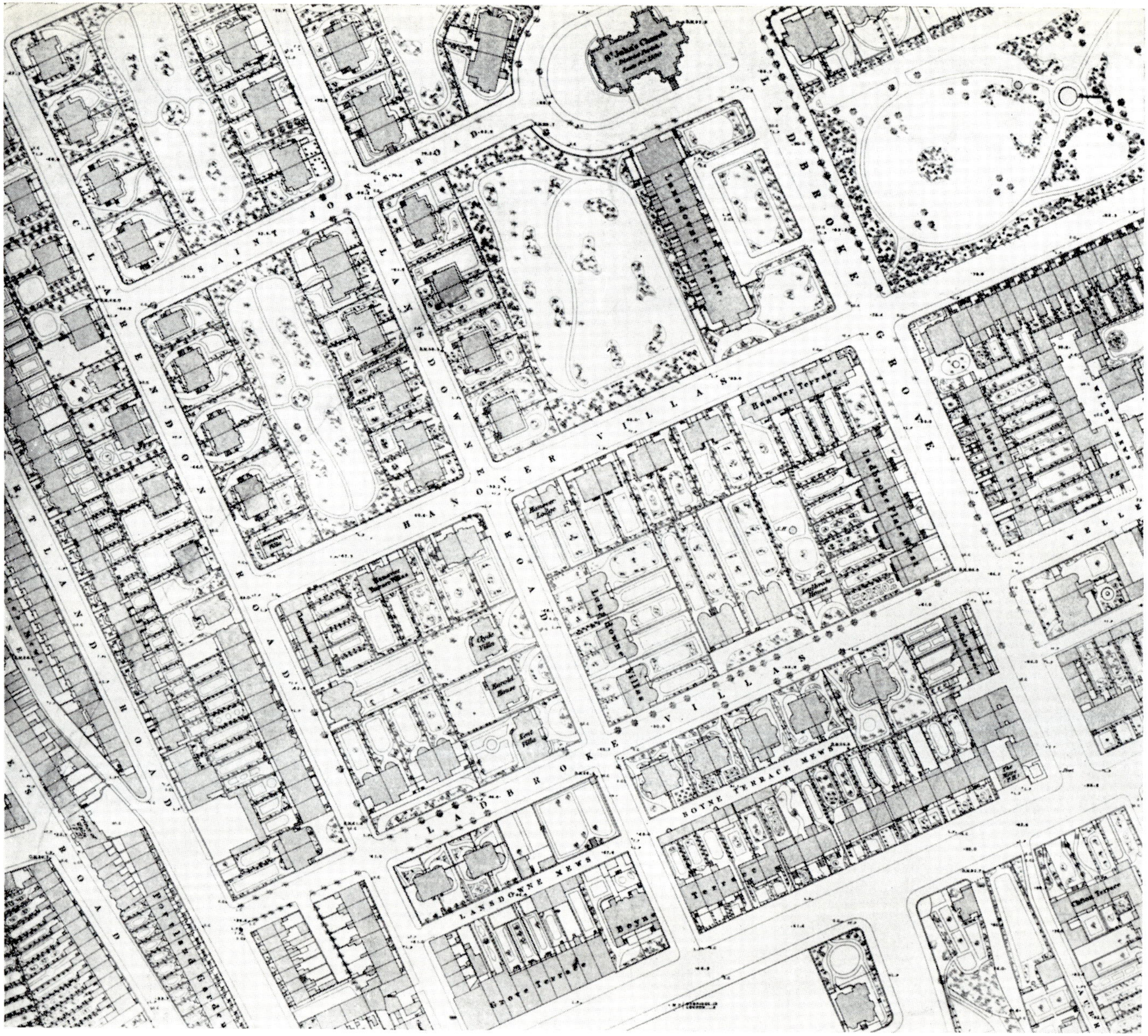

60 **Holland Park.** Although Regent's Park was the climax in England of comprehensive planning on a grand scale, the impulse for urban landscape planning continued with many excellent smaller schemes, such as that at Holland Park. The space design indicates that the backs of houses can be as seemly as the fronts.

61 **Holland Park: View across communal garden.** The individual gardens are small, and the communal landscape strip between the backs is a delightful addition to the urban scene. ▶

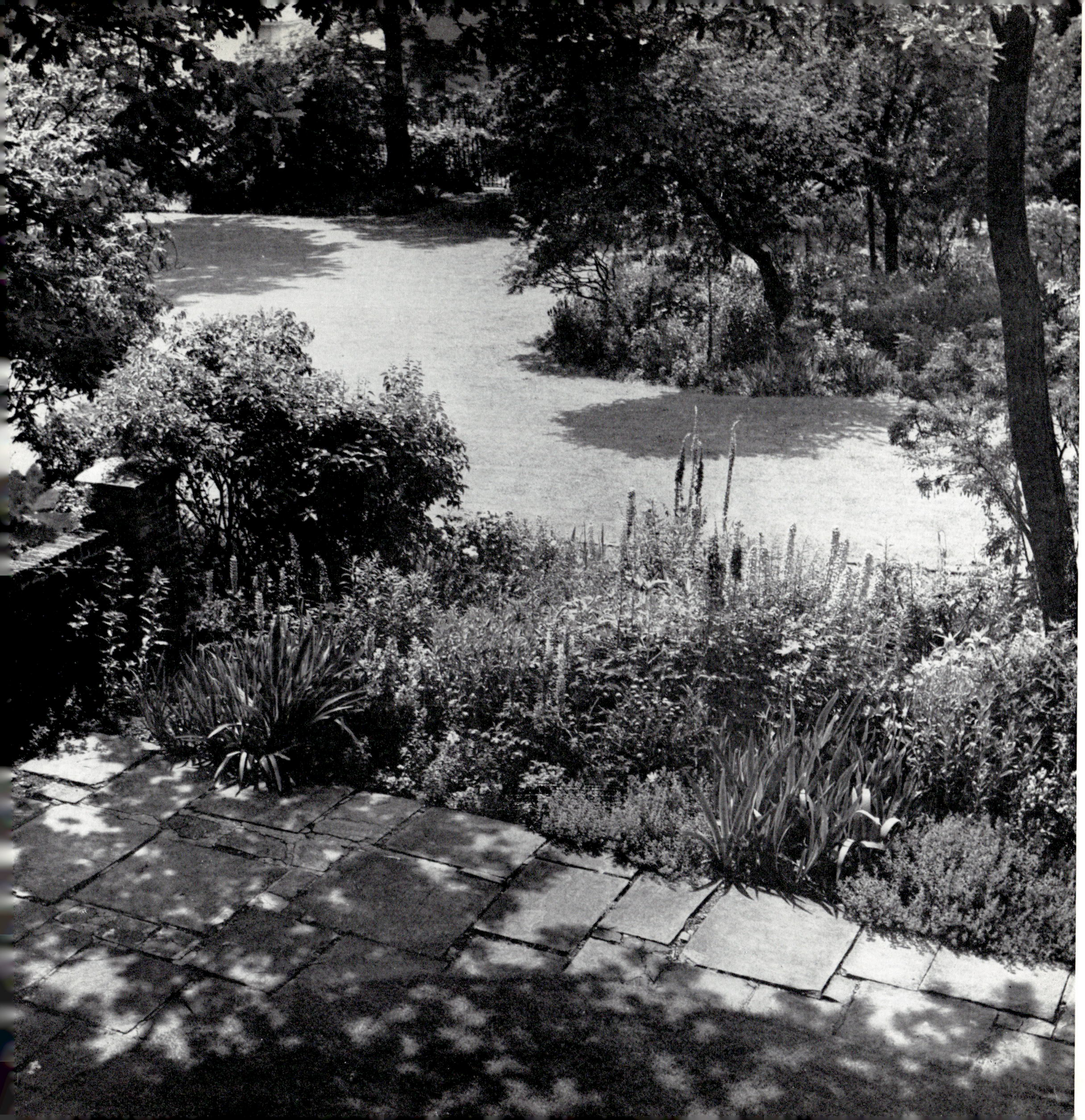

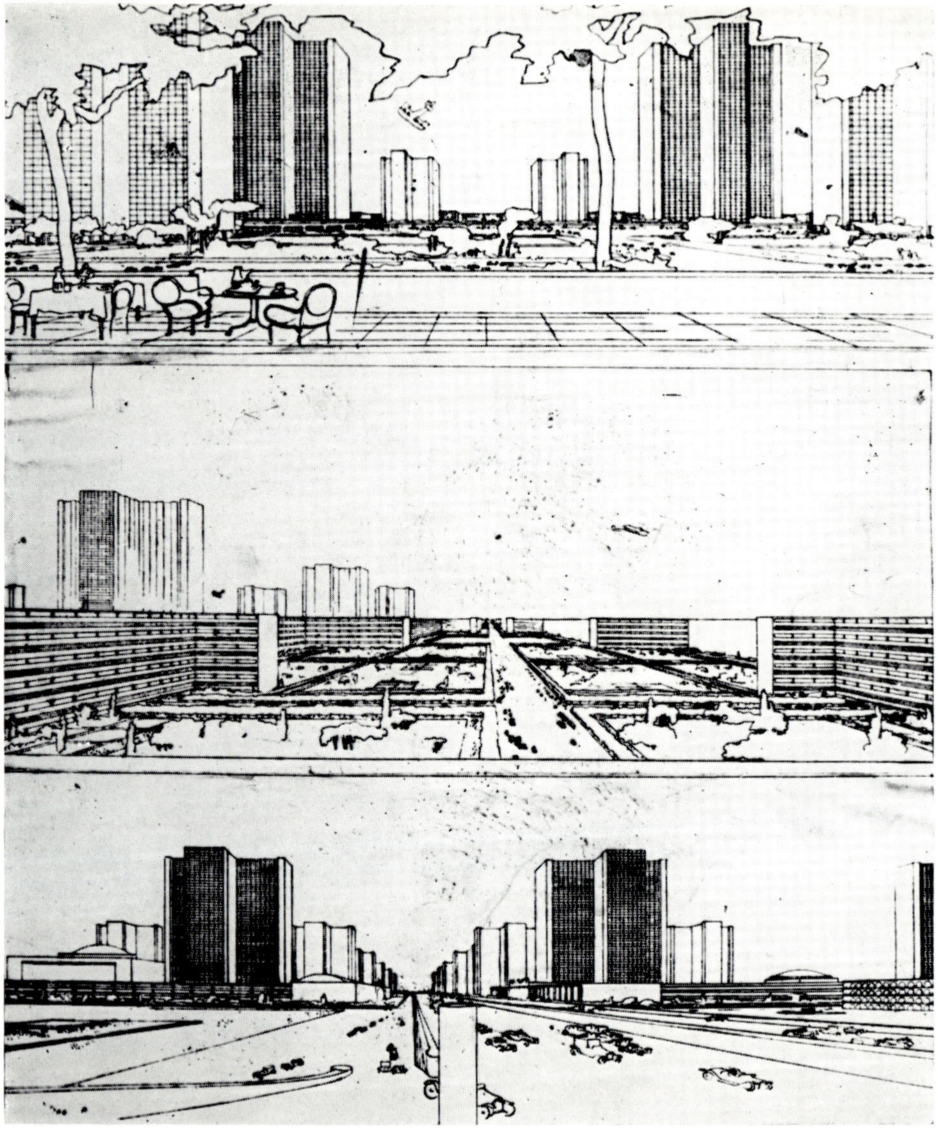

62 **The Vertical City, by Le Corbusier.** The nineteenth-century urban dwelling degenerated into the Victorian terrace or the slum. In contrast the twentieth century began with the garden city movement. A new outlook on urban design was given by the works of Le Corbusier, who approached the problem as a scientist and an artist.

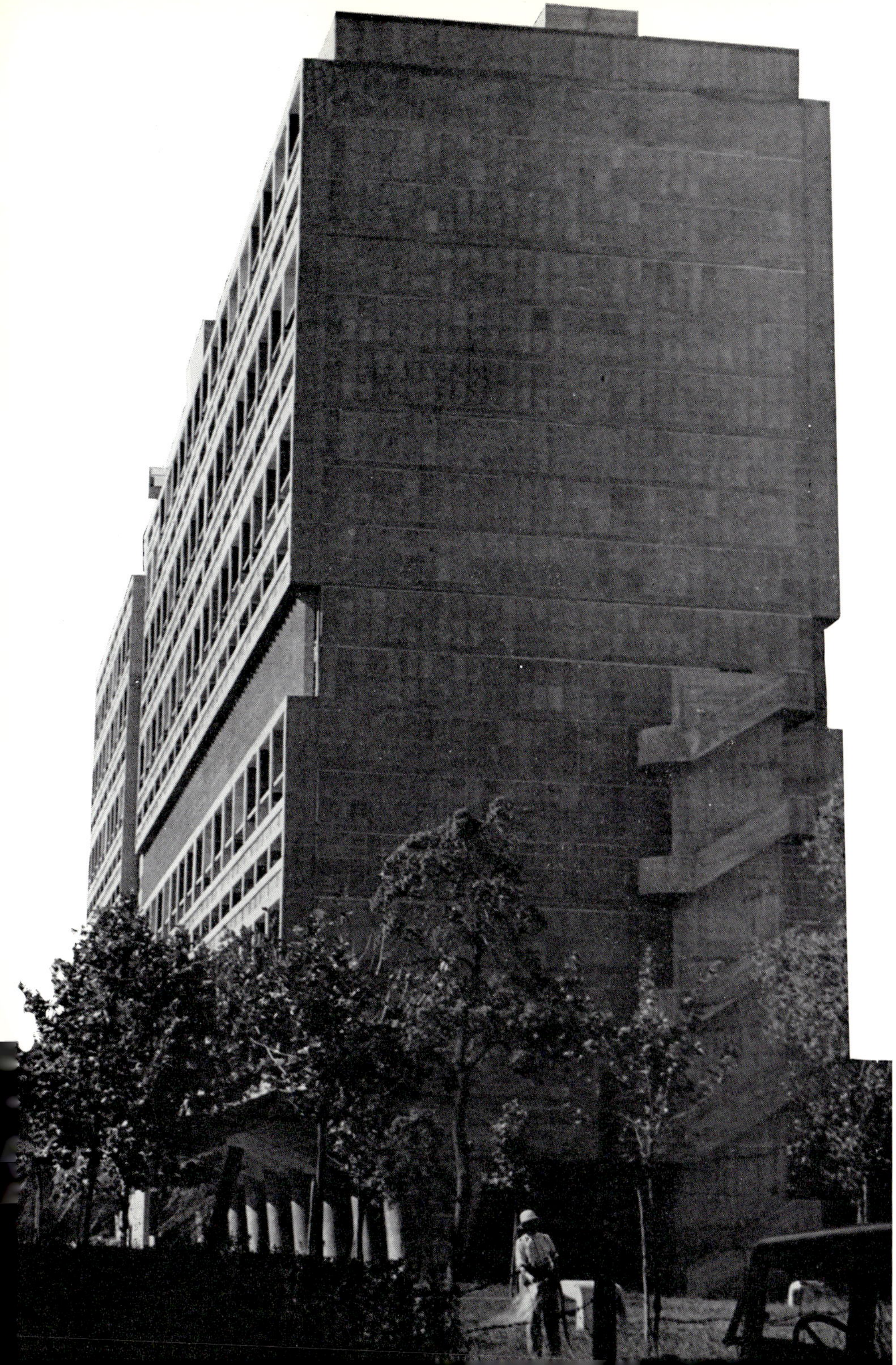

63 **Unité d'Habitation, Marseilles, by Le Corbusier.** Le Corbusier accepted the challenge of the modern age, but it may be that his great and uncompromising works do not answer the problem of the individual.

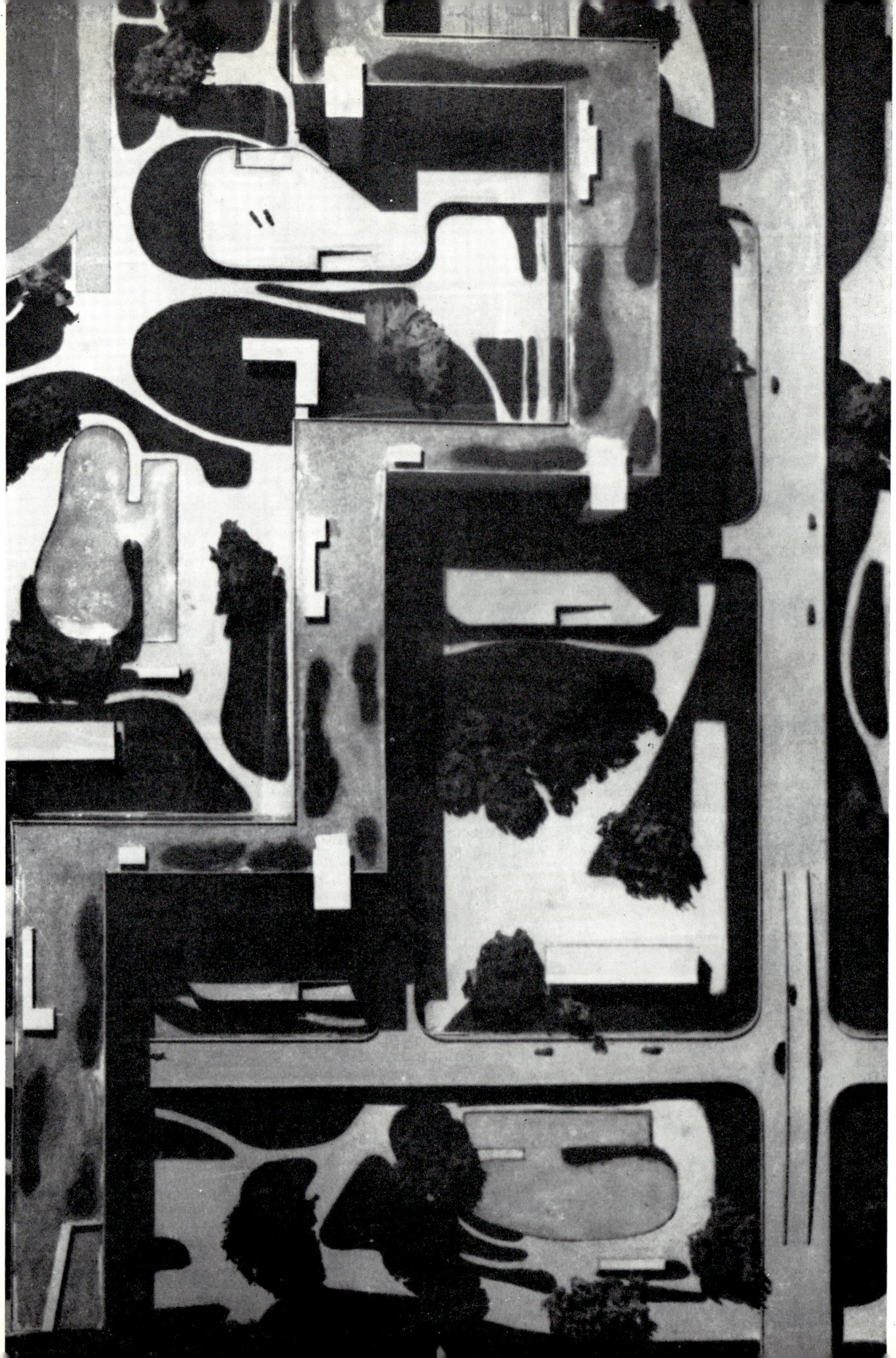

64 **The Vertical City by Le Corbusier, residential detail.** The geometrical terrace and roads interlock and stand upon a 'free' pedestrian landscape.

65 **The Vertical City, residential detail.** The terraces are so high that they dominate the tree and the ground pattern. The pattern of the roads, which are raised, is closely associated with that of the flat roofs, and an obvious development and simplification is a combination of these two elements.

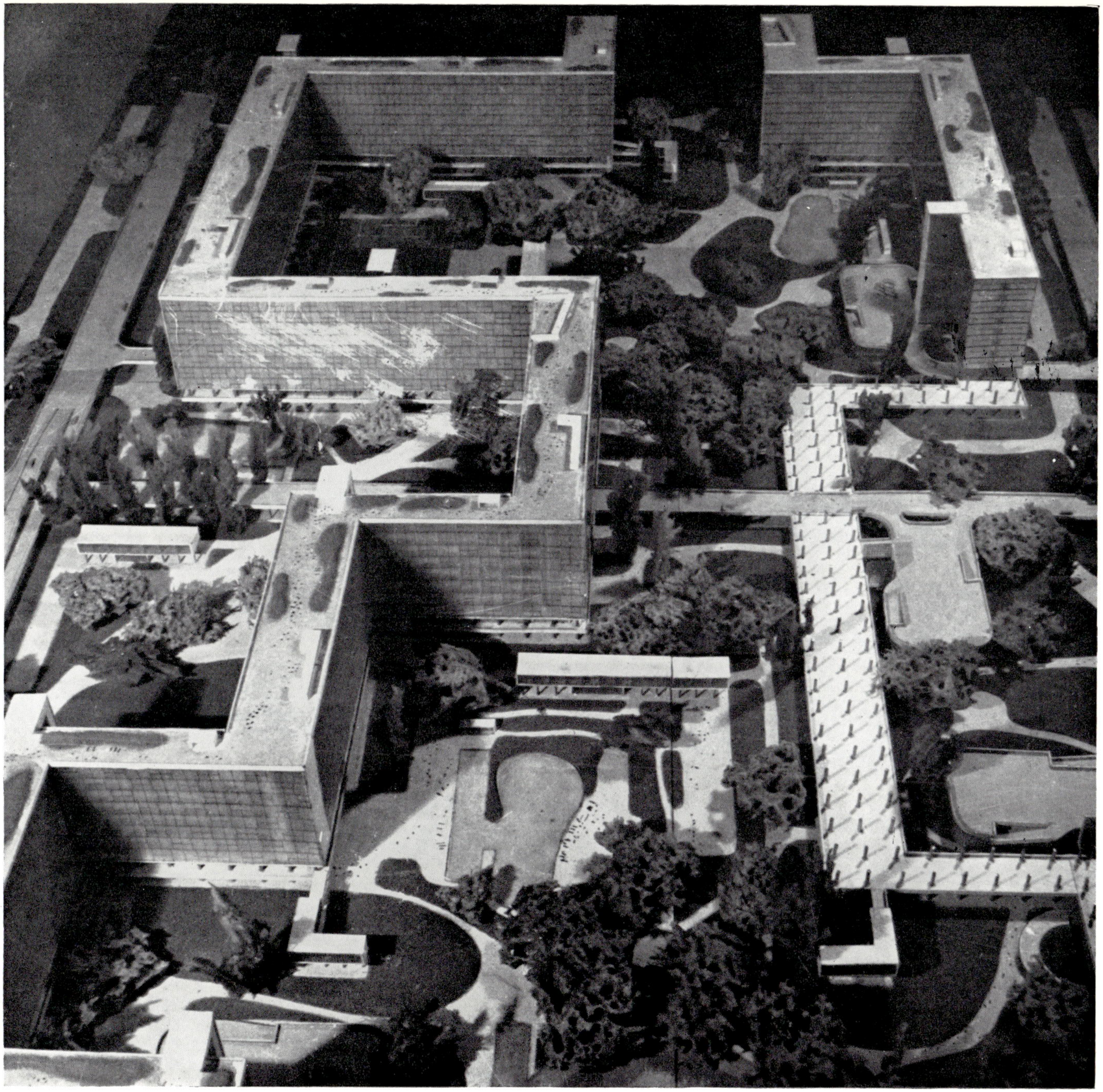

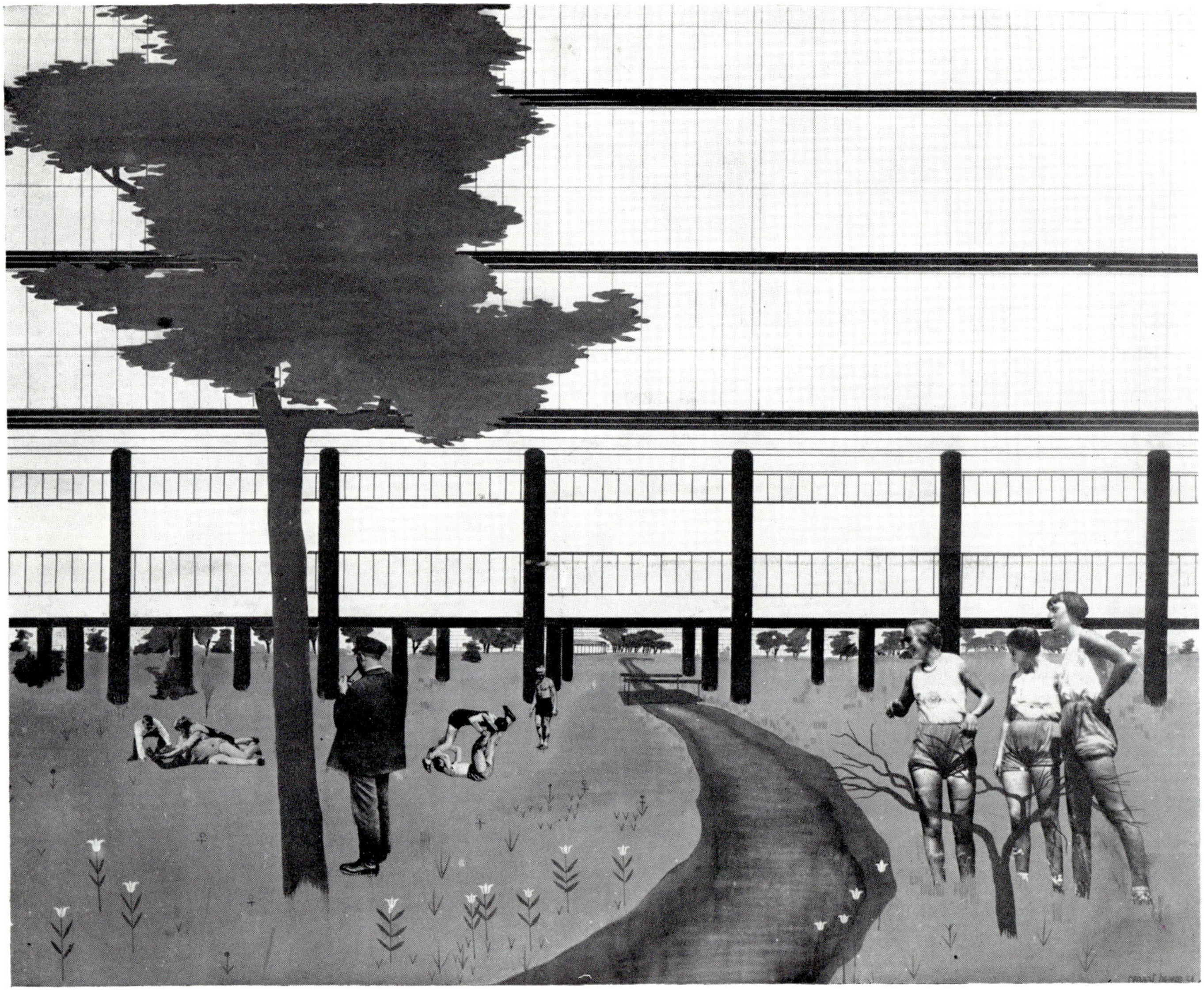

66 **Terrace and Landscape: from the office of Le Corbusier.** Although this is manifestly impracticable, the sketch shows clearly the idea of continuous landscape upon which Motopia came to be based.

THE TOWN CENTRE

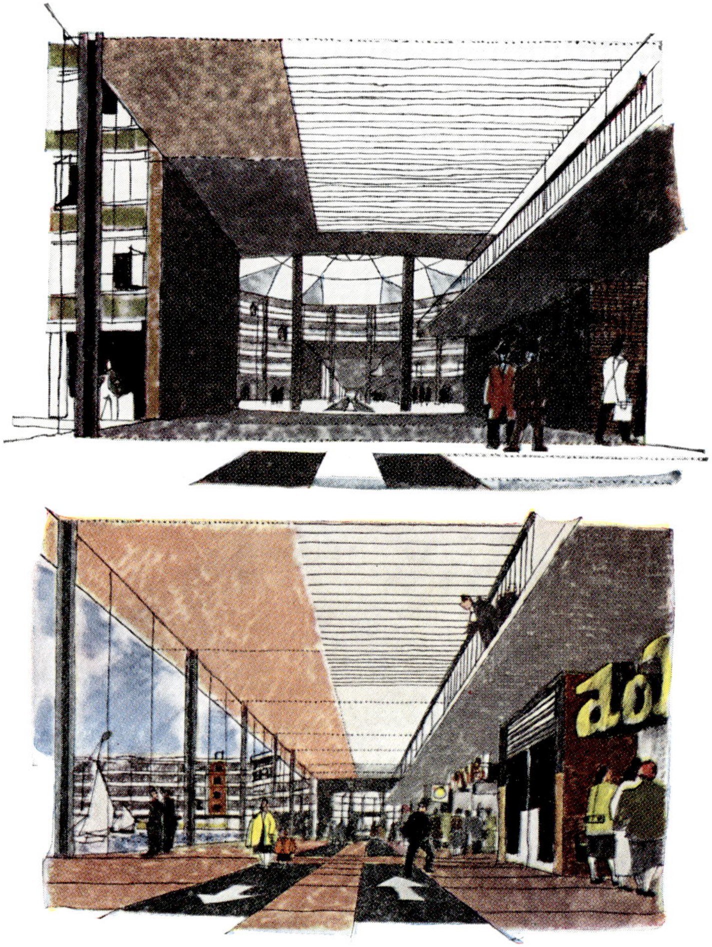

67 **The Stoa of Motopia**
Drawings by Gordon Cullen

For a housewife the natural and most insistent social centre of a modern town is the local shop, the pavement, the bus queue, or any place where she may run into her neighbour without pre-arrangement. After this there are innumerable individual places of congregation and entertainment, but unlike the historic city, there is no public place where all the citizens can intermingle *all* the time (if they so wish) for business and idleness. The reason for this is partly the shape of our towns, partly climate, and partly our use of leisure. It is interesting to compare modern man with a citizen of ancient Athens. In the morning the Athenian would rise, wash and breakfast, all in the space of a few minutes. His work and his domestic life were wholly subsidiary to his presence in the Agora, and with his day's work complete, he was ready for this by the early afternoon. His search for interest and learning inevitably led him from his home to sharpen his wits in discussion. The long colonnades of the Agora contained shops, but their purpose was really purely social. As the home grew in importance, so the public squares became less so; and in such a town as Pompeii, for example, we see a fairer balance between the values of home and community. This balance is maintained through the medieval cities of Western civilization, whose size still allowed a central place of congregation within easy walking distance of any part. In England particularly, however, the climate has been against the idea of the Agora, and it was an event of the greatest magnitude when the Crystal Palace was opened in 1851. Here was an attempt to create artificially the climatic conditions of the Mediterranean, even to the inclusion of full-grown trees under the great glass covering. It was a gigantic social centre. The covered street or arcade developed rapidly throughout northern Europe, and gave rise eventually to the underground ways in many great cities and especially in New York. An eminent scientist, Dr Bernal, has already foretold the time when whole cities will be air-conditioned under one vast shell of glass.

The shape of the Stoa of Motopia is similar to that of the Stoa at Athens; that is to say, it is linear, with one side devoted to shops and the other looking westward over the town lakes and gardens. It is, however, totally enclosed and air-conditioned, and because of its size there is aid to the human feet in horizontal moving bands, and in 'paternoster' lifts to the car parks on the roofs.

68 **The Stoa of Attalos, Athens.** The Stoa has recently been reconstructed, and although the materials are new and unweathered, it is now possible to visualize this noble centre in relation to the adjoining Acropolis. The Stoa is broad, with shops on one side, and was a dignified setting for casual conversation and discussion.

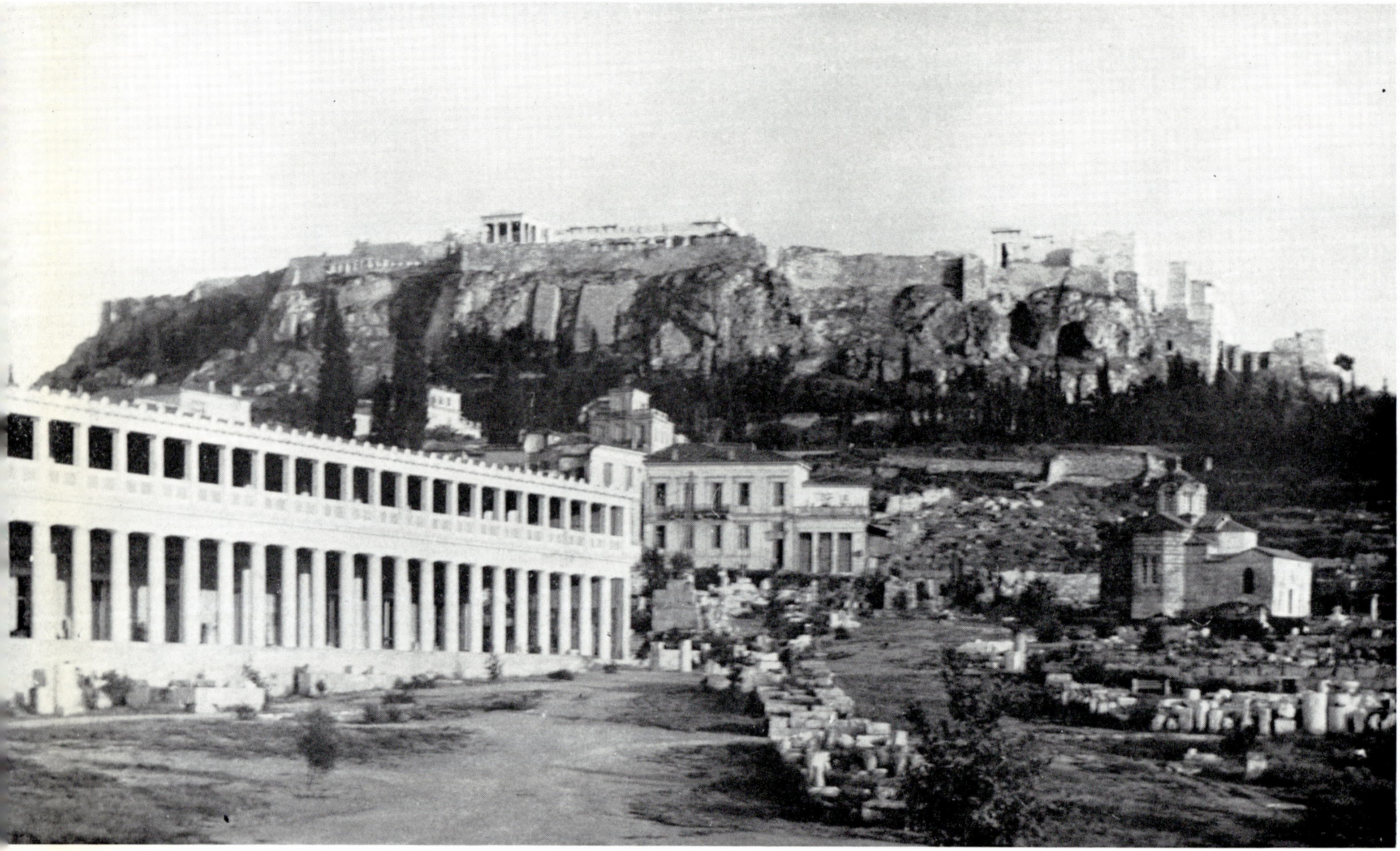

69 **The Forum, Pompeii.** This Greco-Roman forum is the best preserved example of the social centre of antiquity. It is embedded in the city and is composed of the long and splendid classical arcades peculiarly suited to the climate. ▶

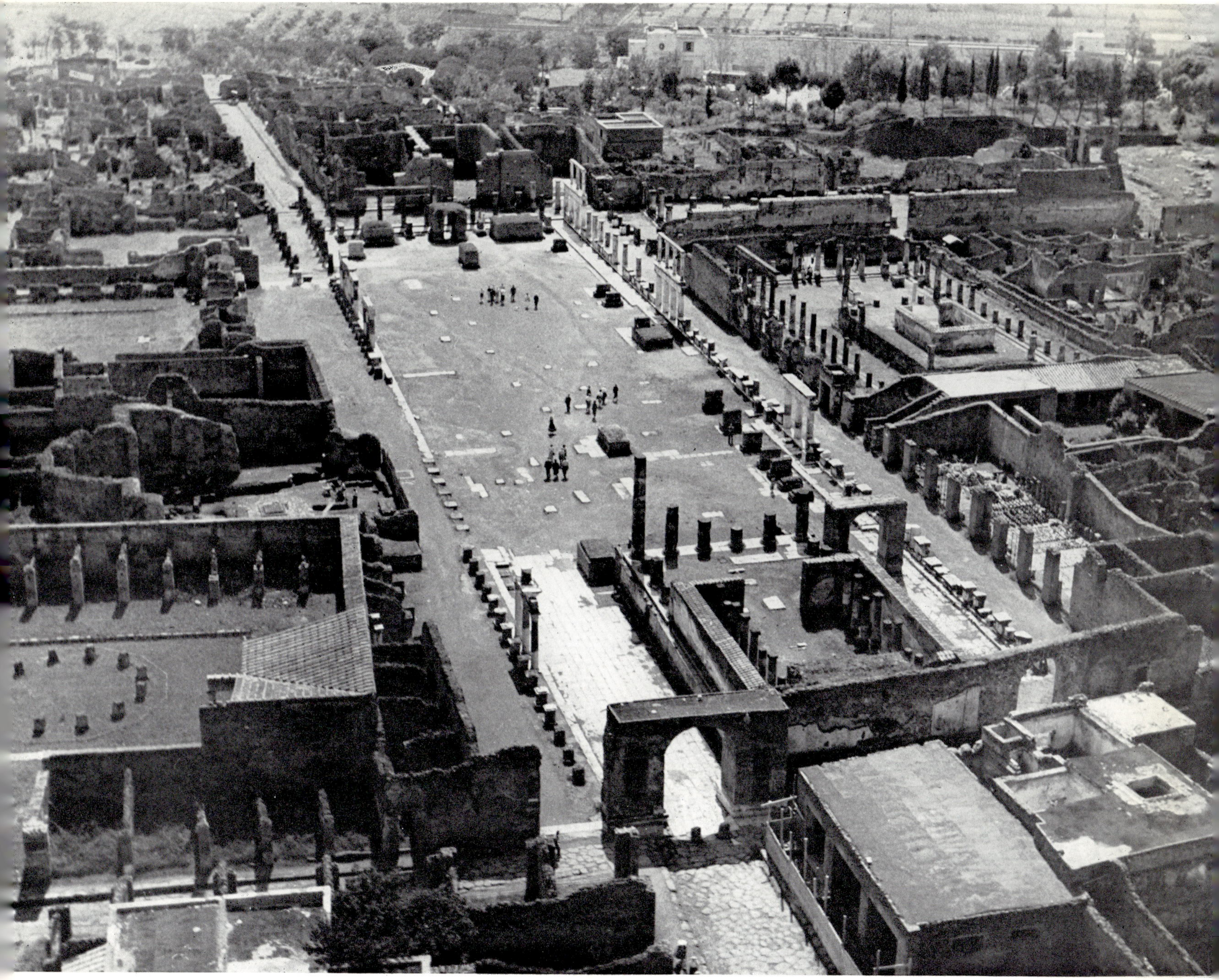

70 **The Binnenhof, The Hague.** A medieval conception of the market square as a precinct before the west doors of the cathedral. The citizen is exposed to the weather without much consideration for personal comfort.

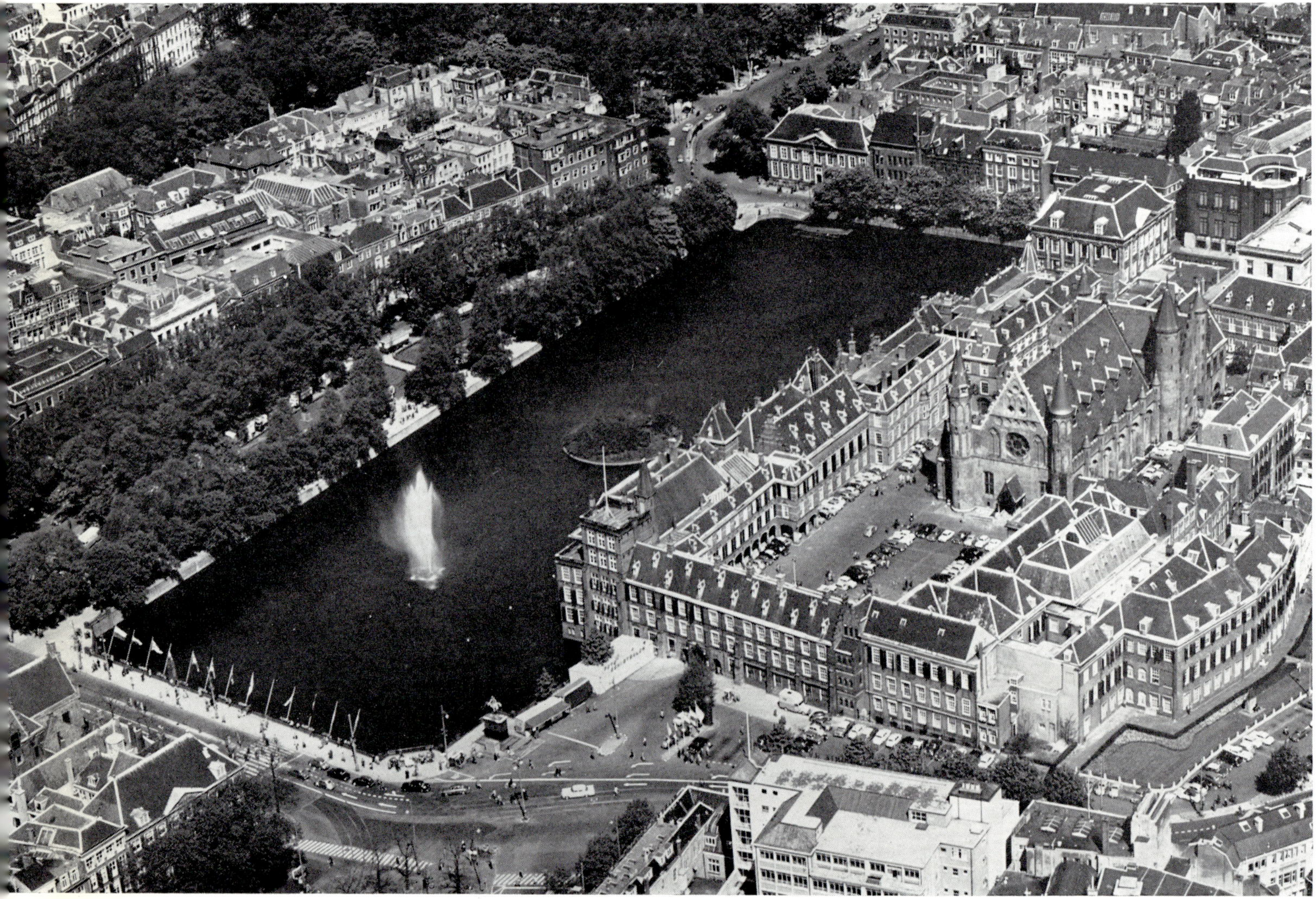

71 St. Mark's Square, Venice. This most famous of all city centres has retained its character over centuries of change of style in building. It proves that a good original idea can remain constant and inspiring even when its external appearance is liable to change.

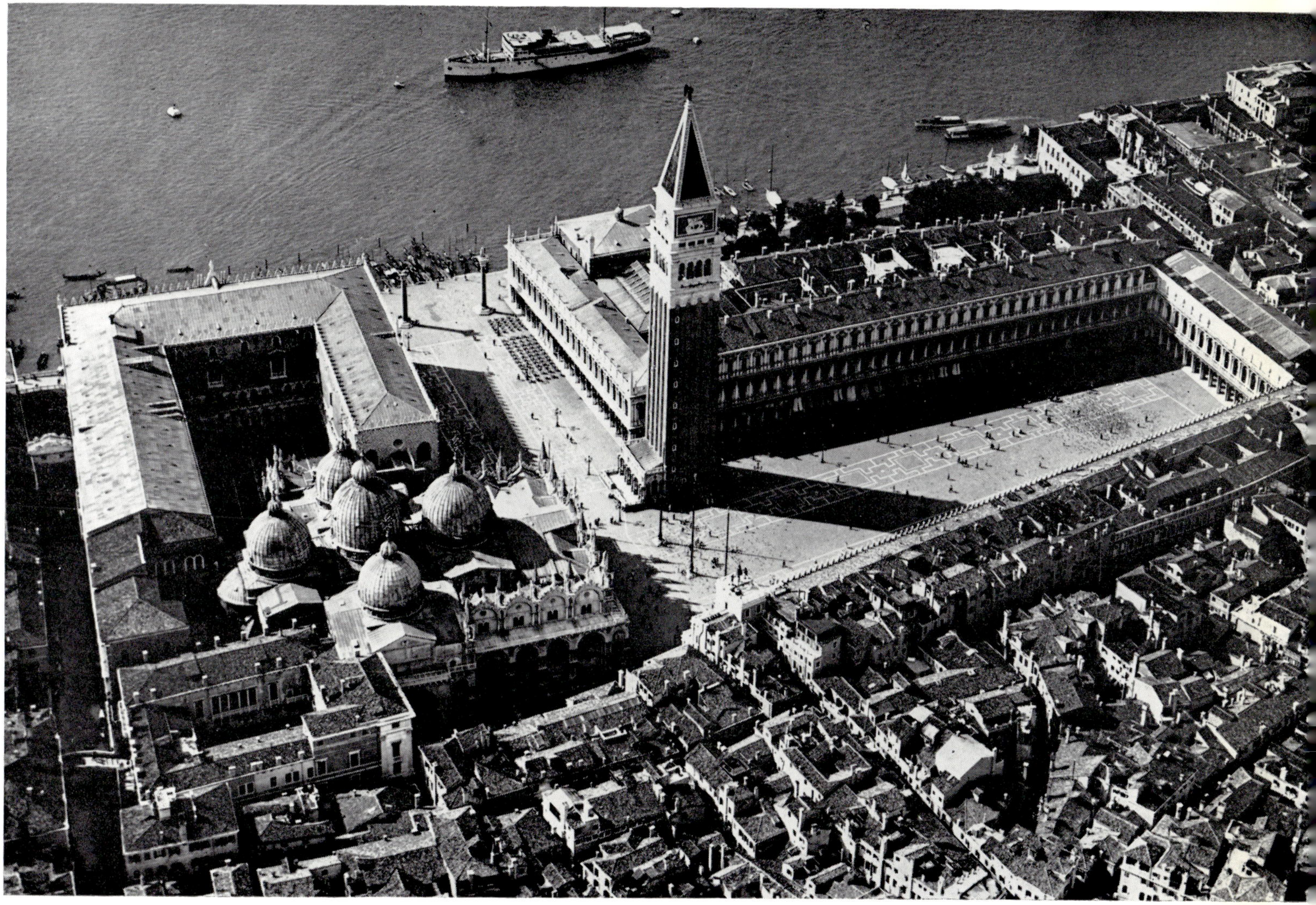

72 **Covent Garden, London (from a print of 1720).** The medieval market place has been formalized. The colonnades of antiquity are re-introduced in the arcade, suggestive of the rise in importance of the individual.

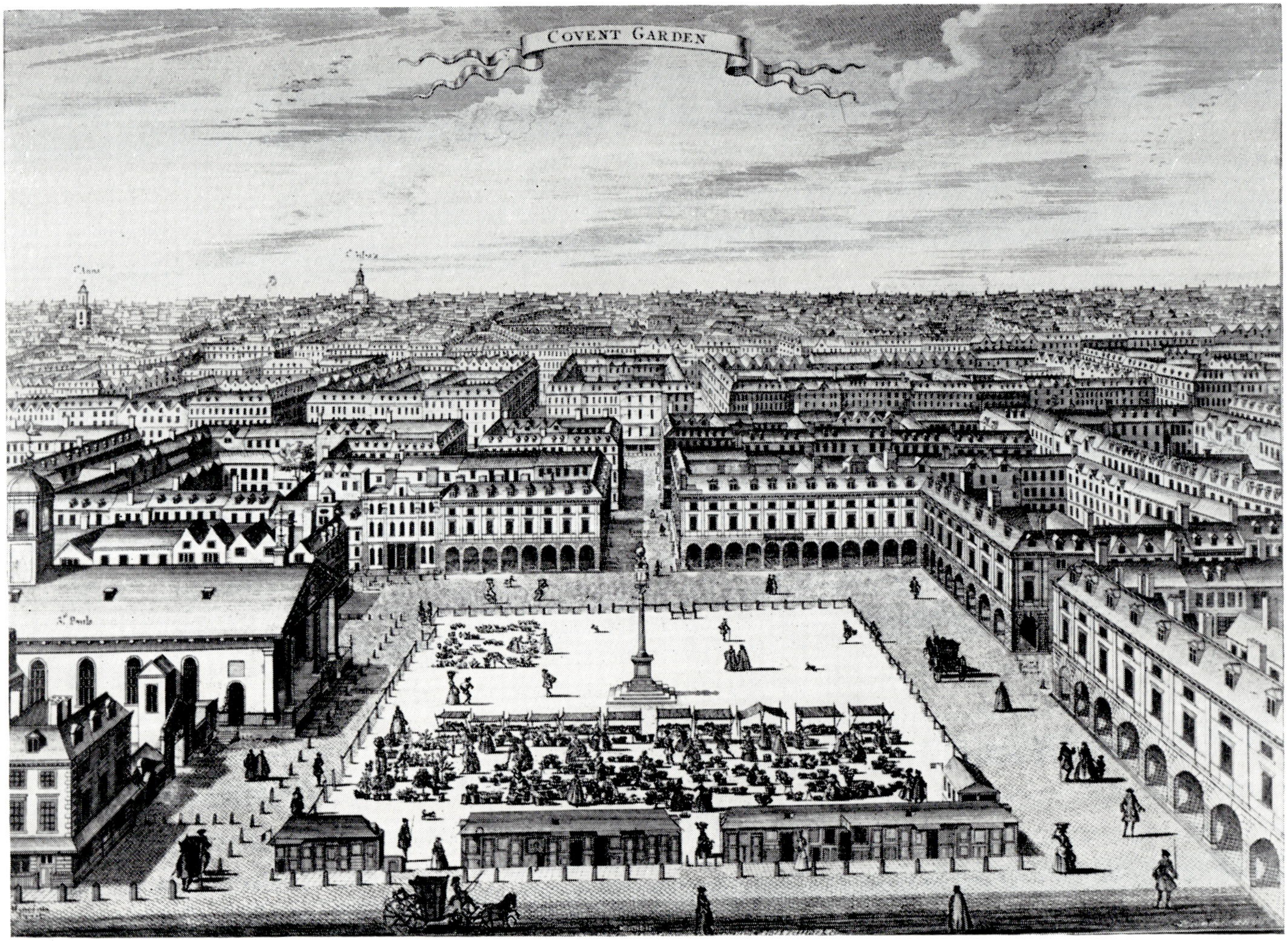

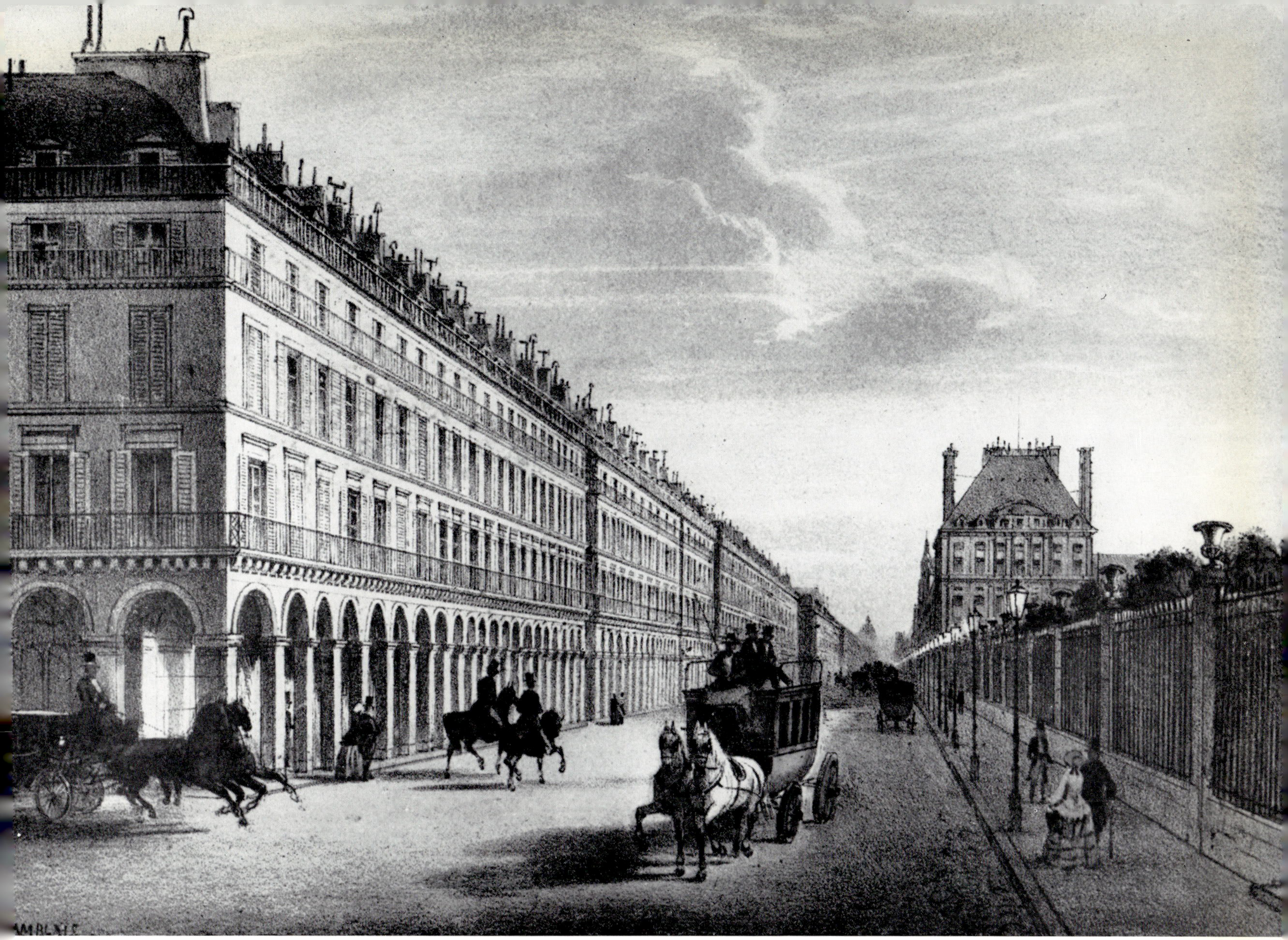

73 **The Rue de Rivoli, Paris.** The most famous of all one-sided shopping streets, now adapted to contain such large stores as *Les Magasins du Louvre.*

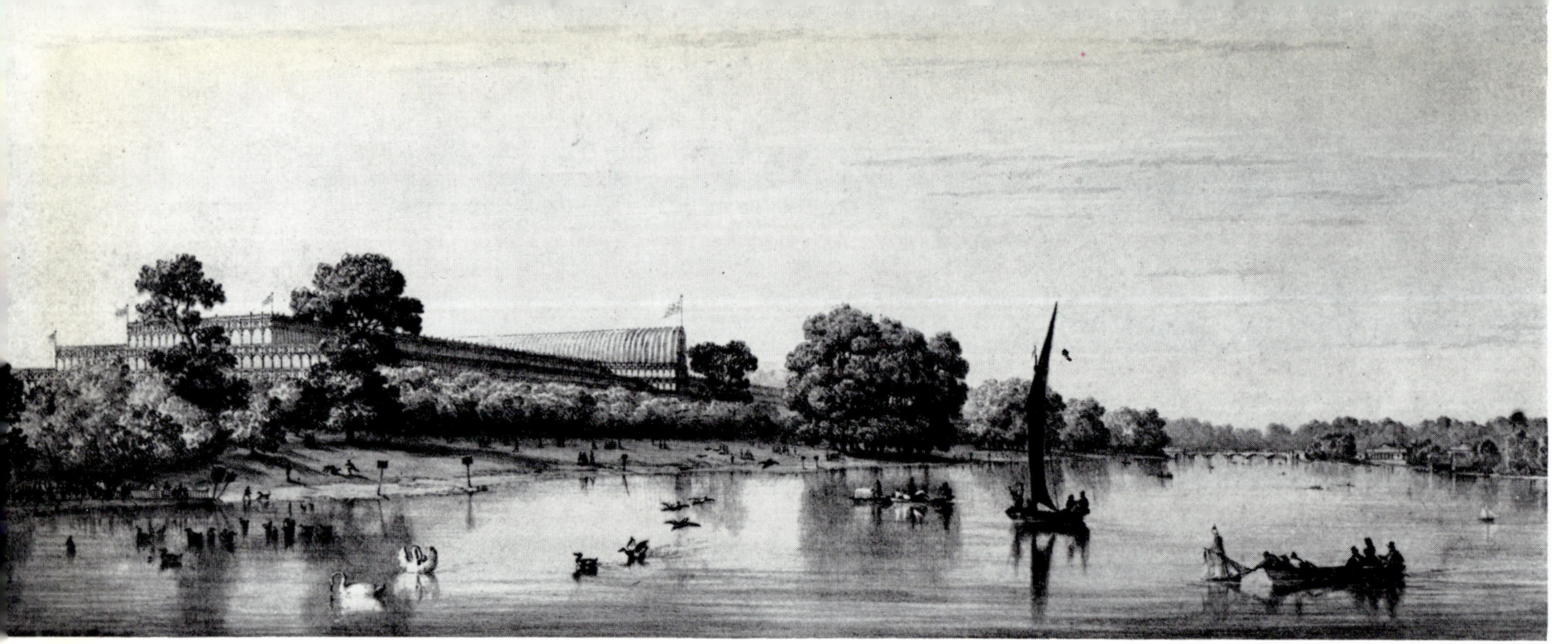

74a **The Crystal Palace, Hyde Park, 1851.** This exhibition building was designed like a vast plant house and settled in position to cover existing trees. It was later dismantled and rebuilt at Sydenham.

74b Ground plan showing the linear character of the exhibition. It was primarily a great social centre and it was the simplicity of idea that made it the most successful and remarkable venture of its kind.

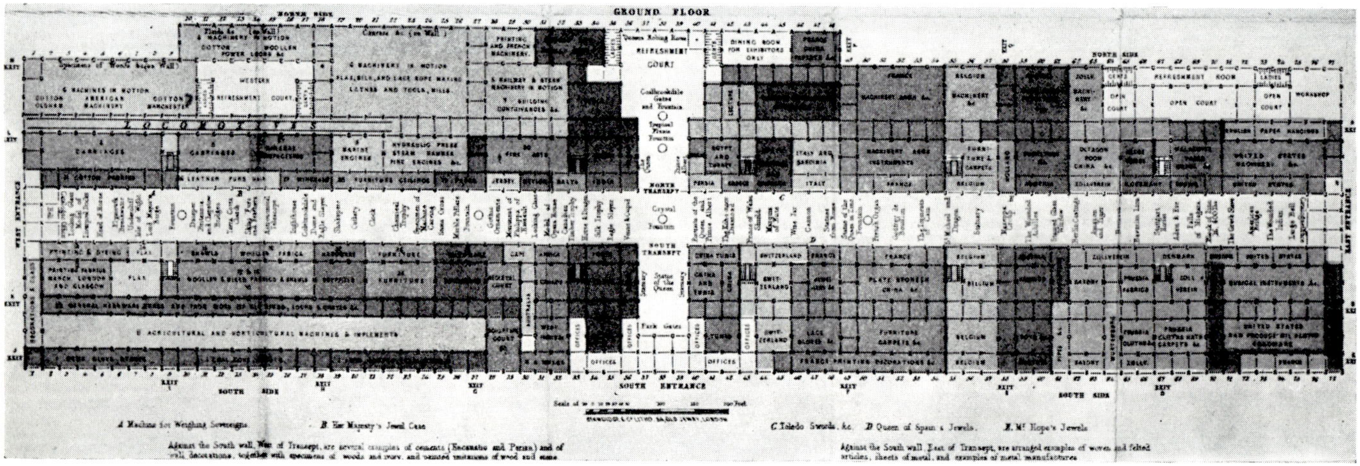

75 **The Crystal Palace, The Interior.** A revolution in the conception of the covered place of assembly, making use of modern techniques of construction. The designer, Sir Joseph Paxton (originally the head gardener at Chatsworth in Derbyshire) also planned a Great Victorian Way to girdle central London with a glass shopping arcade 11½ miles long and on varying internal levels.

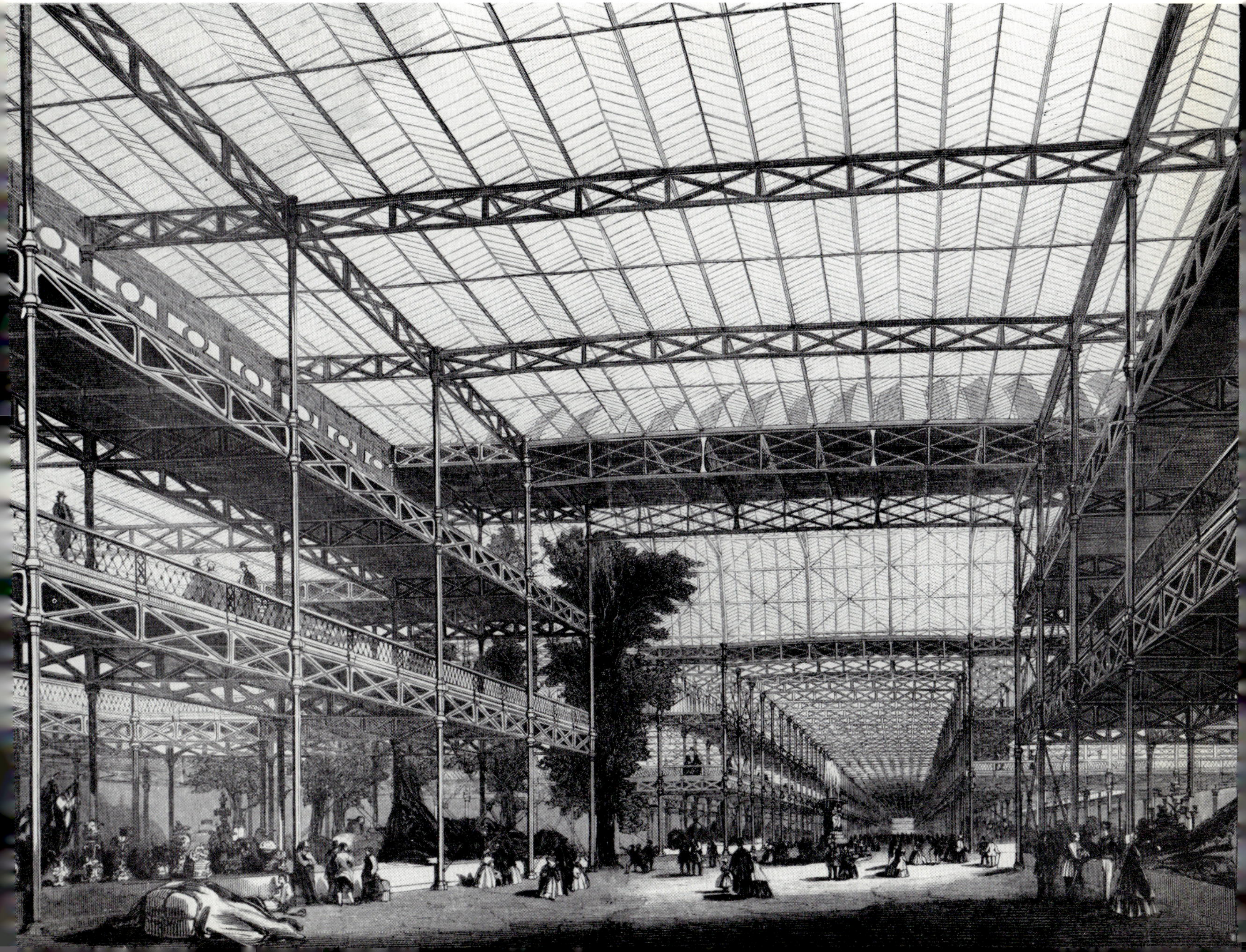

76 **The Galleria, Milan.** A nineteenth-century covered shopping mall, which is also a social centre.

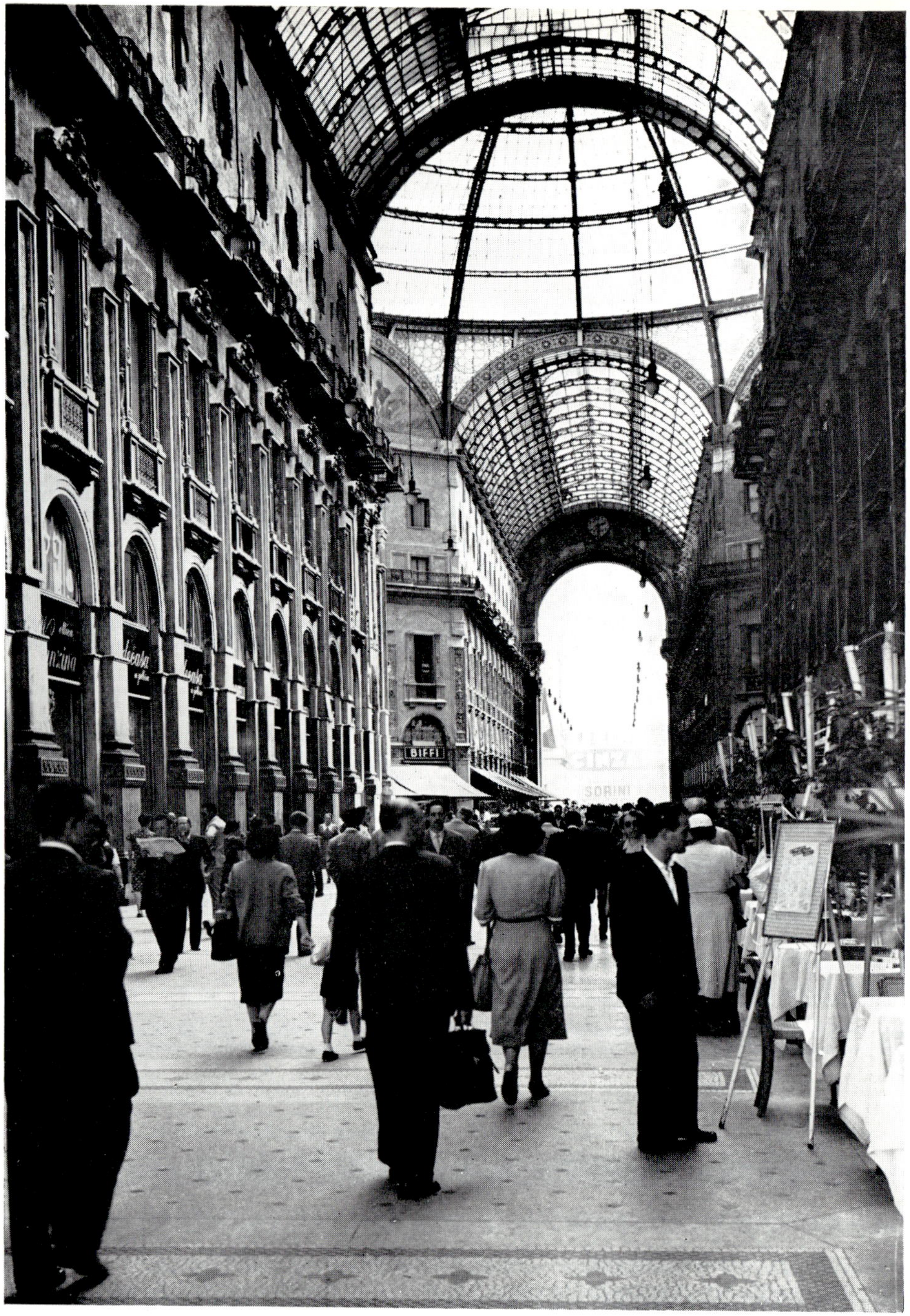

77 (OPPOSITE) **Museum of Fine Arts, Detroit.** Proposed addition by Minoru Yamasaki.

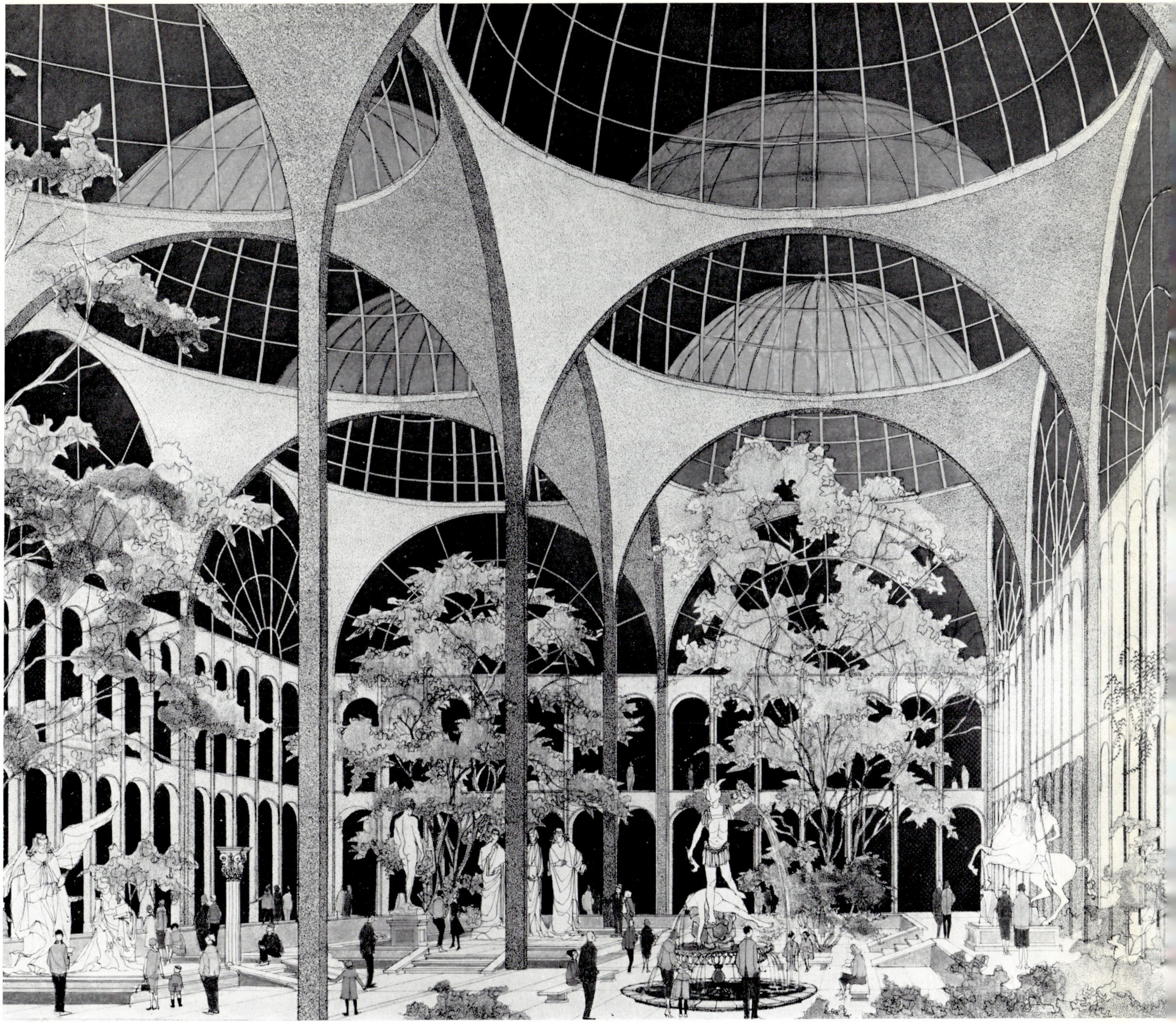

78 **The Rockefeller Centre, New York.** Although mainly devoted to office accommodation, the Centre is interesting for the theory of use of space during the first half of the twentieth century.

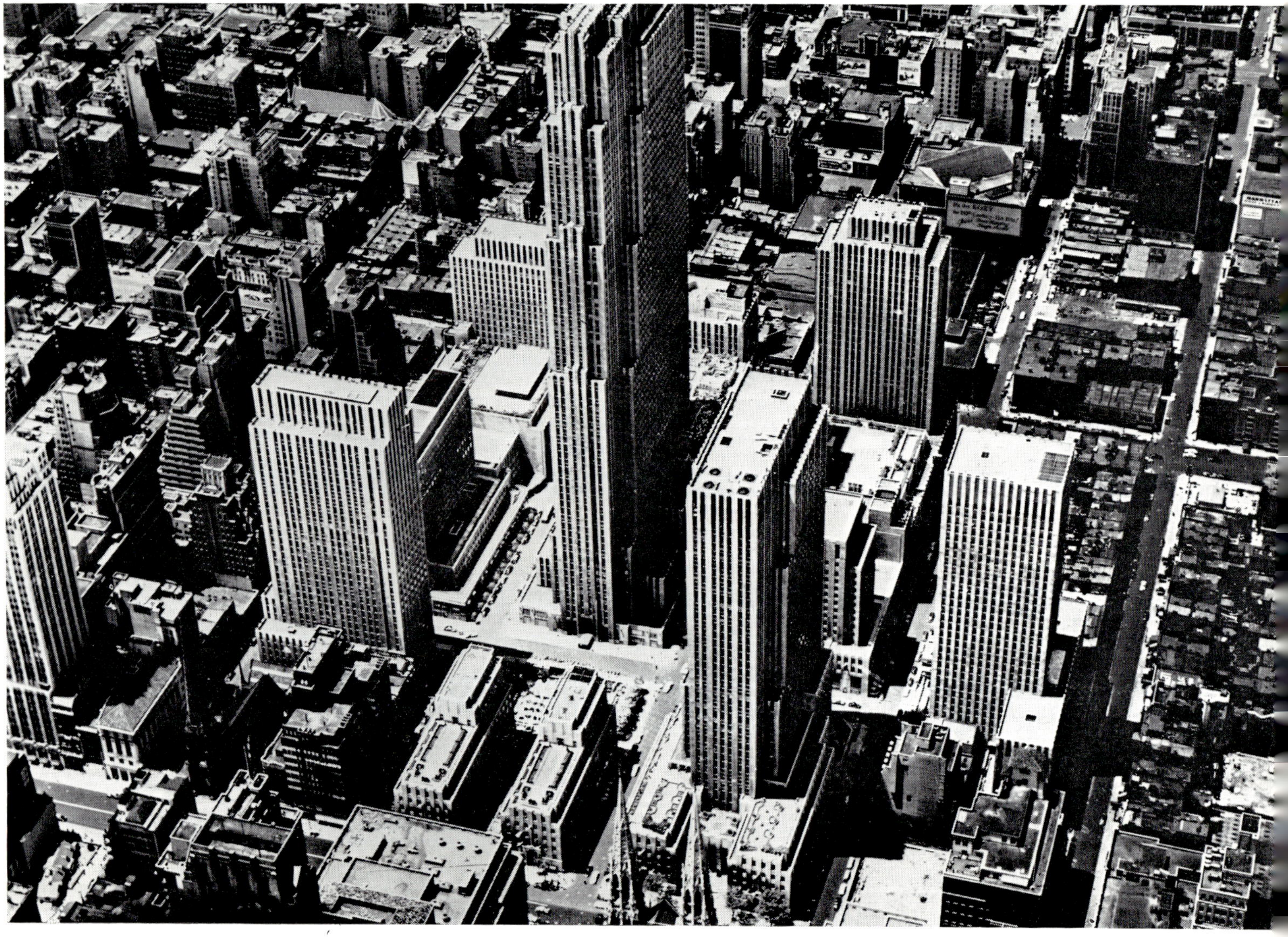

79 **The Rockefeller Centre, New York.** Corresponding to the great height above ground, are considerable ramifications (like roots) below ground. These subways are common in American cities, and provide considerable lengths of enclosed and warmed pedestrian shopping streets. ▶

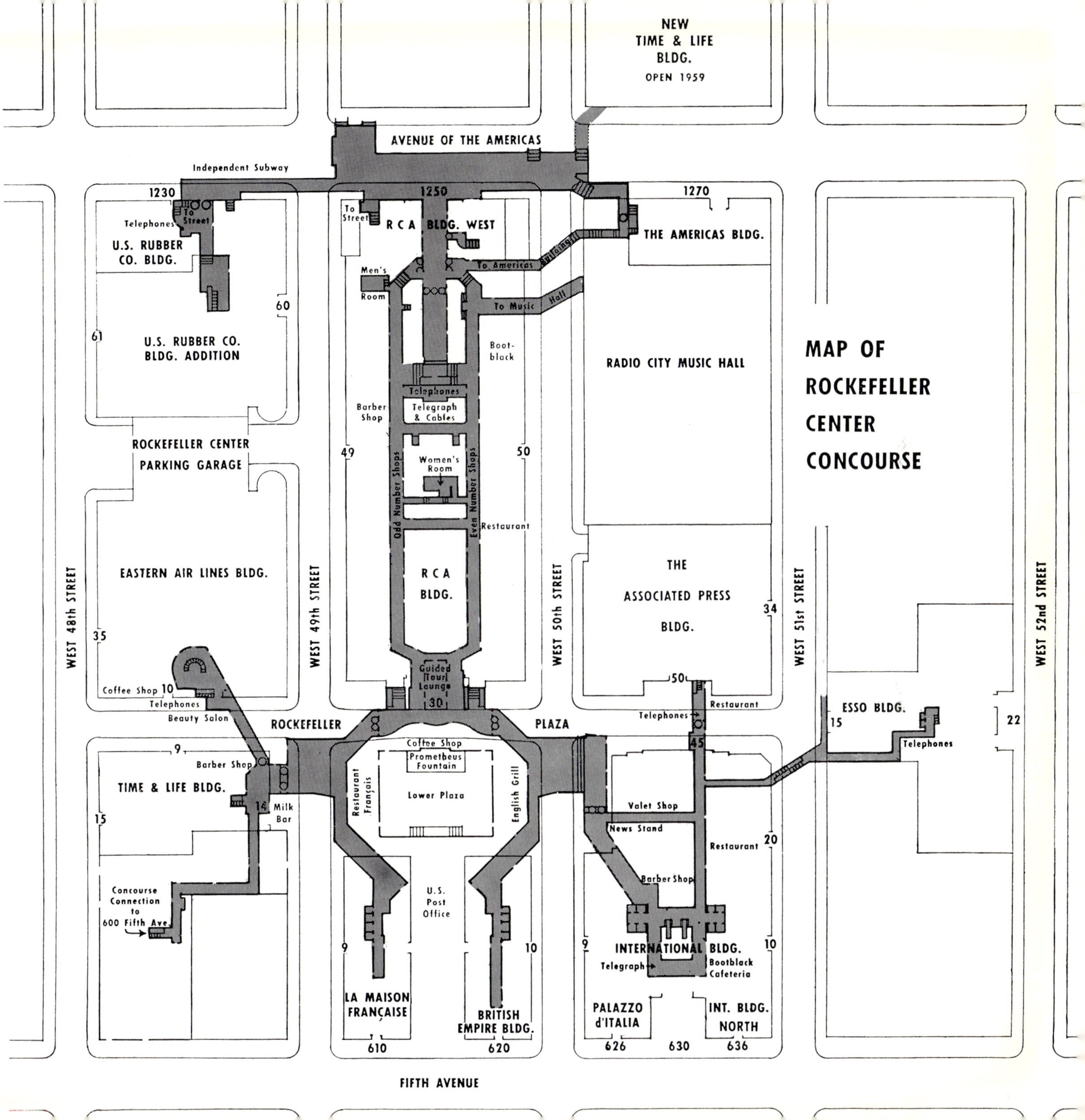
MAP OF ROCKEFELLER CENTER CONCOURSE
NEW TIME & LIFE BLDG. OPEN 1959
AVENUE OF THE AMERICAS
Independent Subway
1230
1250
1270
To Street
Telephones
U.S. RUBBER CO. BLDG.
R C A BLDG. WEST
THE AMERICAS BLDG.
Men's Room
To Americas Building
To Music Hall
60
61
U.S. RUBBER CO. BLDG. ADDITION
Boot-black
RADIO CITY MUSIC HALL
Telephones
Telegraph & Cables
Barber Shop
ROCKEFELLER CENTER PARKING GARAGE
49
50
Women's Room
Odd Number Shops
Even Number Shops
Restaurant
EASTERN AIR LINES BLDG.
WEST 48th STREET
WEST 49th STREET
R C A BLDG.
WEST 50th STREET
THE ASSOCIATED PRESS BLDG.
34
WEST 51st STREET
WEST 52nd STREET
35
Guided Tour Lounge
30
Coffee Shop
10
Telephones
Beauty Salon
ROCKEFELLER
PLAZA
Restaurant
ESSO BLDG.
15
22
Telephones
45
Coffee Shop
Prometheus Fountain
9
Barber Shop
TIME & LIFE BLDG.
Restaurant Français
Lower Plaza
English Grill
Milk Bar
14
15
Valet Shop
News Stand
Restaurant
20
Barber Shop
U.S. Post Office
Concourse Connection to 600 Fifth Ave.
9
10
9
INTERNATIONAL BLDG.
10
Telegraph
Bootblack Cafeteria
LA MAISON FRANÇAISE
BRITISH EMPIRE BLDG.
PALAZZO d'ITALIA
INT. BLDG. NORTH
610
620
626
630
636
FIFTH AVENUE

80 **New Town Centre, Stevenage, Hertfordshire.** In English new town planning the pedestrian shopping precinct is an accepted fact. Car parks are placed as close to the centre as possible.

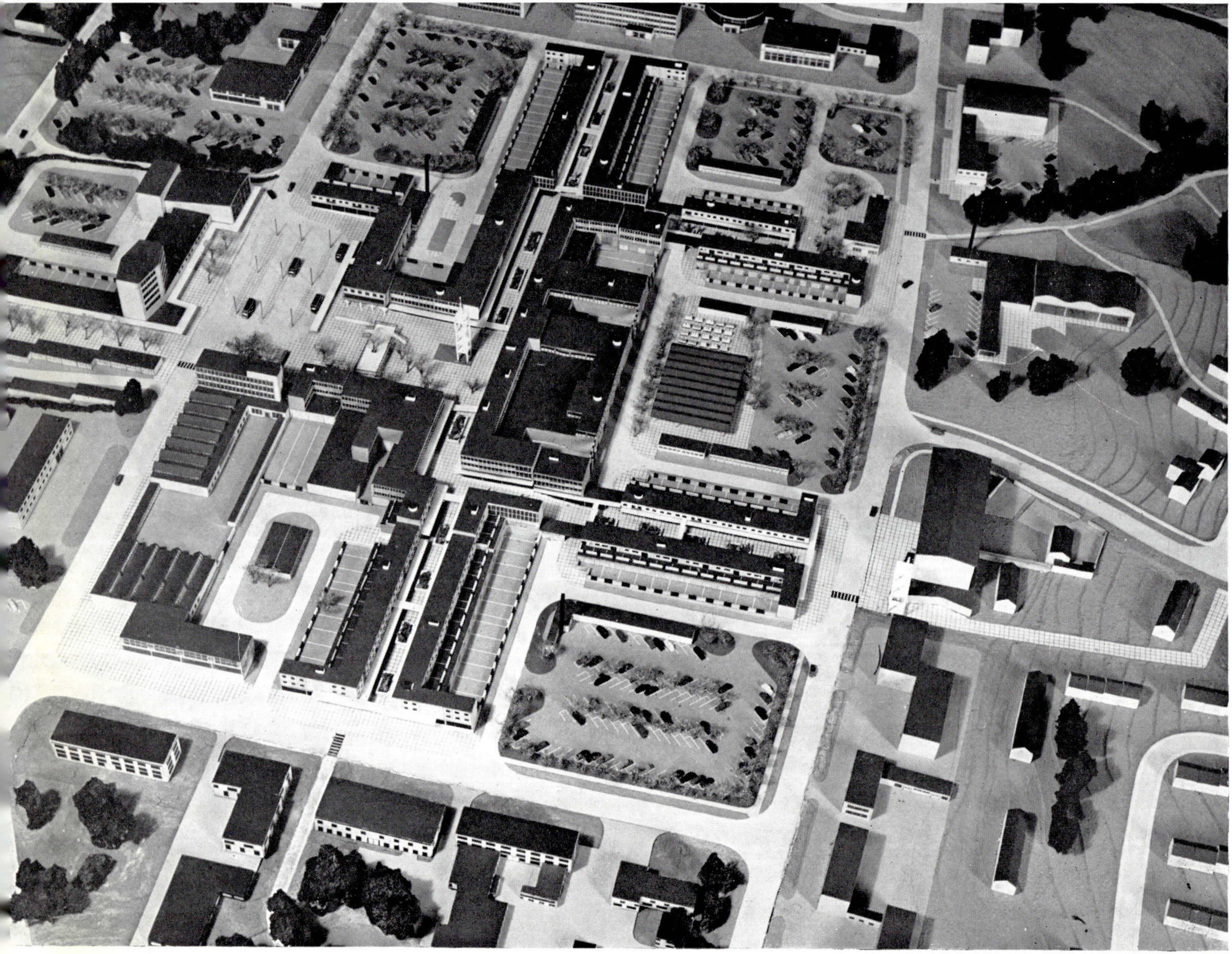

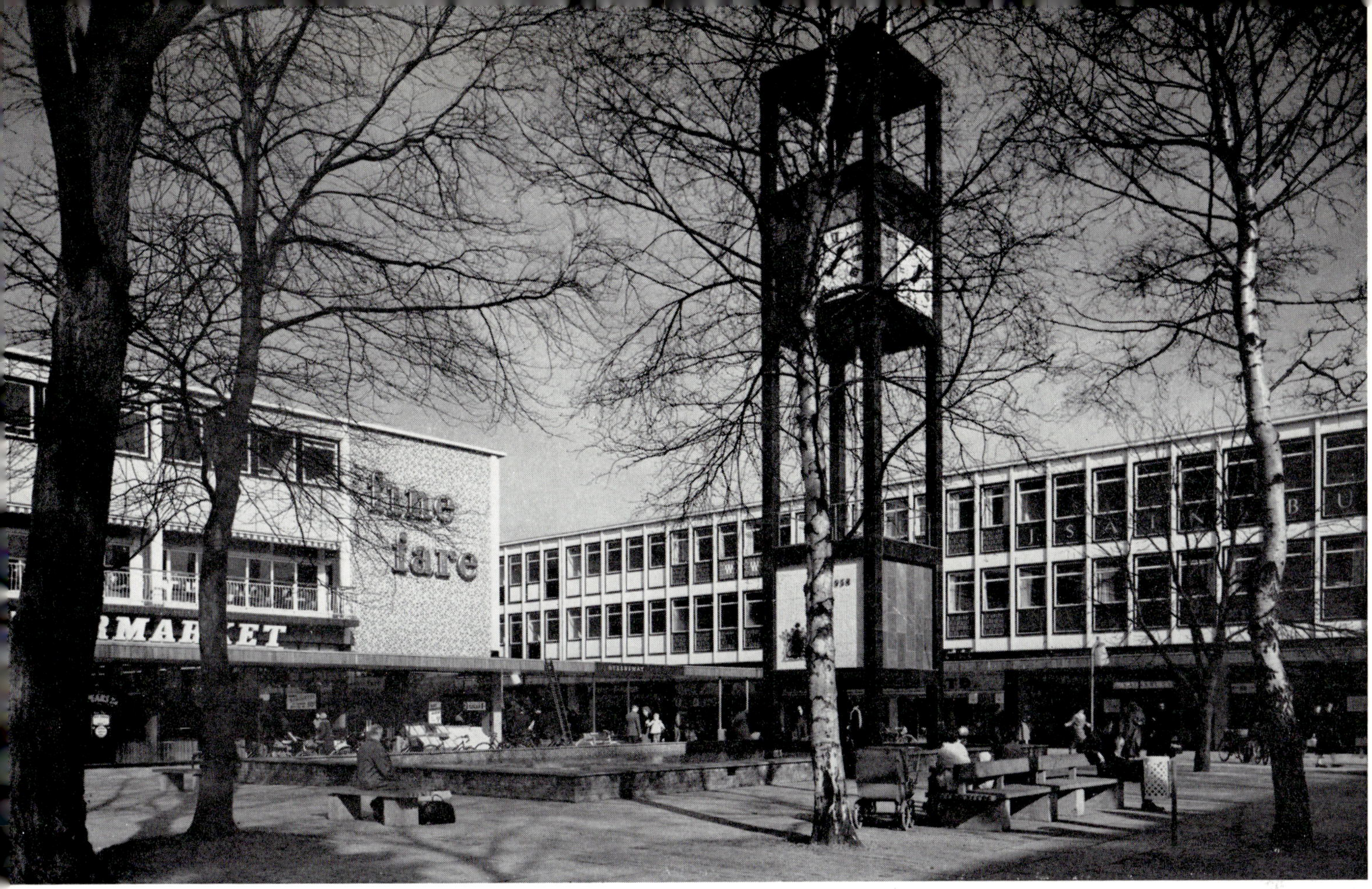

81a The Town Centre, Stevenage

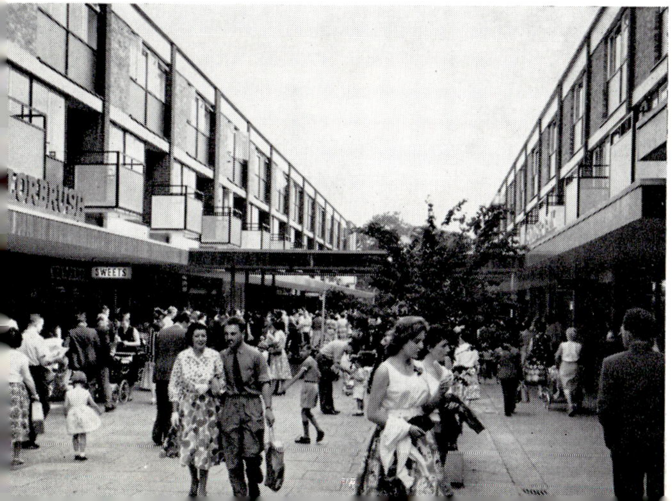

81b The Shopping Mall, Stevenage

82 **Model of the Town Centre, Coventry.** Note the use that is to be made of roofs for car parking. On the right of the picture a continuous roof road-pattern begins to take shape.

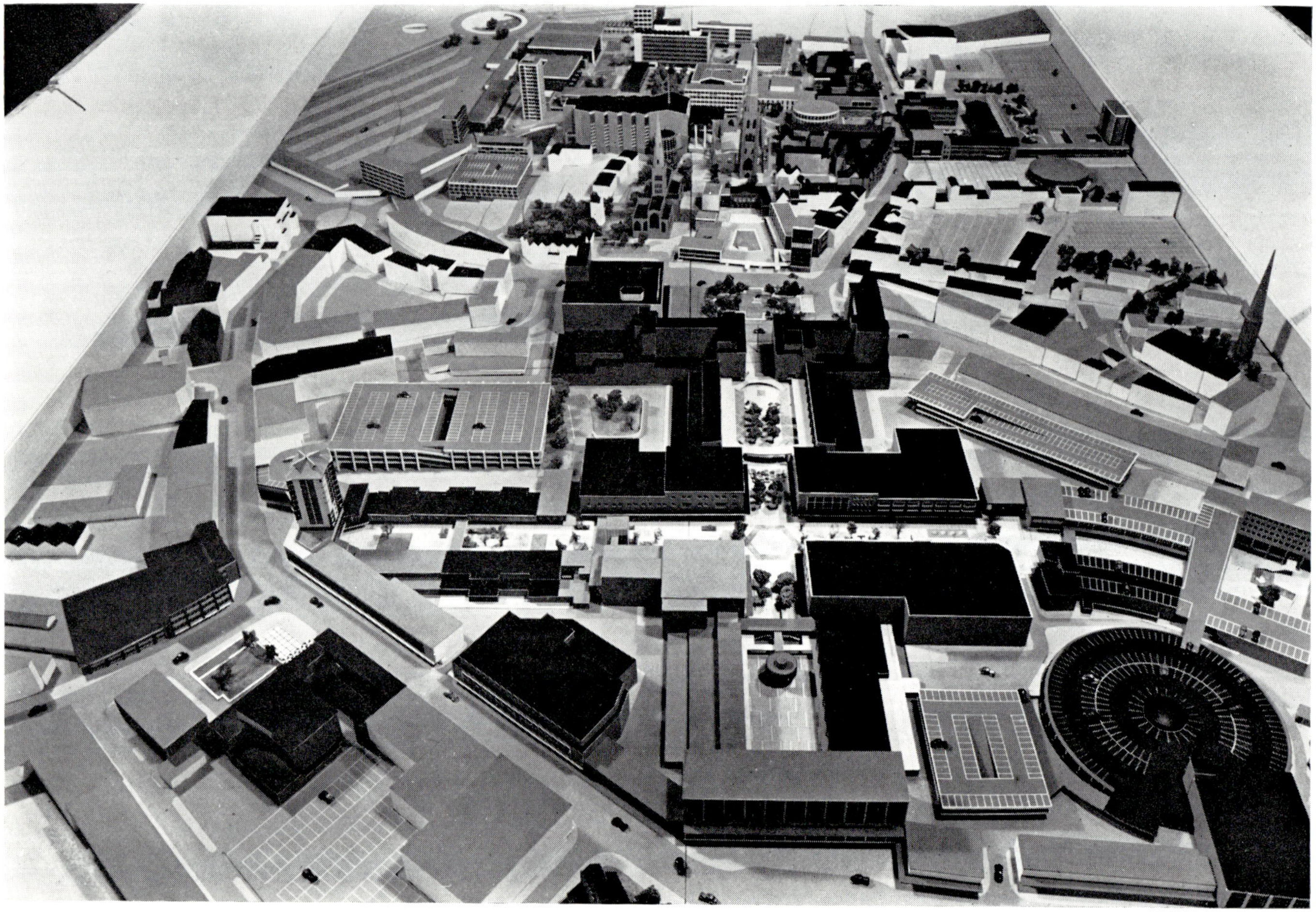

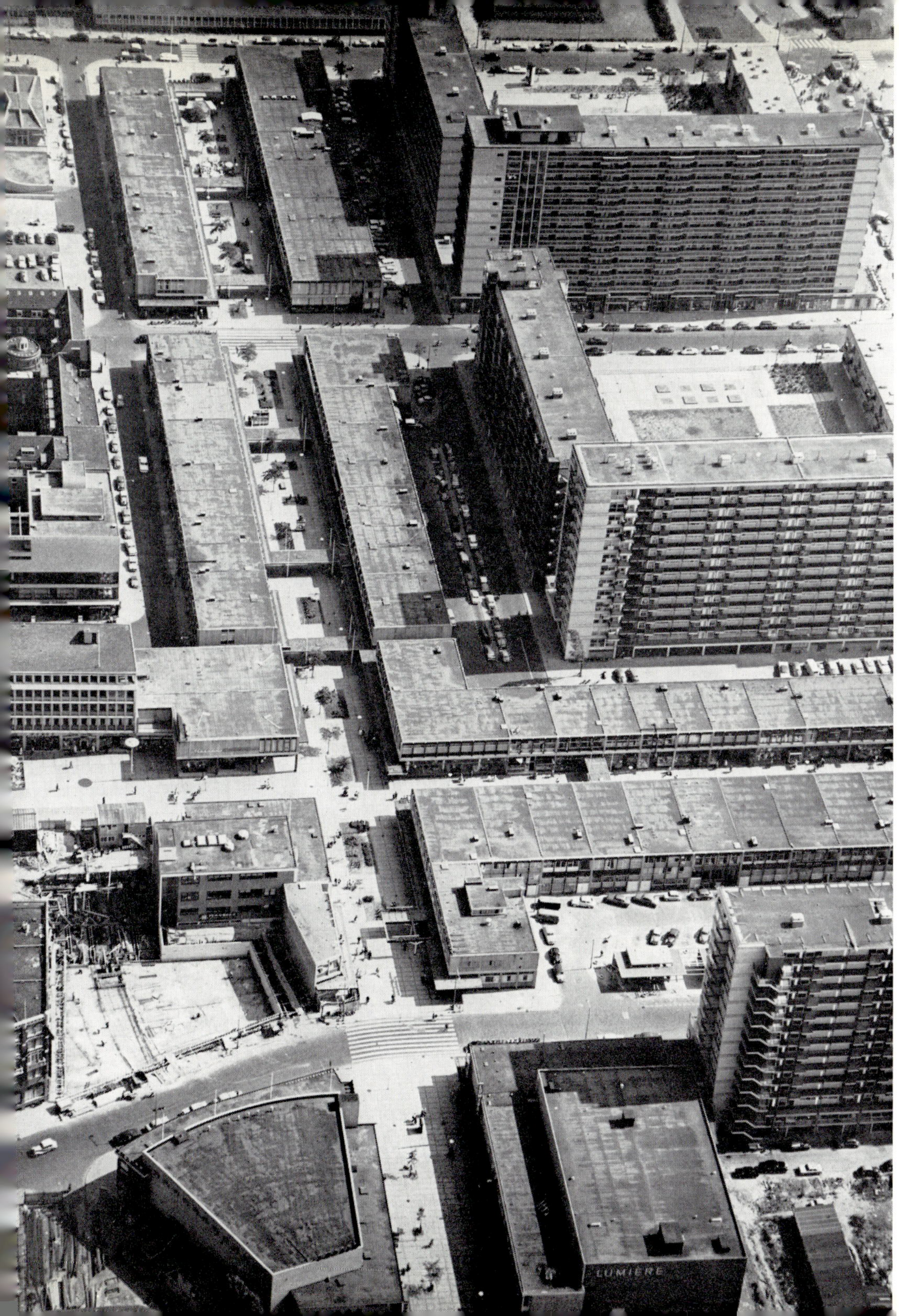

83 **The Shopping Centre, Rotterdam.** The centre way is pedestrian only. This air view is interesting as indicating that one half of the total valuable space is wasted by unused roofs.

84 **Shoppers' World, near Boston, U.S.A.** A centre set in the country that can only be approached by car. The total capacity of the car park is 6,000, and the walk from the extreme car to precinct is no mean feat.

85 **Shoppers' World, near Boston, U.S.A.** In contrast to the exterior, the market interior is small in scale and delightful with flowers and garden sights. ▶

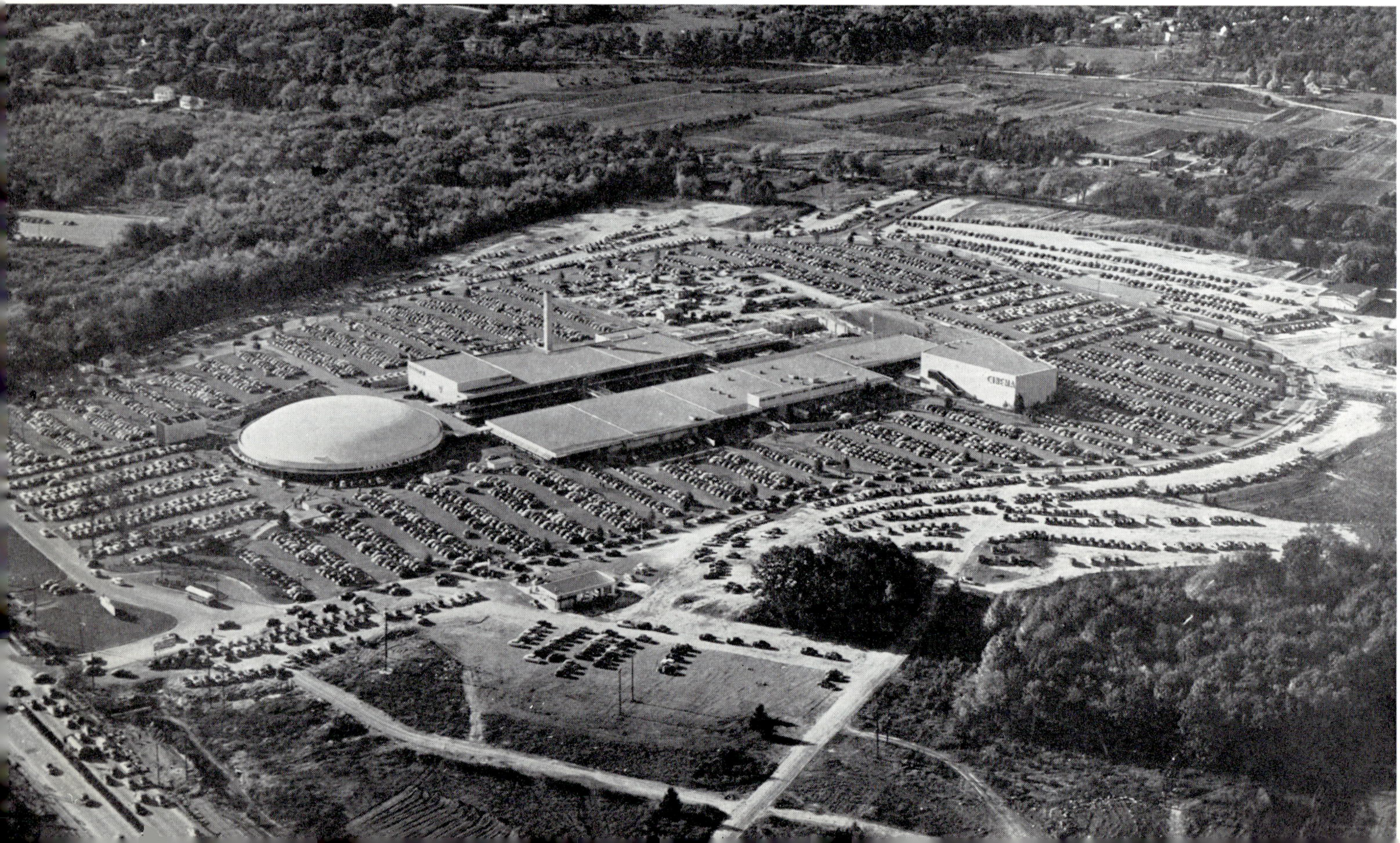

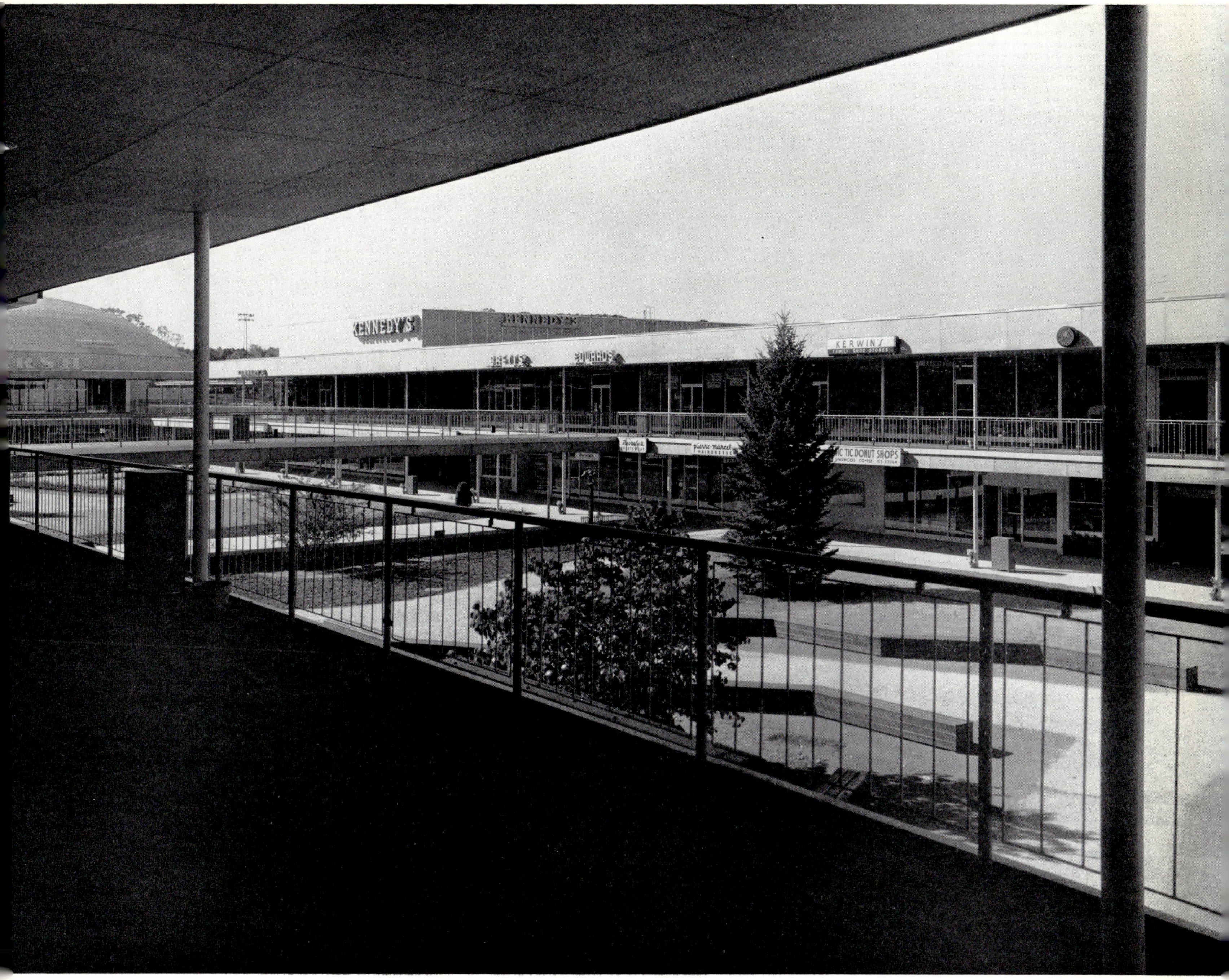
KENNEDY'S
KENNEDY'S
BRETTS
EDWARDS
KERWIN'S
pierre-marcel
TIC TIC DONUT SHOPS
SANDWICHES COFFEE ICE CREAM

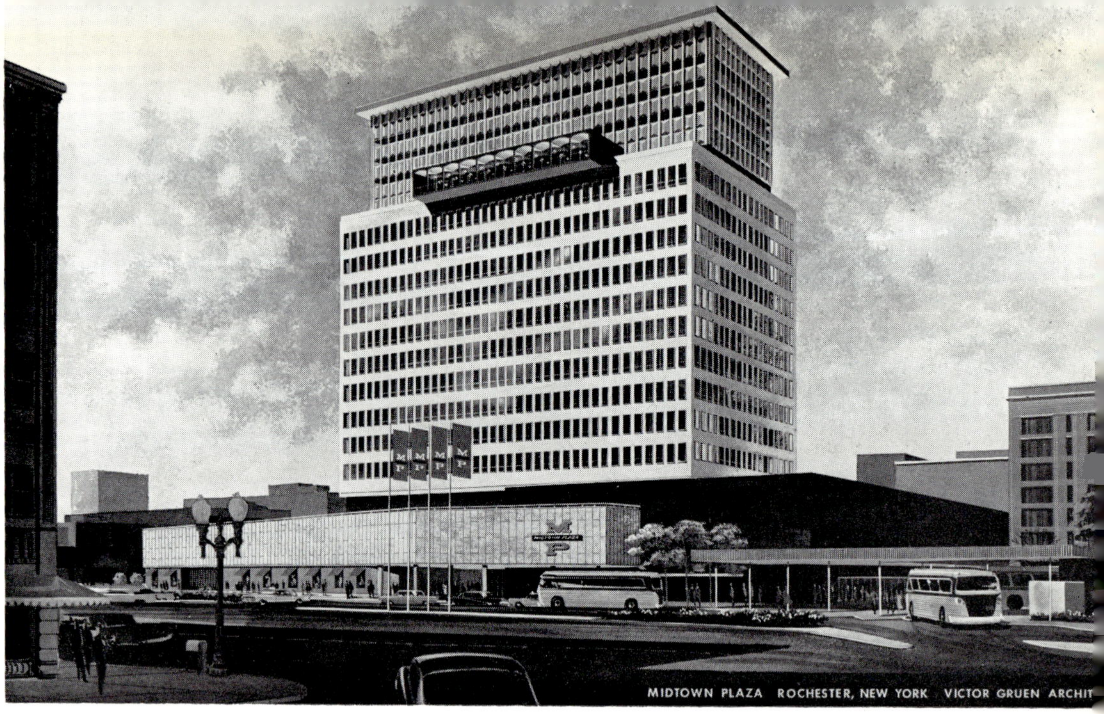

86a **Midtown Plaza Shopping Centre, Rochester, New York (Victor Gruen, Architect)**. Now under construction. In England the plans for the Elephant and Castle area, published in July 1960, show a similarity of idea and an advance in architecture.

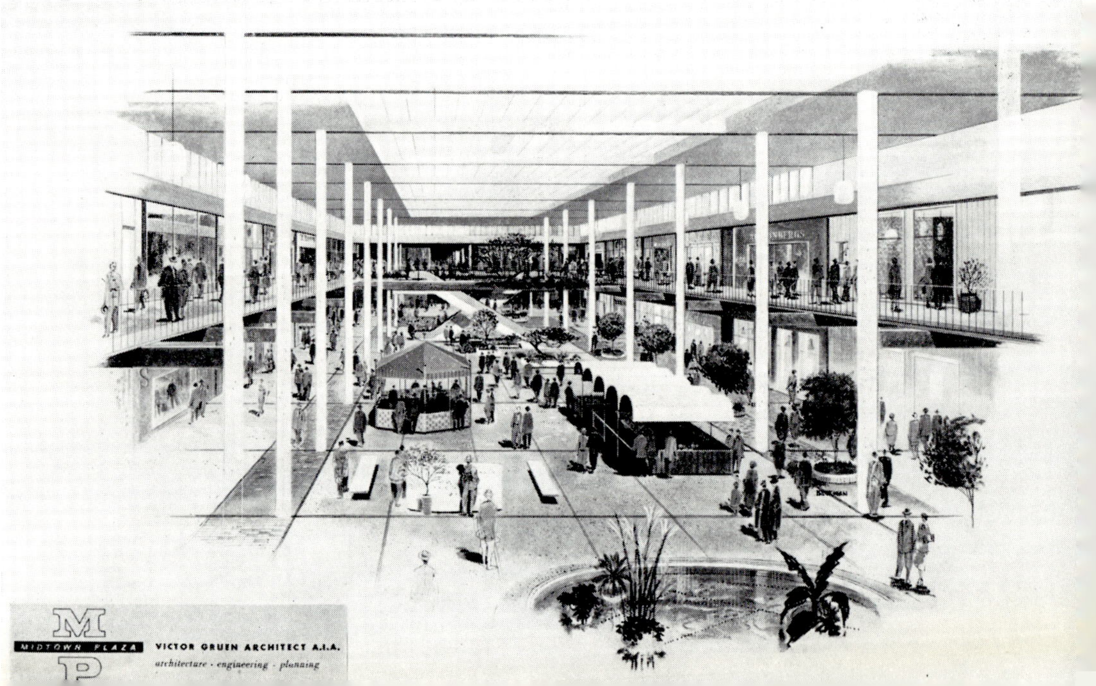

86b **Midtown Plaza Shopping Centre, Rochester, New York. (Victor Gruen, Architect)**. The interior of this shopping mall is illustrative of the tendency that has been developed since the Crystal Palace in 1851. The customer parks his car in the basement and reaches either level effortlessly by escalator. He need never go into the open air.

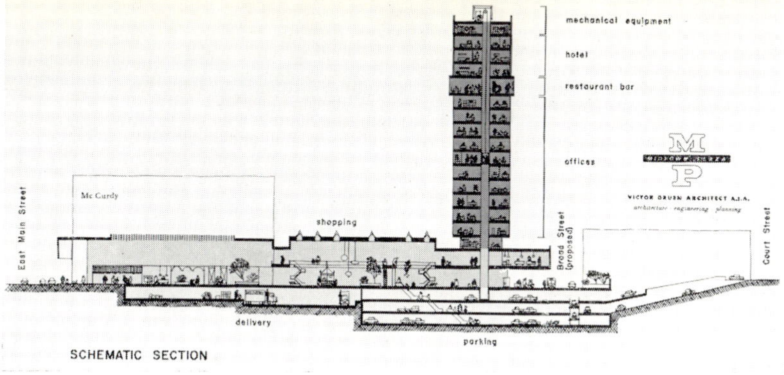

87a Section showing particularly the basement parking, and access by escalator.

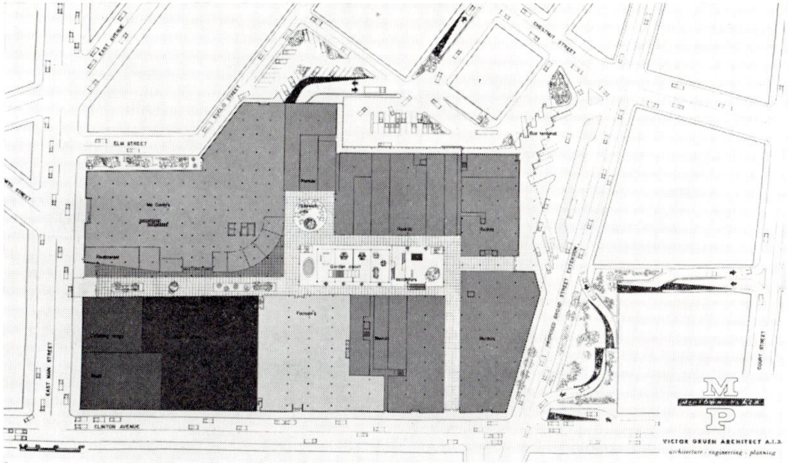

87b Plan of ground floor, showing shopping mall.

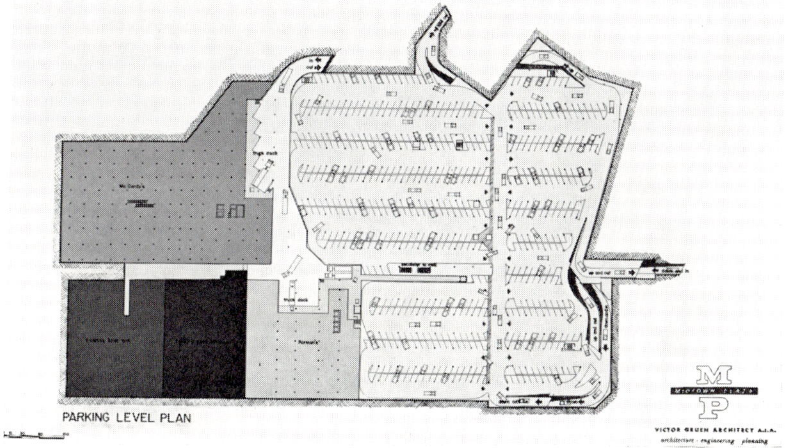

87c Plan at basement level.

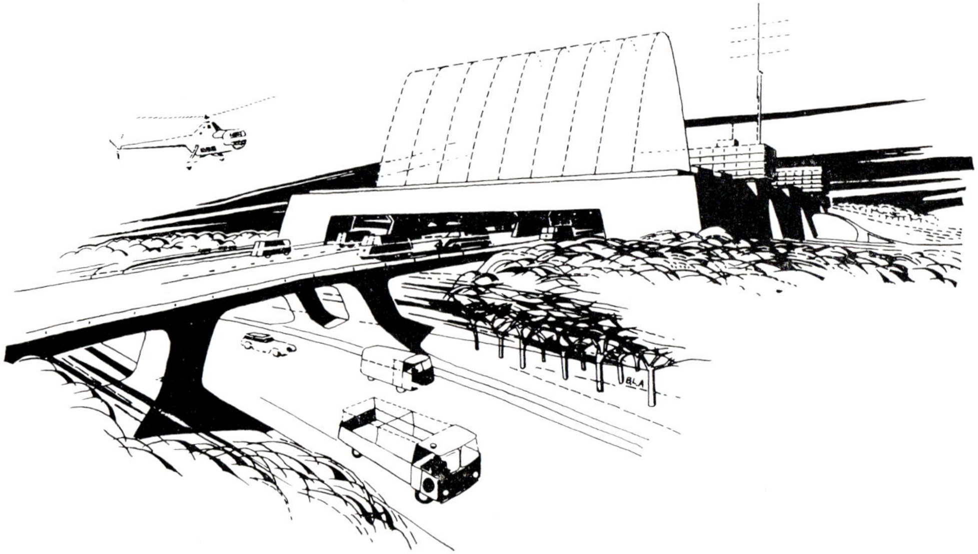

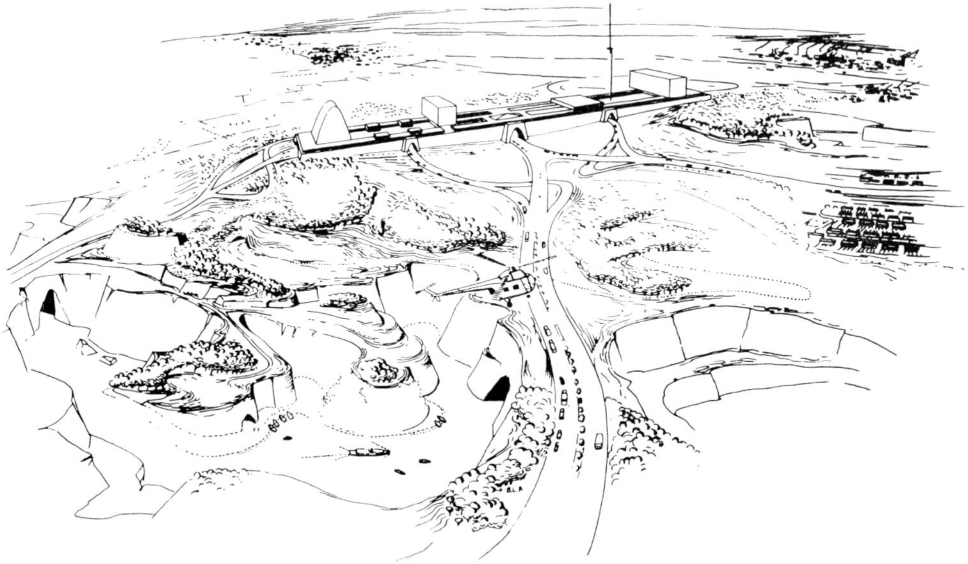

88 **High Market, between Dudley and Oldbury.** A project by Gordon and Eleanor Michell for a 'shoppers' world' in the area adjoining the Black Country of the Midlands.

SEGREGATION OF TRAFFIC

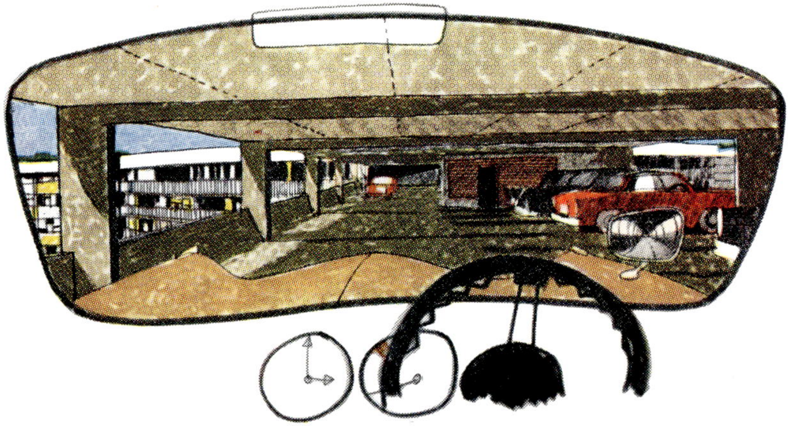

89 **Motopia: Three levels of Traffic**
Drawings by Gordon Cullen

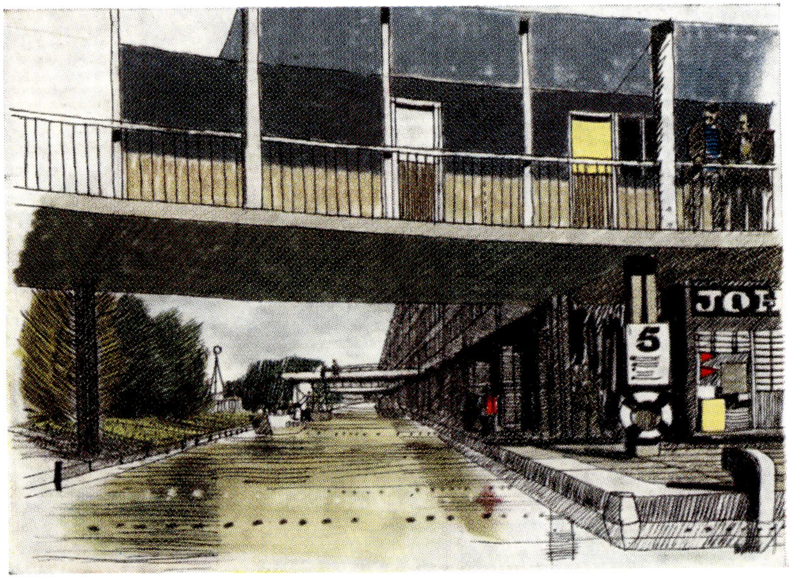

The traffic problem is by no means a modern phenomenon. It was certainly an anxiety, for instance, in classical Rome, for there are records of measures for keeping vehicles clear of the city at certain periods. Priene, with its steps, must clearly have solved its problem agreeably for the pedestrian, but of course there is no equal in history to the canals of Venice (and in a scarcely less satisfactory way, to those of Holland). Here the segregation is not only physical; it is concerned, too, with sound. Leonardo da Vinci, adventurous and imaginative as always, envisaged a two-level road system, one for gentlemen and one for tradesmen; but it was not until the nineteenth century that major attempts were made to design the movement of traffic on two or more levels. This idea was primarily stimulated by the coming of the railways, and we cannot but admire the tremendous scale on which the railway projects were undertaken. The overhead railways, entering London to reach the main line stations, transformed and lowered the residential values within their neighbourhood. Probably it was the Inner Circle railway, completed in 1863, that was the greatest historic landmark in the unobtrusive and efficient system of shifting the population. Man had been put into a sewer. At ground level, however, planners made no serious attempt to deal with the coming complex of street traffic until the twentieth century. At Radburn, in the U.S.A., Clarence Stein made domestic-planning history by segregating pedestrians and cars, and since that time all English planning in the new towns and elsewhere has been directed towards this end. The words 'pedestrian precinct' became much in use, and meant what they intended: safety from the danger and disagreeableness of the streets. In 1960 the full impact and significance of the car had been appreciated by laymen as well as professionals and it was apparent that a revolution must take place in the concept of road building, or much of our way of life would be in jeopardy. Many planners had followed in the footsteps of Leonardo da Vinci by foreseeing the traffic dilemma many years before it came to a head. Foremost among these was Le Corbusier, whose many projects have become classics of their kind, not because they propose an engineer's solution, but rather because each is informed with the feeling of the artist. Le Corbusier will surely go down in history as the man who showed that we could in fact be liberated from the appalling circumstances we had ourselves created. From him have flowed all the theoretic schemes, mostly by students of architecture, that help to stimulate the imagination of the weary practitioner and the responsible authority.

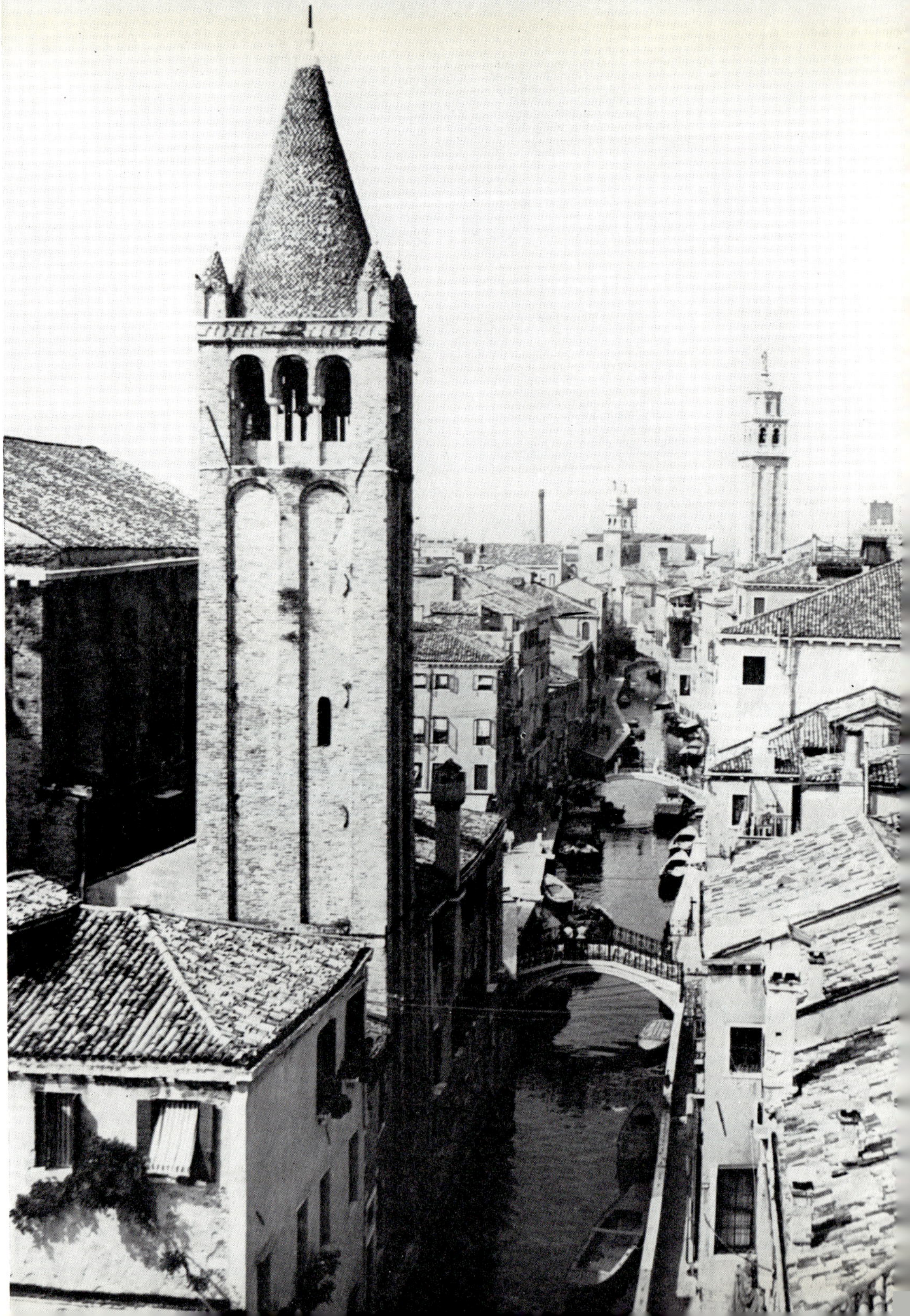

90 **Venice.** The earliest of all forms of segregation was water and land.

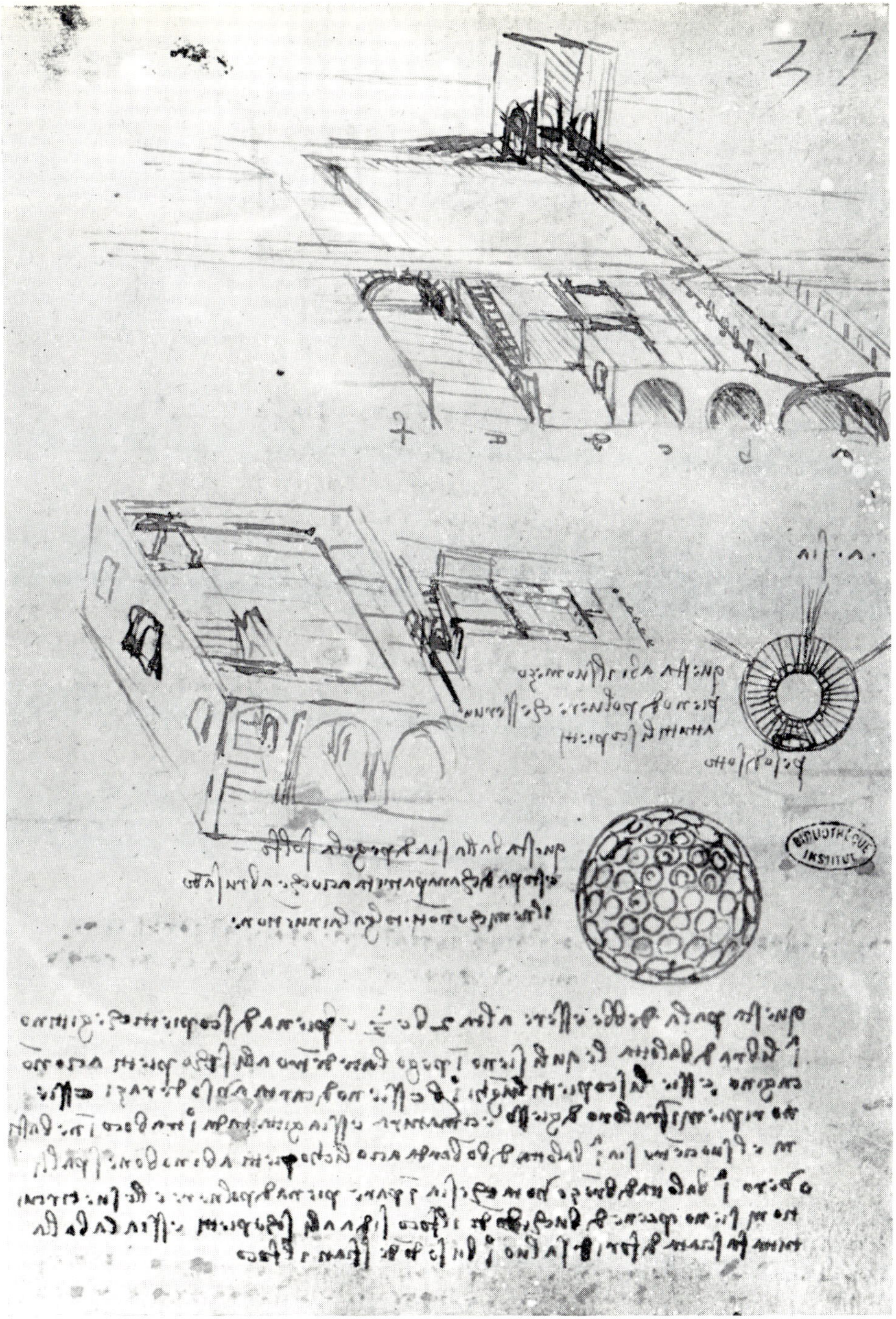

91 **From the Notebooks of Leonardo da Vinci.** The top illustration shows a two-level road system. Leonardo conceived the idea of an upper level for the exclusive use of gentlemen, and the lower for service.

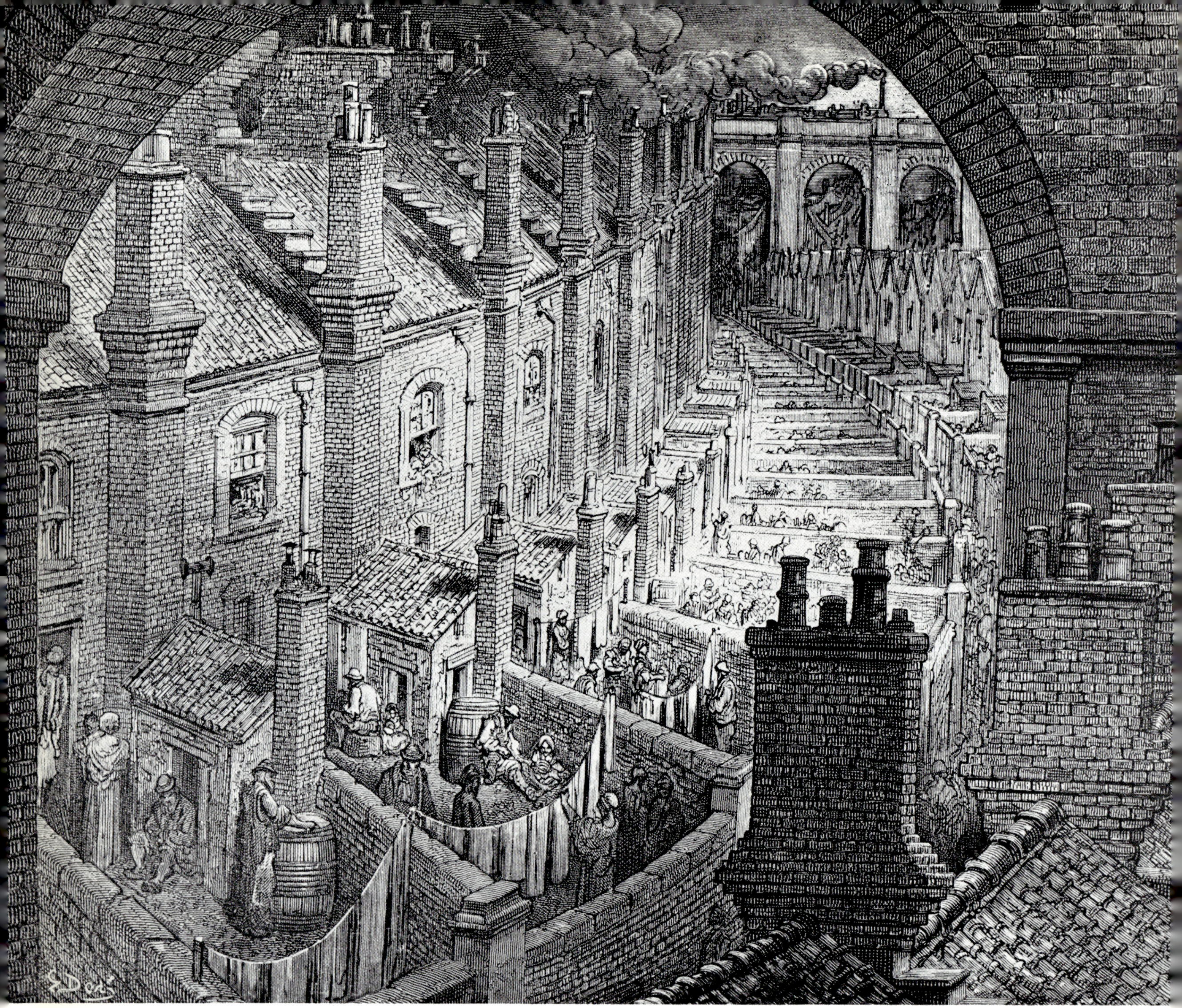

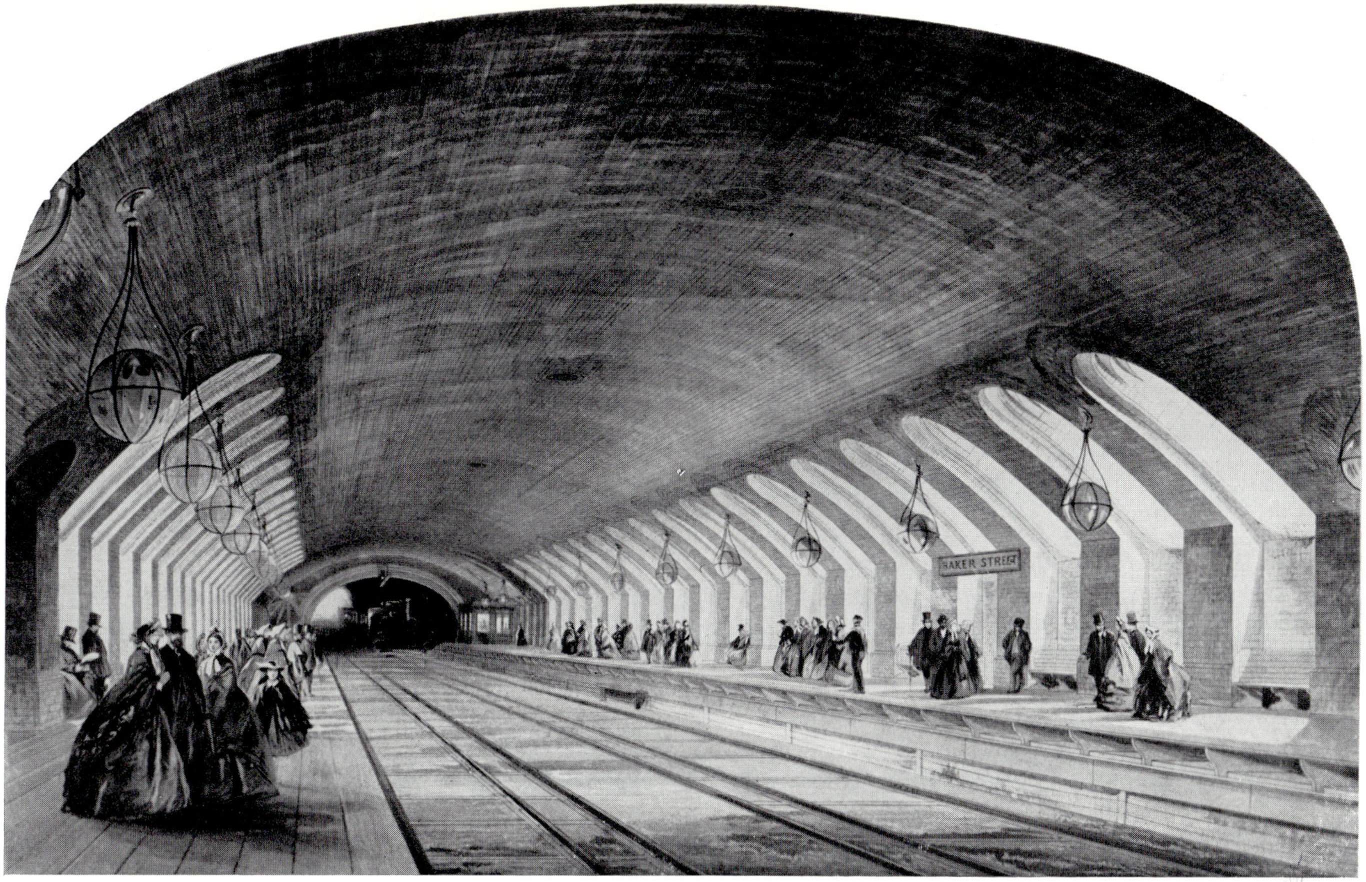

93 **The underground railway, Baker Street, London.** While the most immediately economic form of segregation was the overhead railway, it tended to depress values and create slums. More satisfactory was the underground railway, whose initial cost was considerable, but which was comparatively harmless to the existing town amenities. The Inner Circle railway of London must have been a truly heroic conception.

◀ 92 **The overhead railway, London.** The impact of the railway upon nineteenth century London must have been overwhelming, for, unlike the car, the railway train accepts no compromise on total segregation.

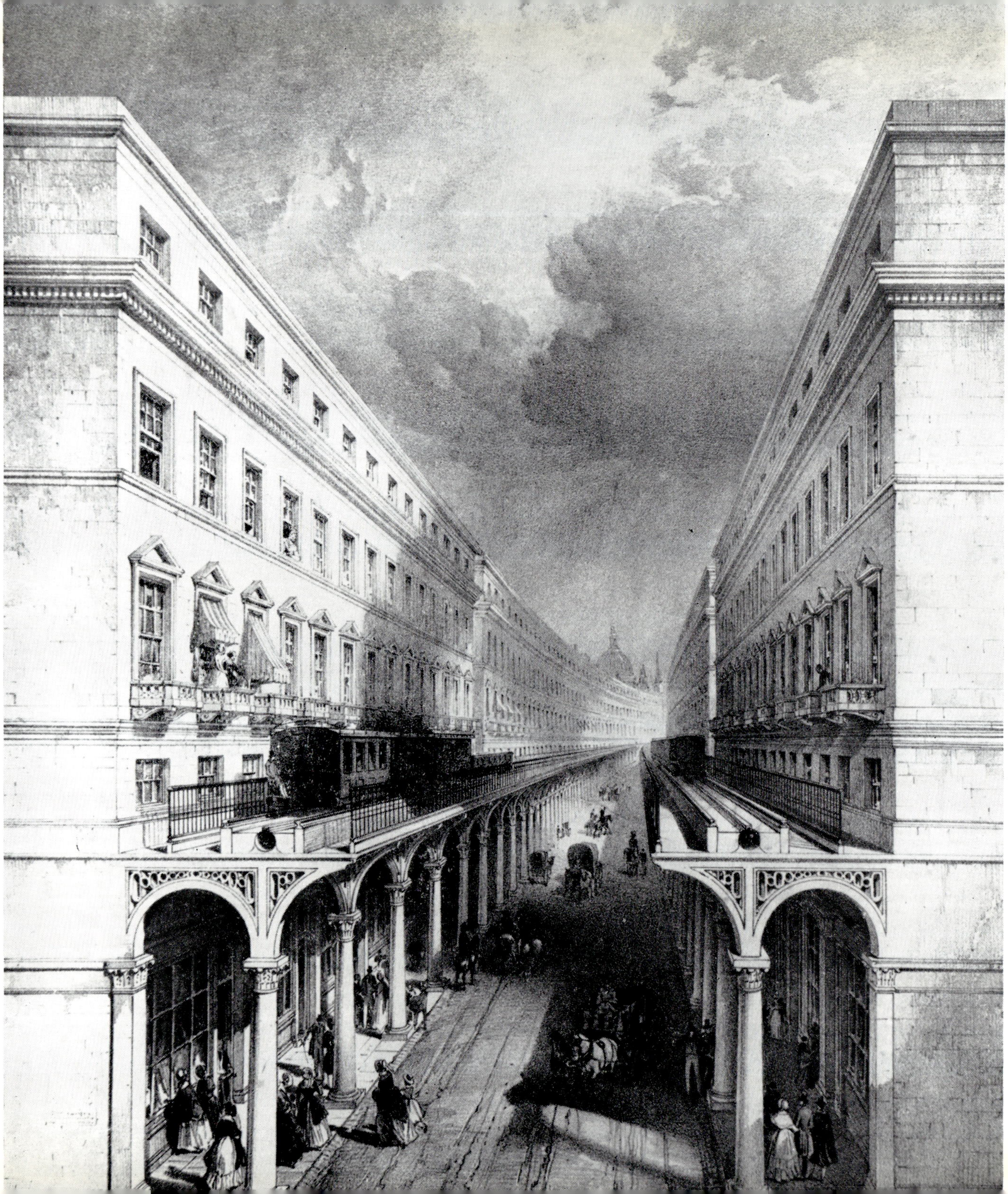

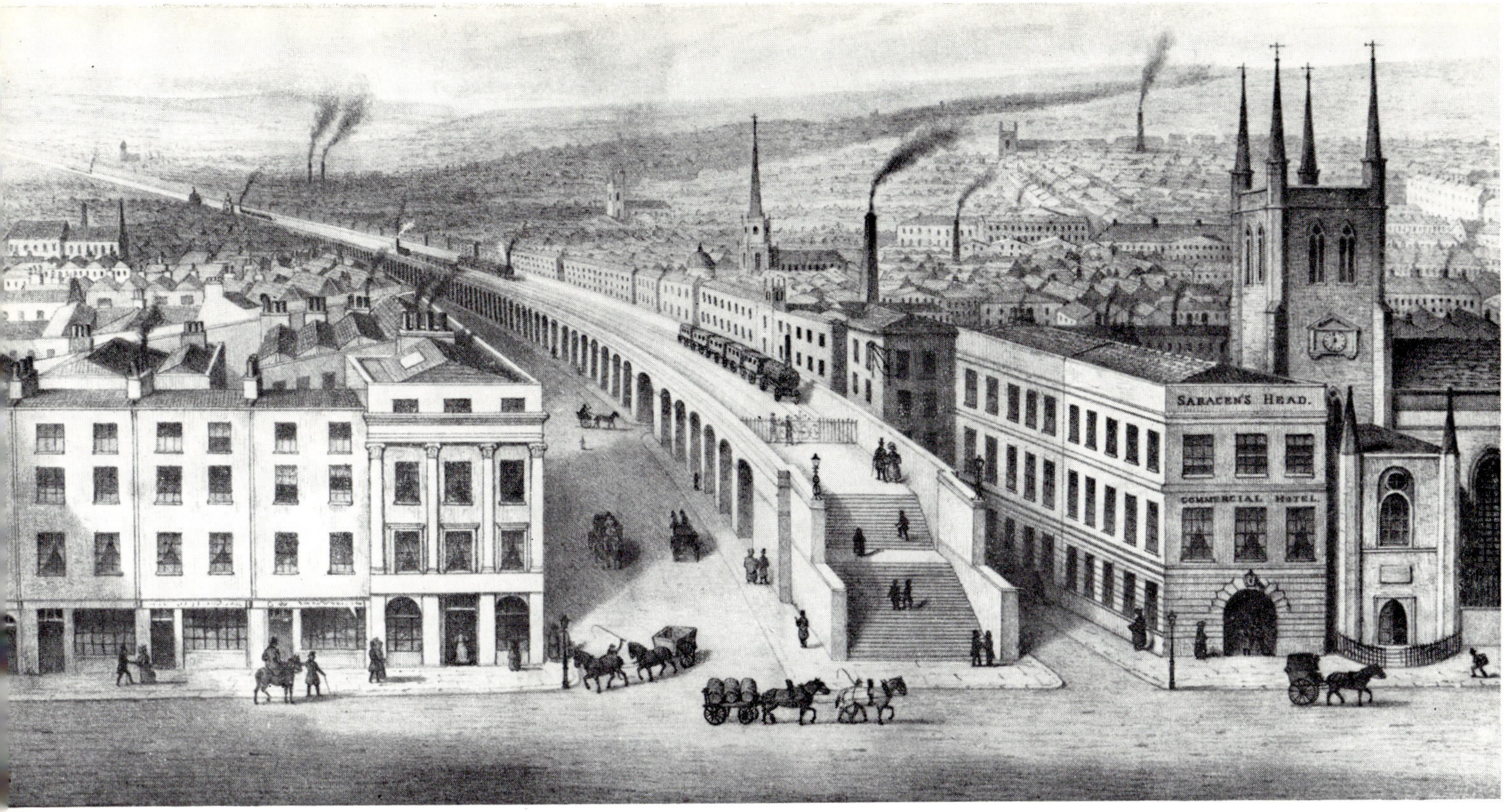

95a **The London Grand Junction Railway.** It is surprising to think what a large number of overhead railways were in fact built along urban streets, and that it is only recently that they have begun to be dismantled.

◀ 94 **The London Railway.**

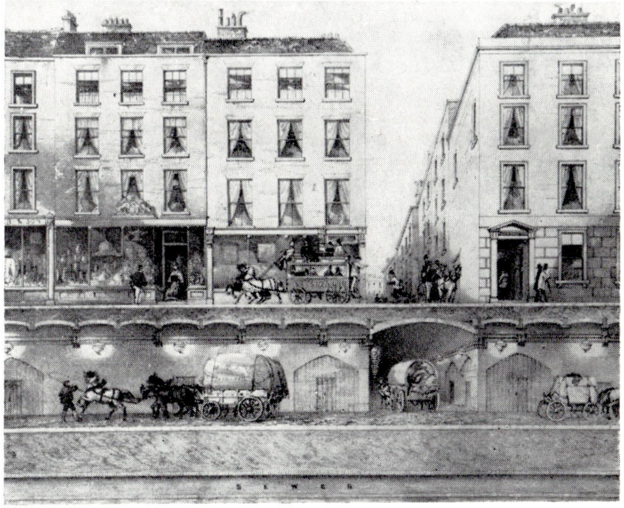

95b **Metropolitan Traffic Relief.**

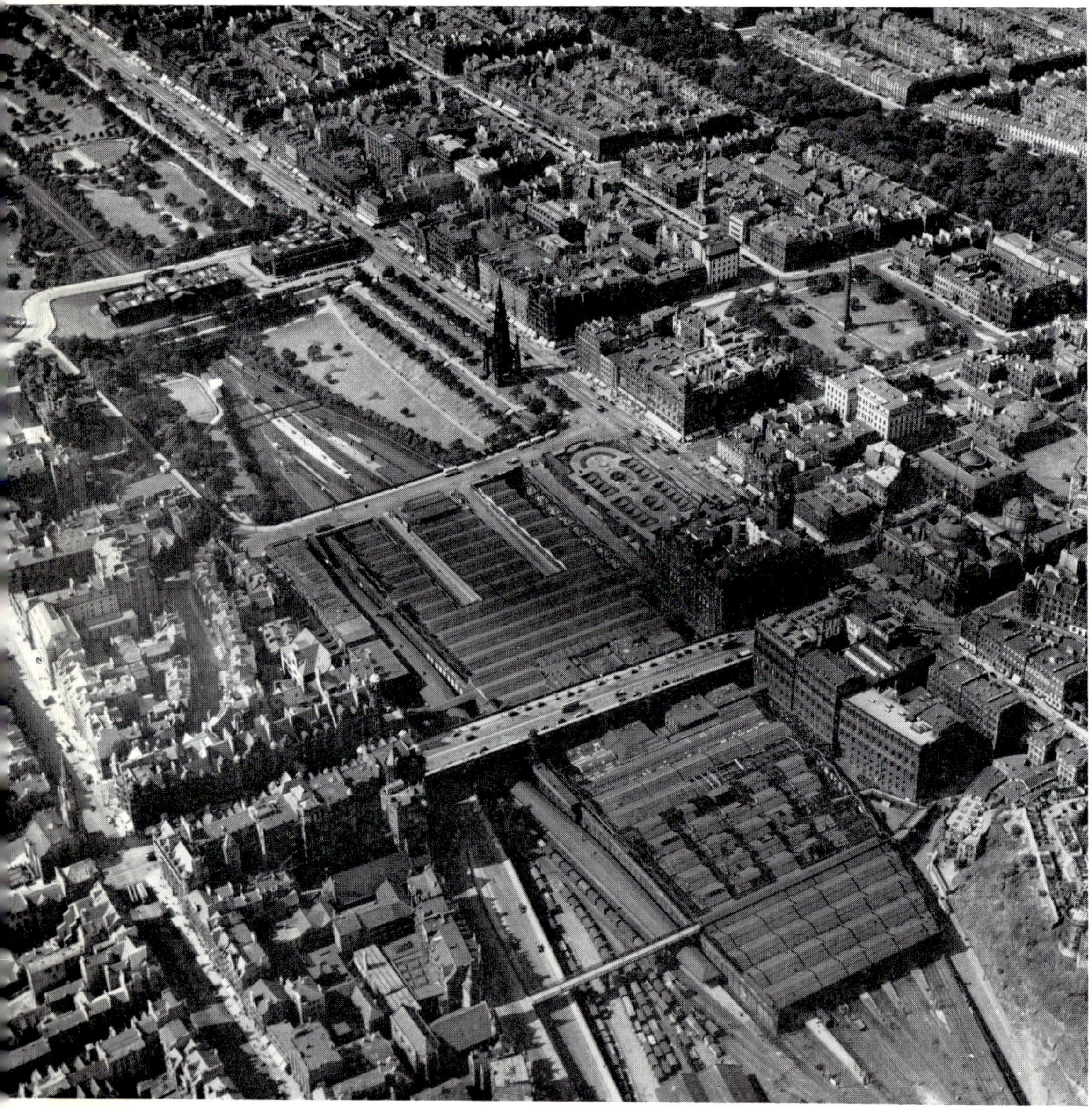

96 **Edinburgh.** The railways slipped into Edinburgh between the medieval and the Georgian towns and in many ways were a model of discreet urban planning—only made possible by the existing ground levels.

97 **Central Station, Rome.** Rome station is also a model of its kind. It is a work of modern architecture superbly sited in relation to historic Rome, but, unlike that at Edinburgh, is a positive contribution to civic design.

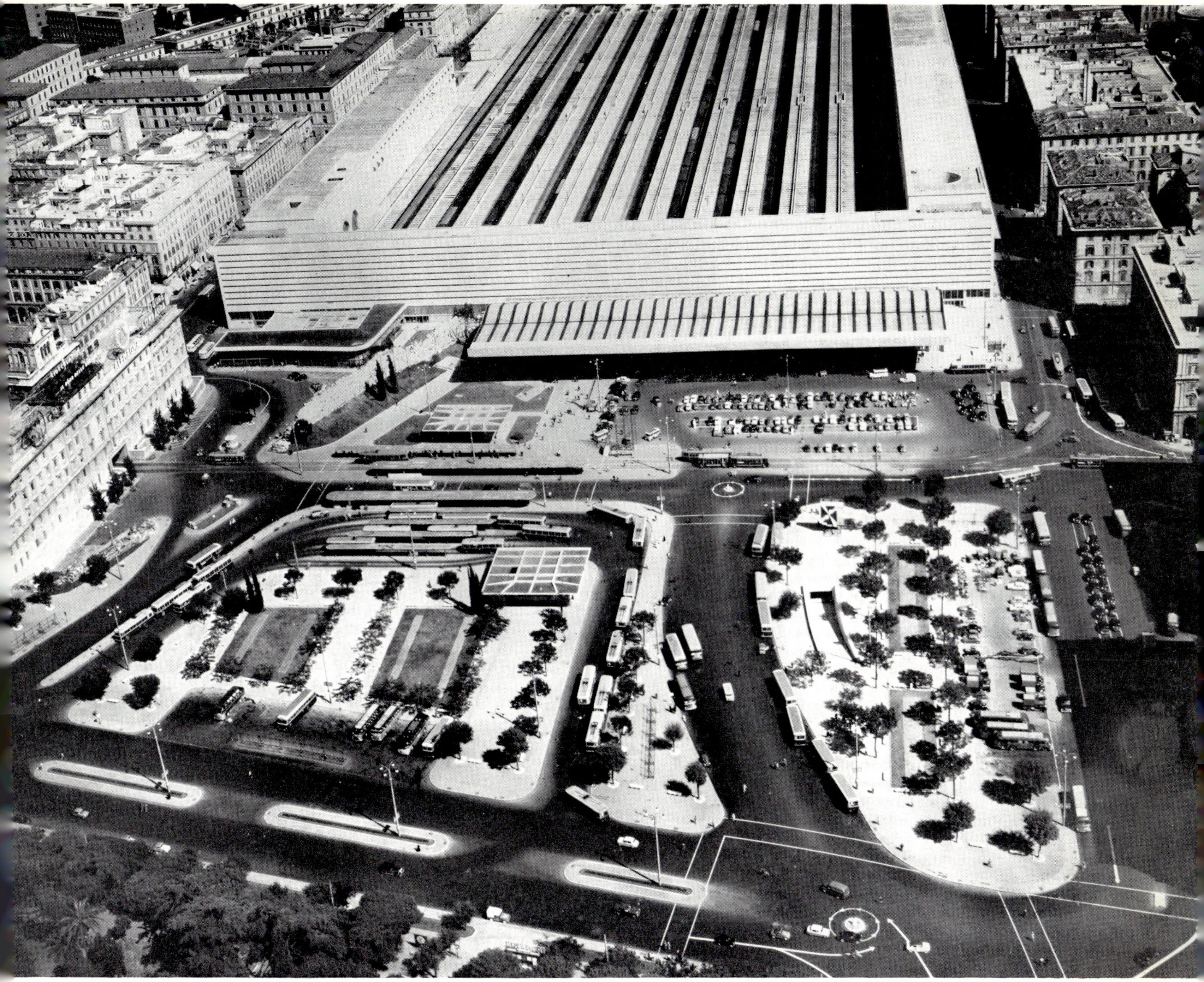

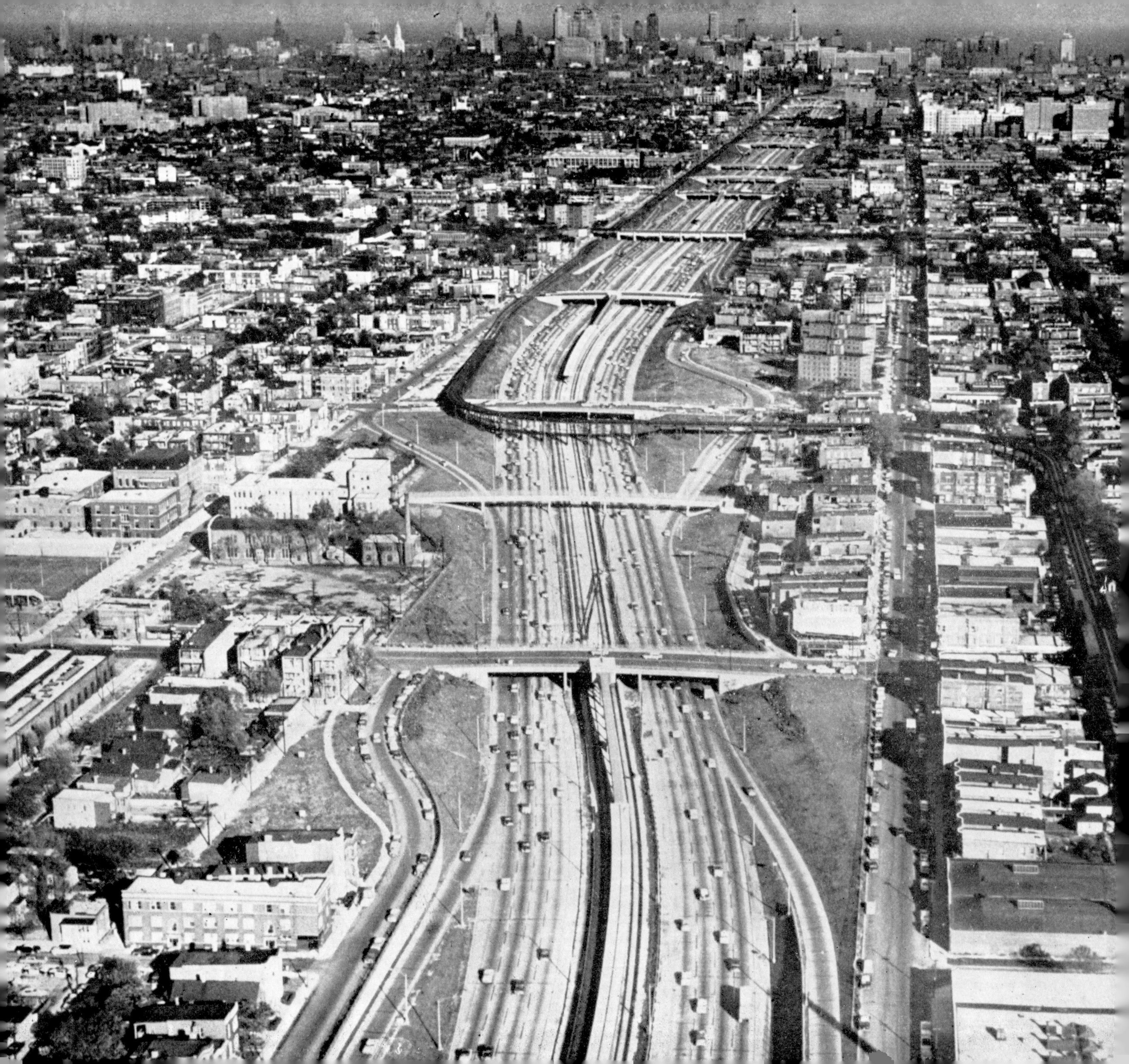

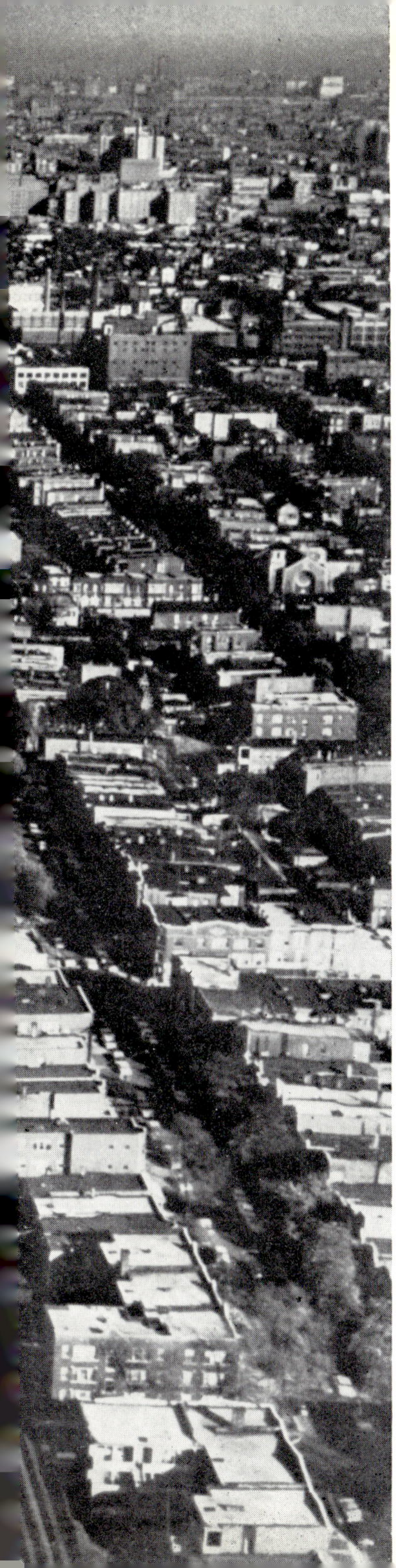

98 **A Sunken Freeway, U.S.A.** The principle of the sunk railway at Edinburgh applied scientifically to the road approach to a city centre.

99 **Triple Parkway intersection in New Jersey, U.S.A.** On the other hand, this form of road junction leaves one with the sense of total chaos as the ultimate goal.

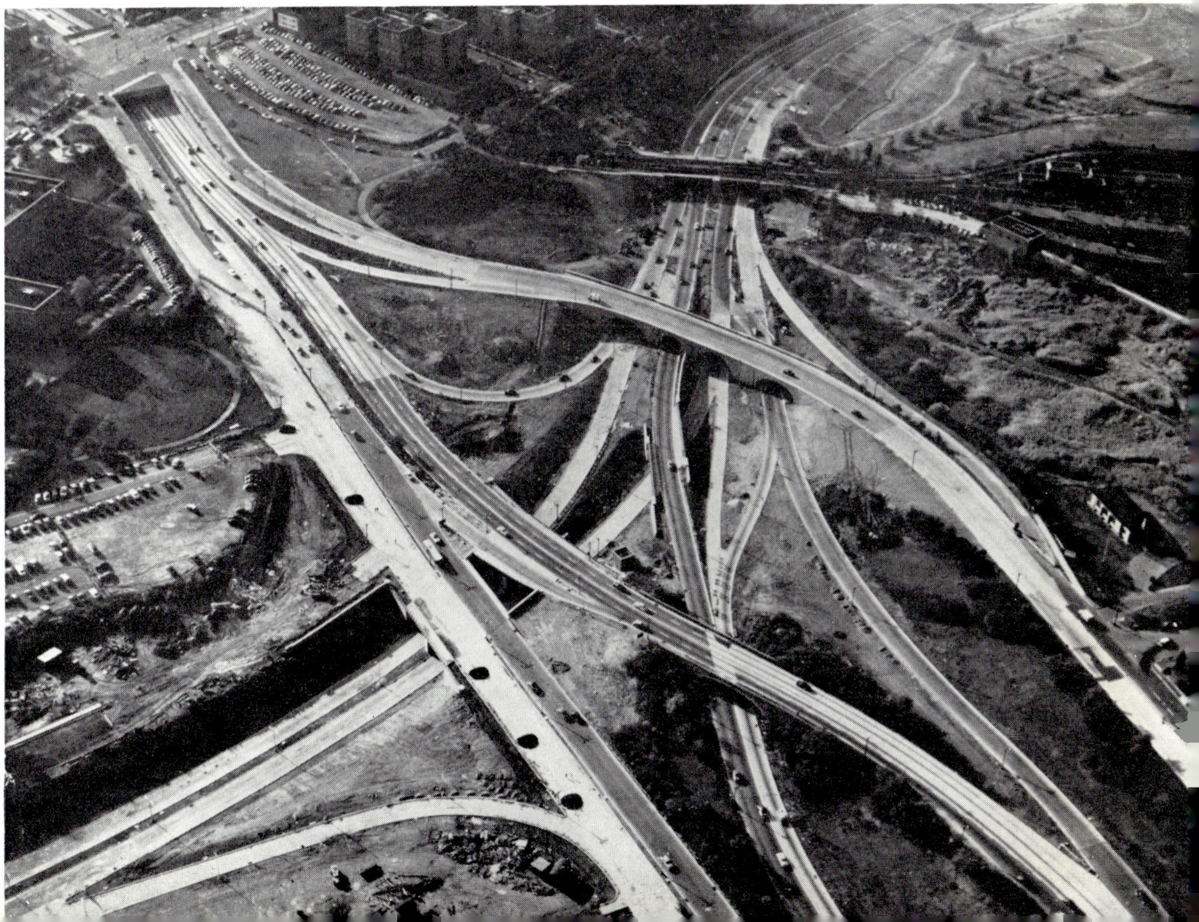

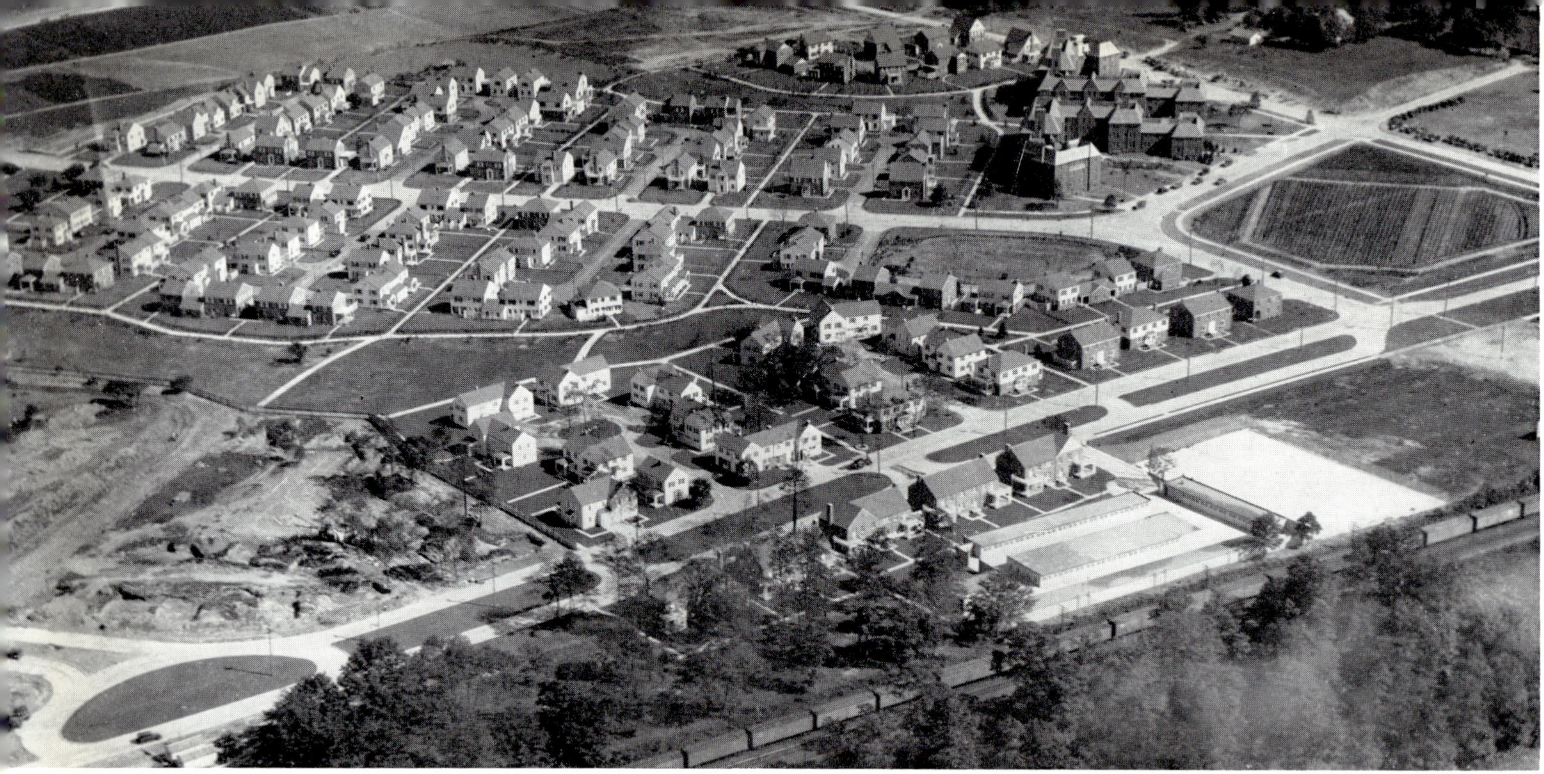

100a **Radburn, New Jersey, U.S.A., 1929: Clarence Stein and Henry Wright.** This fragment is part of a design to reconcile garden city principles with those of planning for a motor age. Note the continuous pedestrian landscape at the rear of the houses.

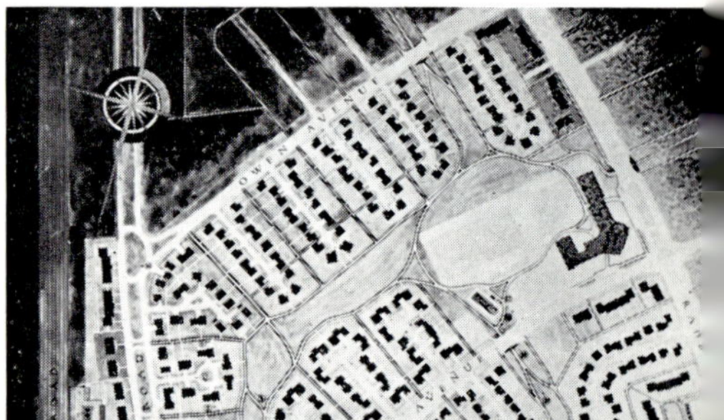

100b Detail of part of plan

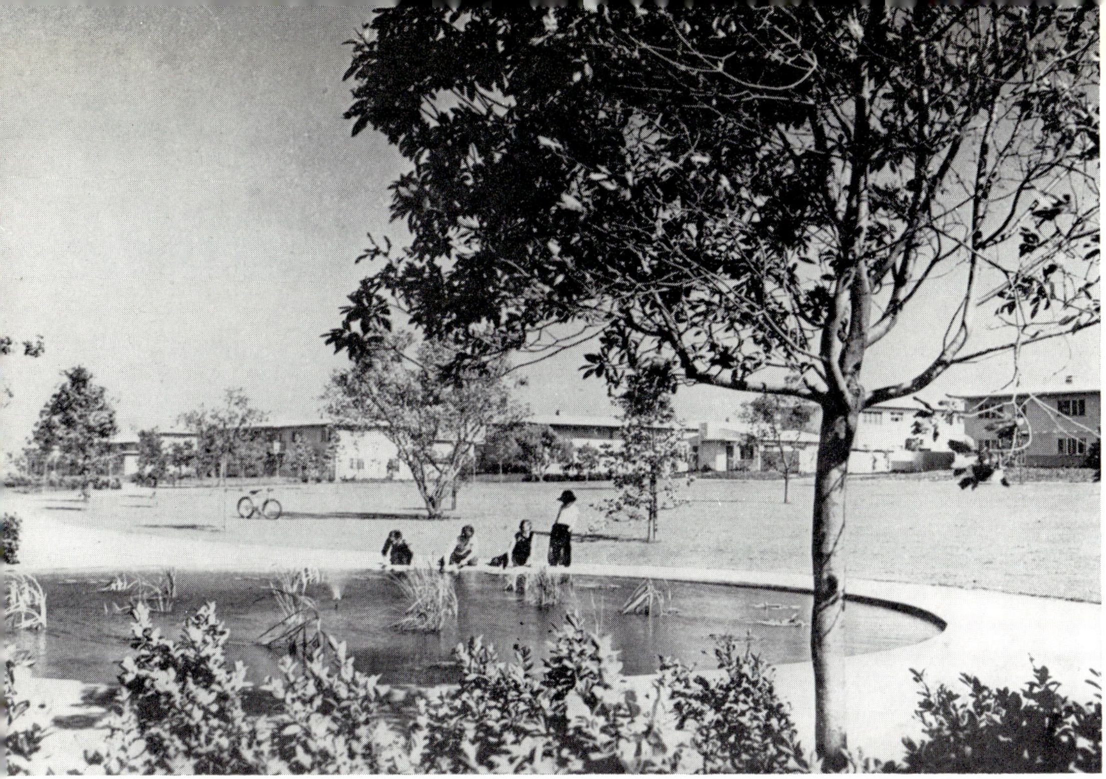

101a **Baldwin Hills, near Los Angeles, 1940.** A view within the landscape between houses.

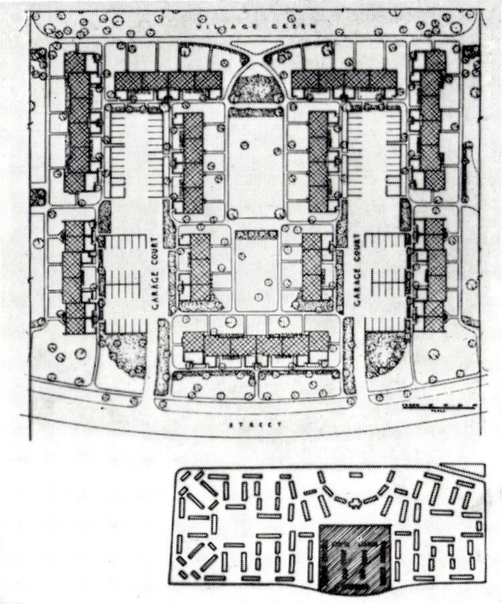

101b **Baldwin Hills.** The Radburn principle carried a further stage with 'back access'. The car is confined in a seemly court and the house is approached through a walled patio garden. Remaining space is given to landscape.

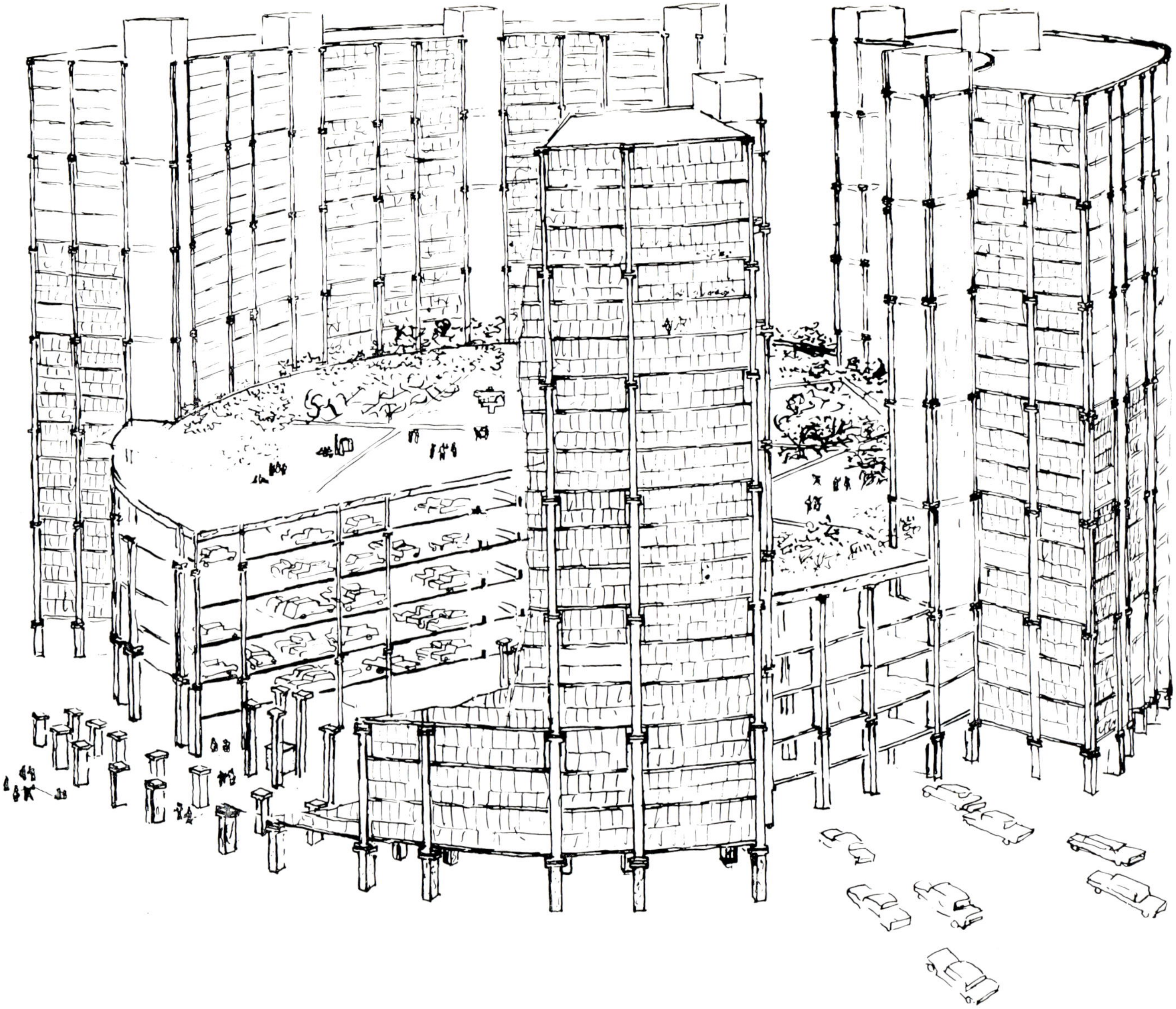

102 **Philadelphia.** Suggestion by Louis Kahn to provide circular multi-storey car parks within a circle of offices.

103 **Philadelphia.** The proposal applied to the centre of the city, showing the imposition of the circle upon the gridiron pattern.

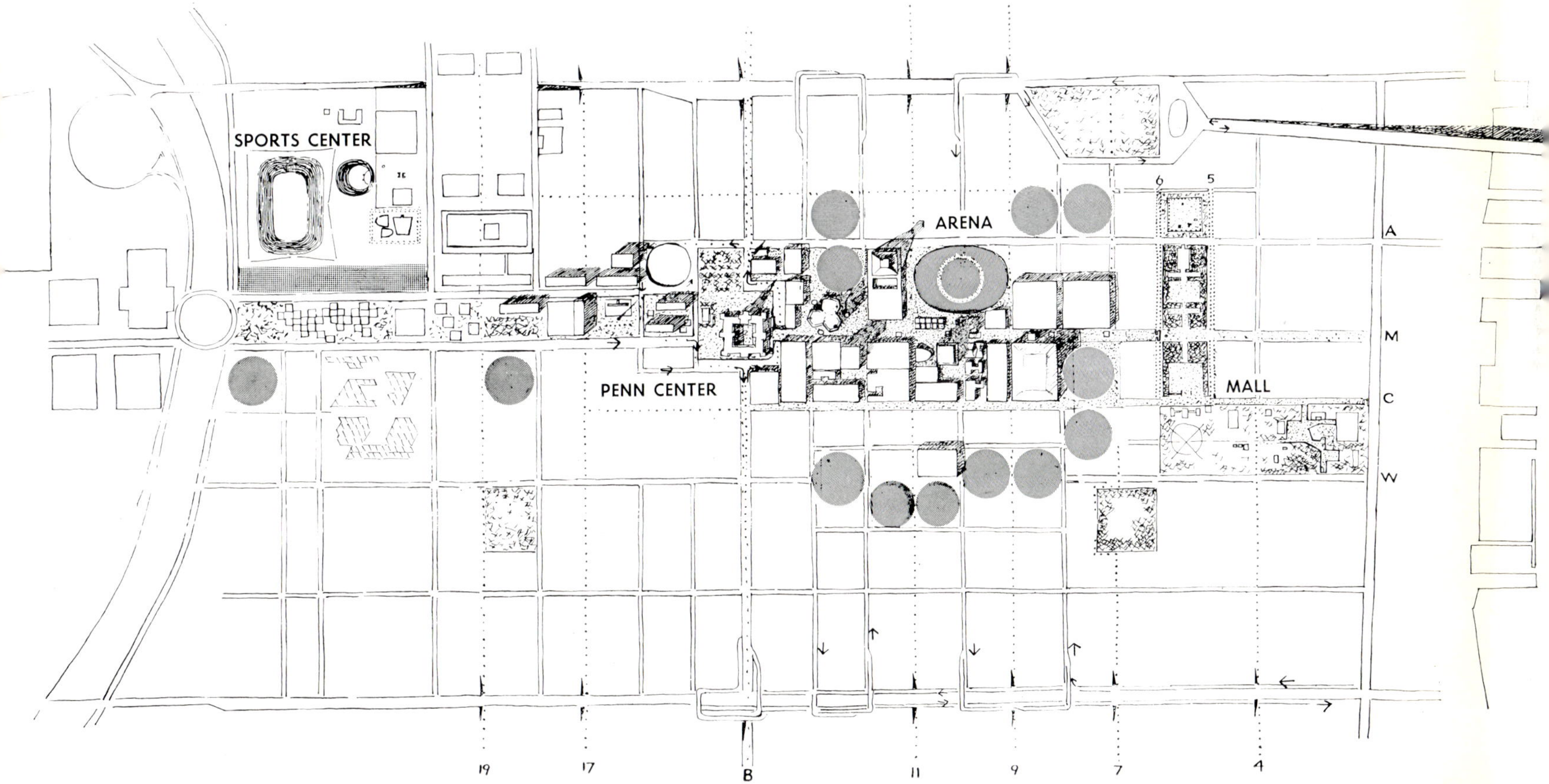

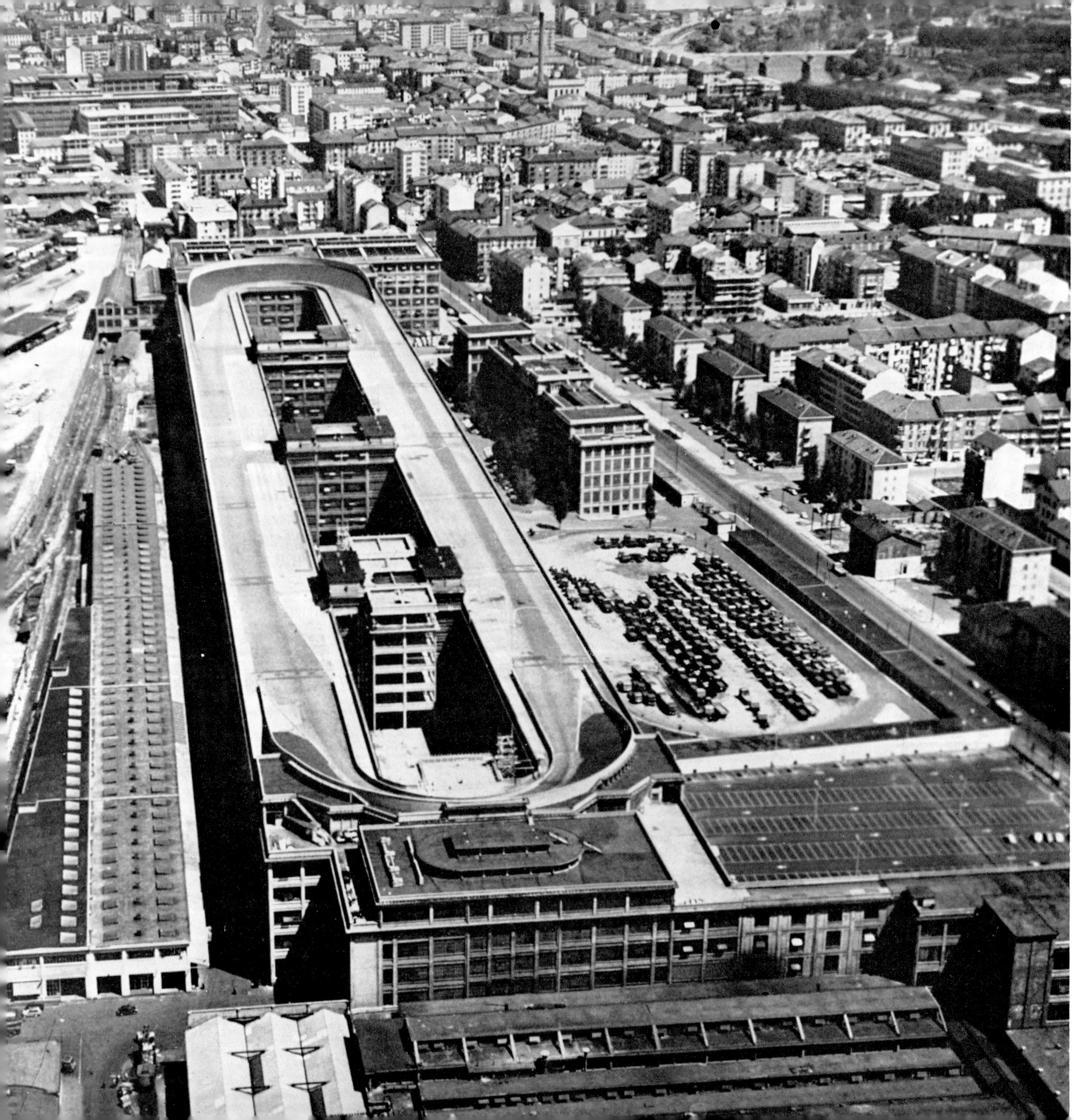

104 **The Fiat Works, Turin: the Former Testing Track.** Probably the earliest example of a reinforced concrete flat roof used for cars.

105 **Parking Garage, by E. M. Khoury, Consulting Engineer, Canoga Park, California.** The model illustrates a hyperbolic-paraboloid type of construction. The upper floors are cut away to show warped floors on far section. This is one of the latest car park designs, the purpose of which is to avoid ramps.

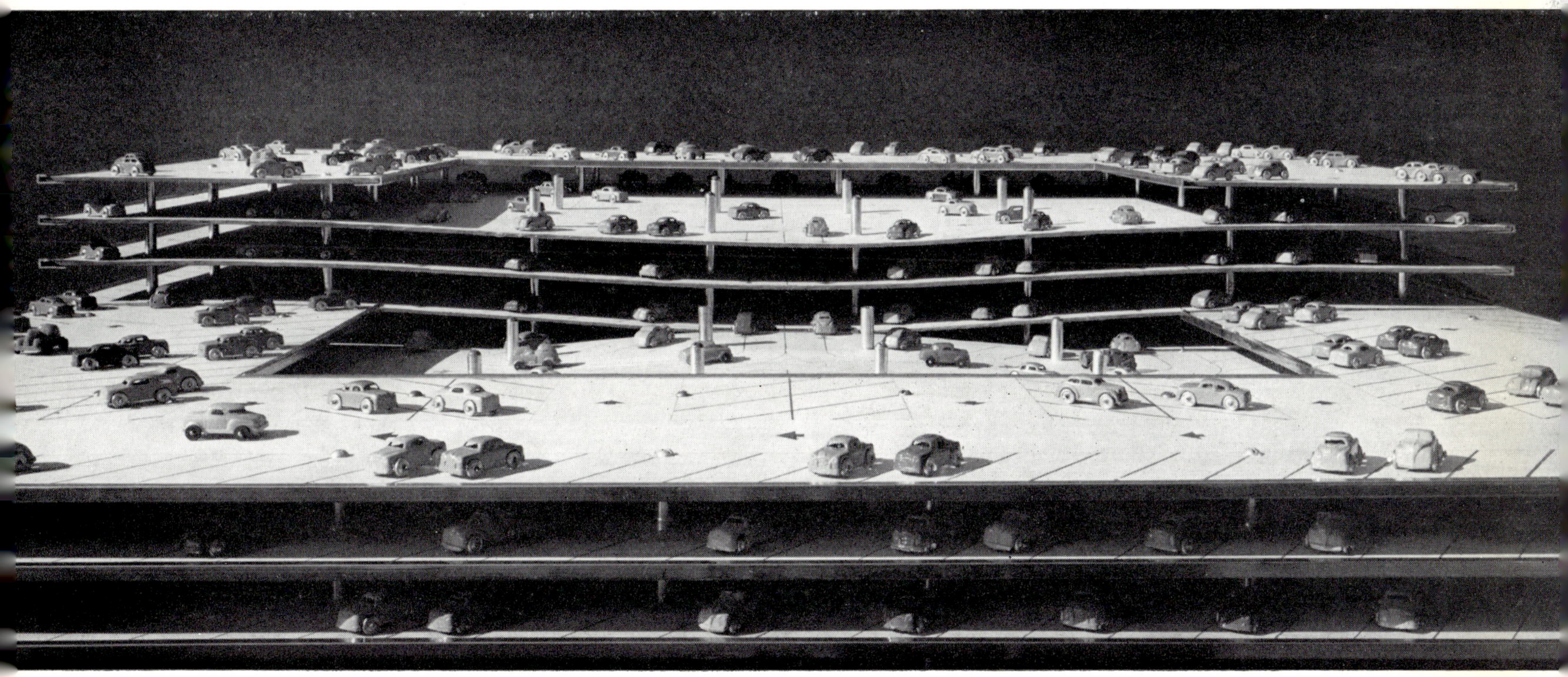

106 **A roof road designed by E. M. Khoury.** The designer says: 'a photograph of Los Angeles with the urban areas master-planned for the future in block bands knifing through the heart of the city in selected areas and tied in with the outside freeways . . . an entirely new and independent traffic system is added to the existing street traffic system.'

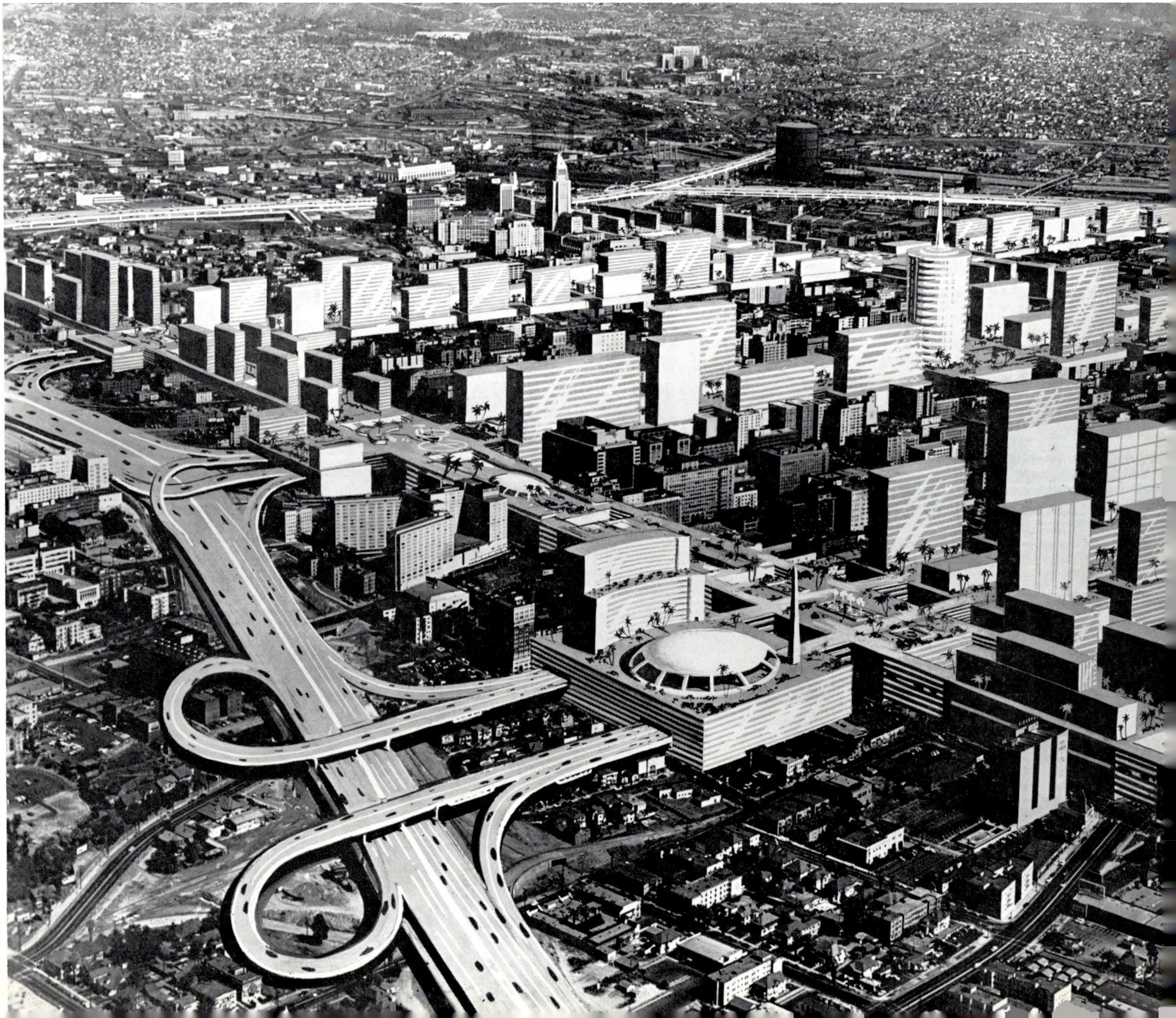

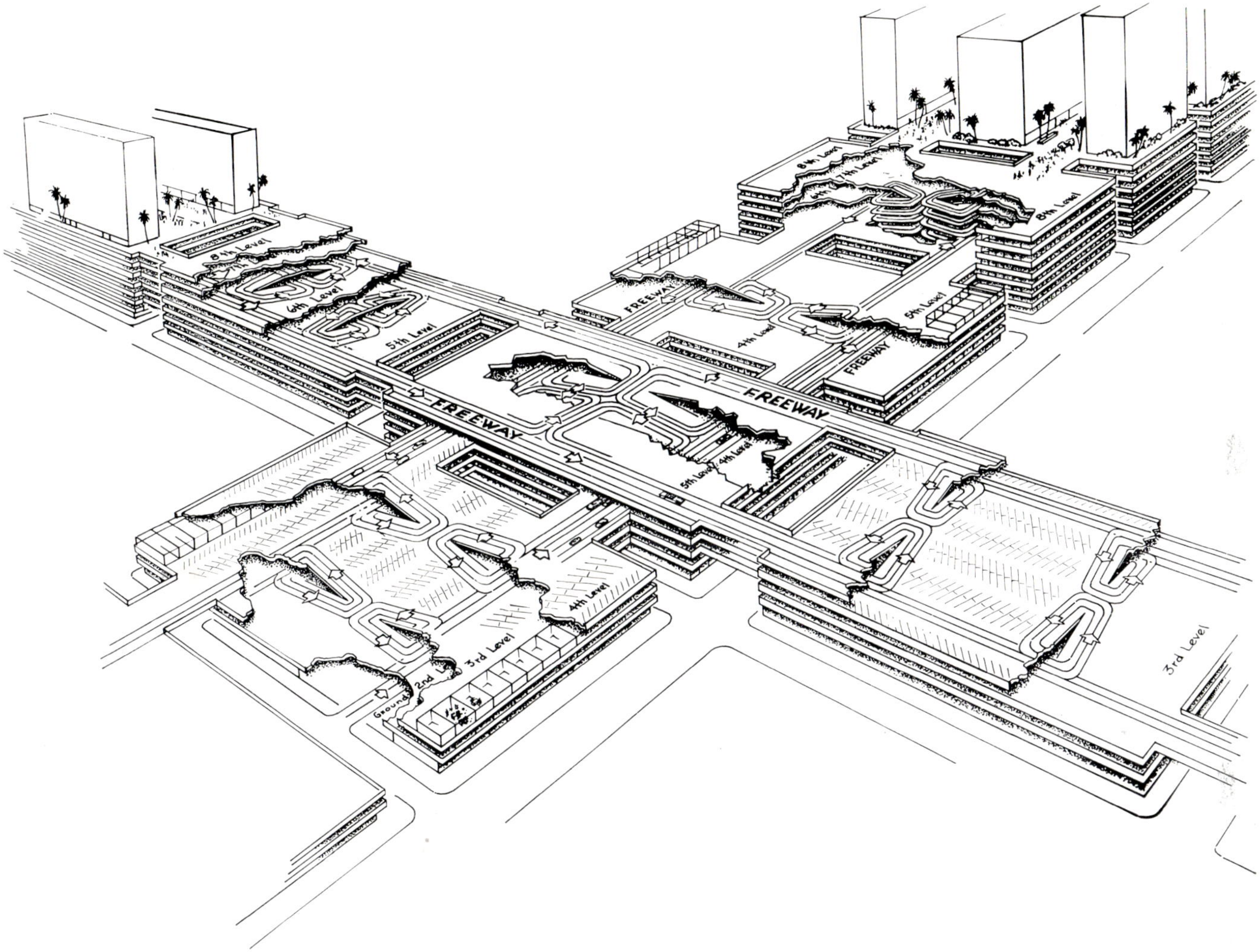

107 **A Roof Road design by E. M. Khoury.** The designer says: 'a schematic showing how two intersecting blocks are functioning. Note the fourth floor freeway in the wide block and the fifth floor freeway in the narrow block. Note the simple interchange in the area where the two blocks come together. Note the parking areas, the office areas, and the buildings on top.'

108 **Le Corbusier: Plan for Algiers.** The roof roads give the 'freeway' character to the town. Note especially the complexity of the various levels.

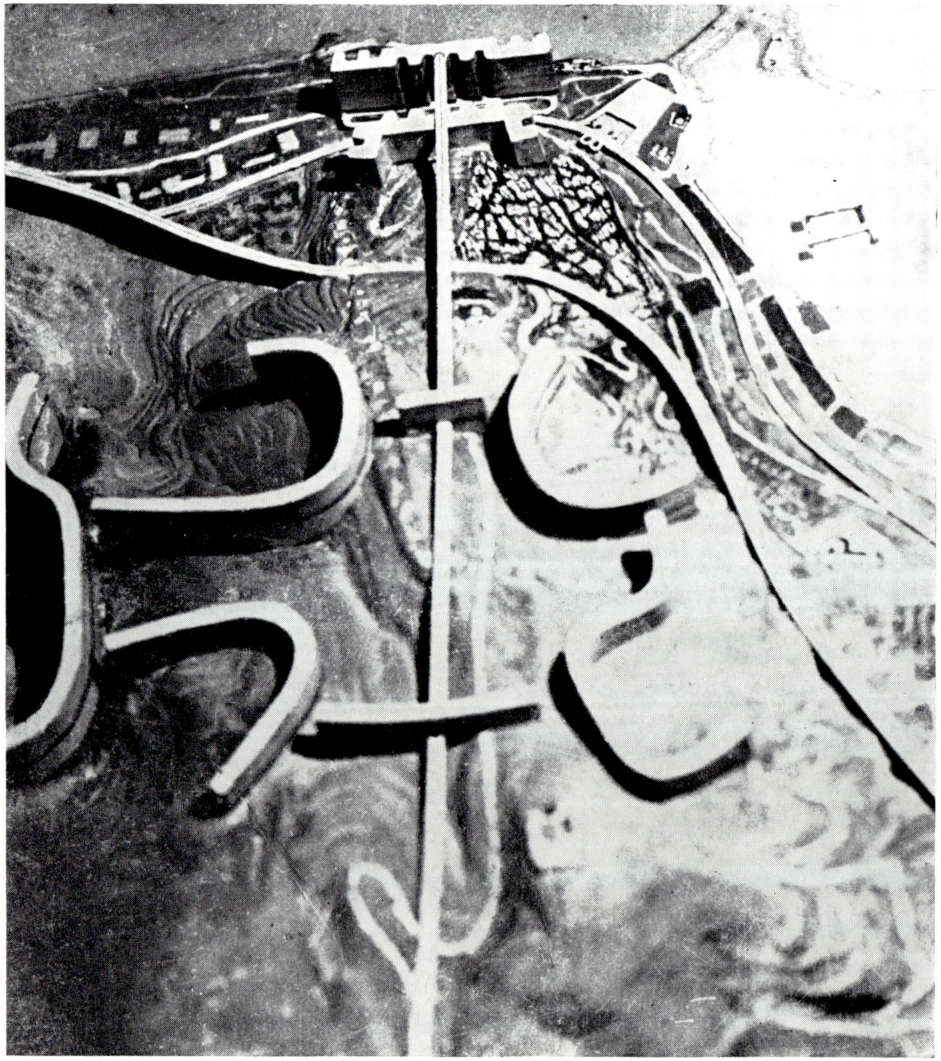

109 **Le Corbusier: Plan for Algiers.** It is probable that this entertaining and imaginative design would have distinct drawbacks, such as vehicular access to the long terraces. These would also tend to cut off the town-on-the-ground from the sea. Nevertheless it is an inspired and stimulating proposal.

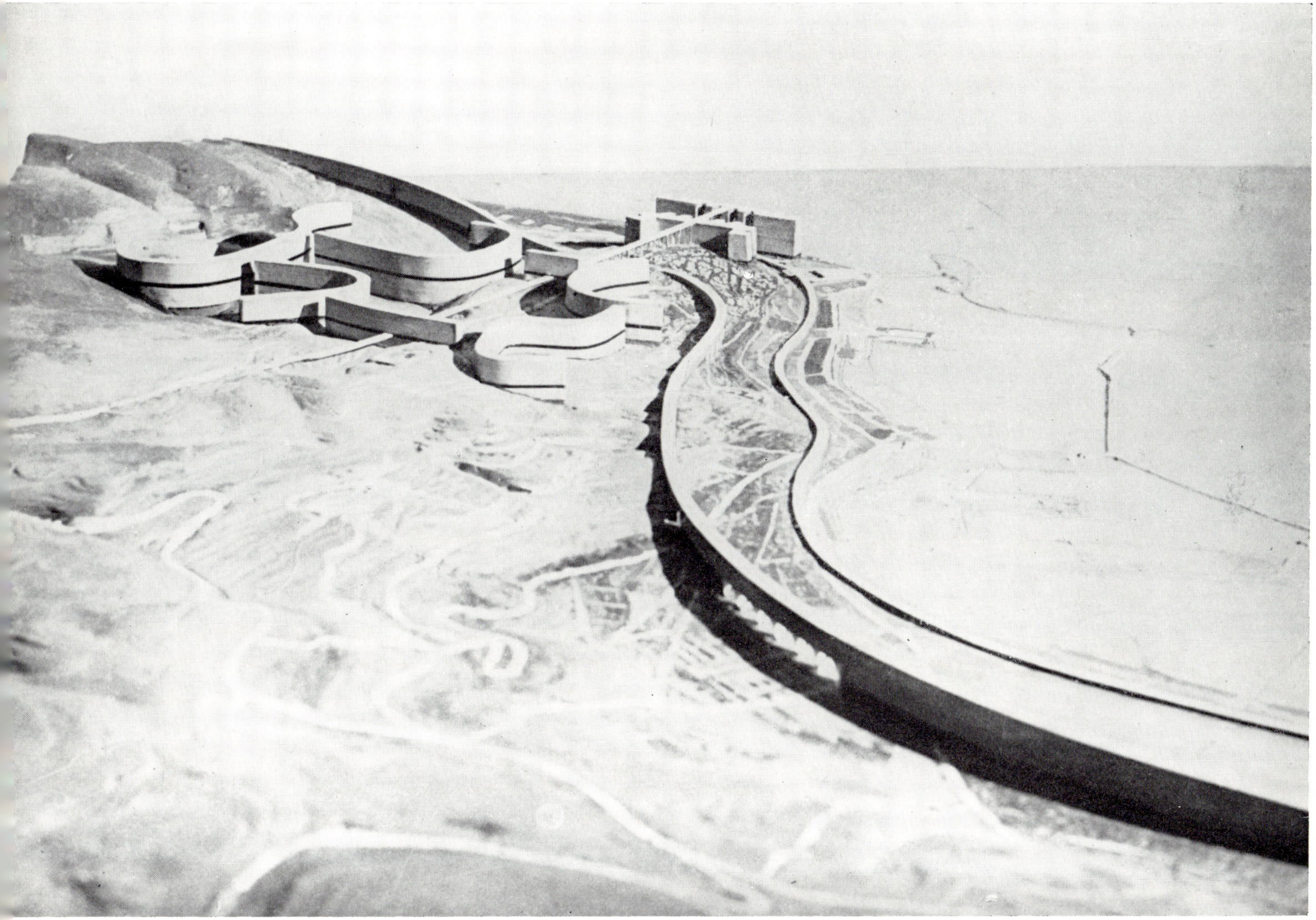

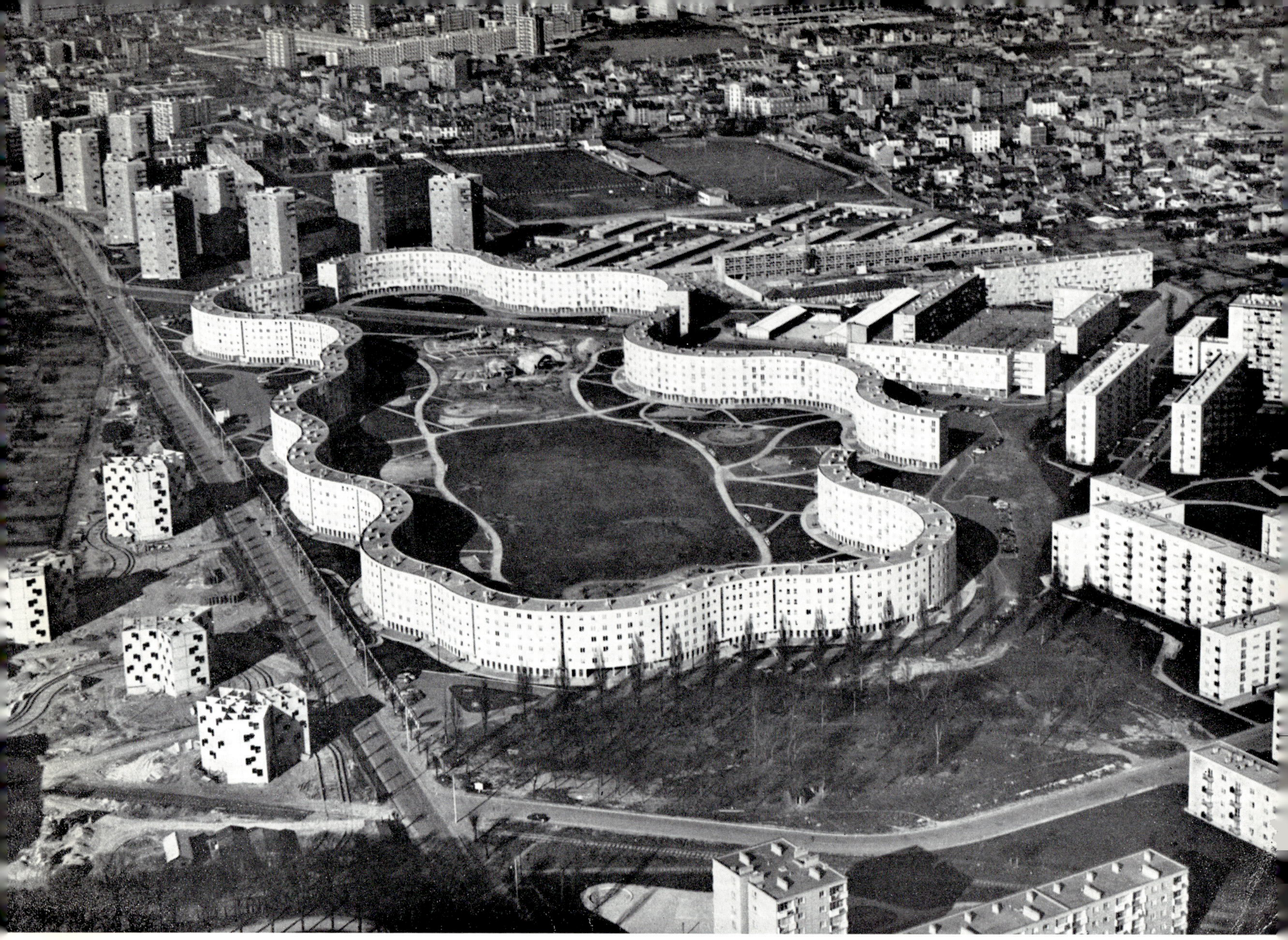

110 **Flats at Pantin, France.** This project was completed in August 1960, and is the modern conception most near to that of Motopia.

MOTOPIA

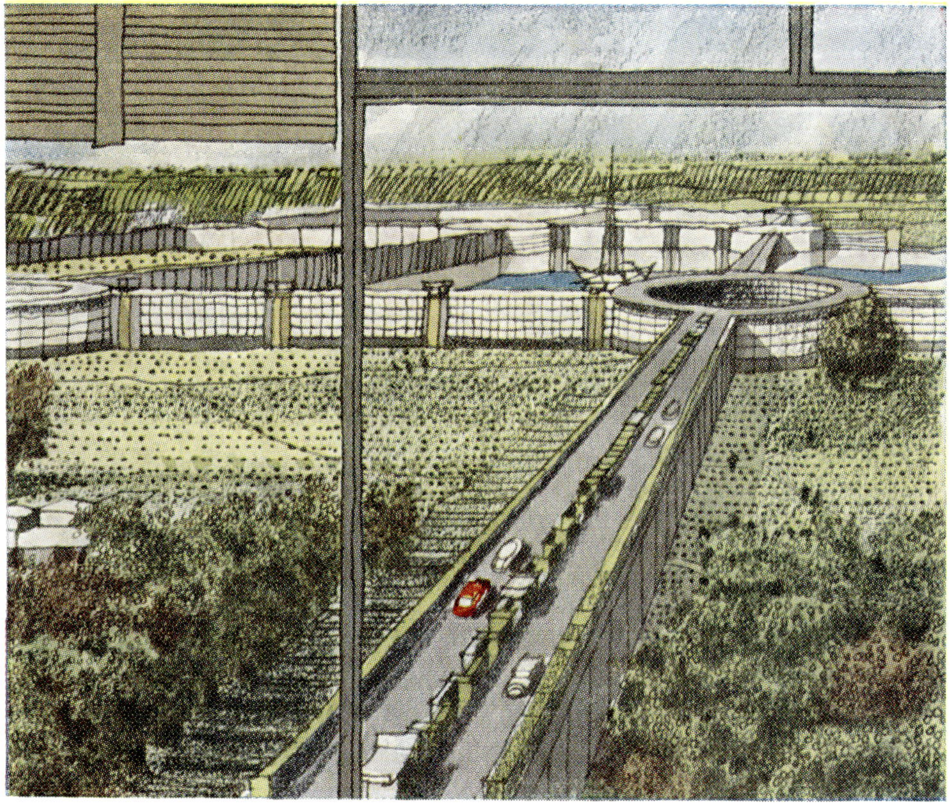

111 The idea of Motopia can be comprehended in a glance
Drawing by Gordon Cullen

The design for Motopia is diagrammatic only. The principle could be applied to any reasonably level site, but one adjoining higher land is obviously an advantage for access. The land itself can be waste, for in any case a wholly new landscape is created. It can be extended indefinitely. It can form more complex shapes than has been indicated, for the diagram has been simplified to state the case clearly. One glance at the model is enough to comprehend the two principles, one scientific and the other romantic: (a) the roads are placed on the roofs and leave the whole ground free for the pedestrian, and (b) the maximum contrast is made between the geometry of the buildings and the free and natural shapes of the ground landscape. Within these two principles certain minor principles have been established. The Town Centre should be at the side and not at the centre of the layout, in order to allow direct access of service vehicles and all those extra persons who come from outside; and to allow for extension. The height of the terraces is governed by the number of parking spaces available in a mews road. A higher terrace would, however, mean a second tier of mews road, the design becoming proportionately more urban with a higher density; the problem of ramp access is more difficult and becomes unreasonable except for a very large new city; the relation between terrace and forest tree is no longer agreeable.

The site for this example is on the flat land adjoining the Thames near Staines Reservoir. It is in the Green Belt, and has been chosen therefore as an exercise only. It adjoins London Airport and is on the natural extension of the road system out of London to the west; the Chiswick fly-over already prepares the visitor for rooftop sensations. The ground is first-class agricultural land, seriously encroached upon by worked-out gravel pits which are today partly used for yachting. Rivers cross the site from north to south to join the Thames. This crossflow has been emphasized by the artificial planting of forest trees, cutting across the gridiron patterns. The population chosen is 30,000 persons and all the buildings requiring open spaces, such as schools, are to the present accepted standards and are contained within the town or on the immediate perimeter. The dwellings are mixed within the grid standardized for each terrace, and normally have two aspects. There are 1,113 dwellings with private gardens. There are arcades at ground level which link the dwelling to the neighbourhood circle, with its local facilities, and to the main shopping centre. Ground transport is normally by water bus. The estimated cost is £60,000,000, of which one half is for the residential terraces, including roads. The approximate rent, inclusive of heating and car parking, would be about £100 per head per annum.

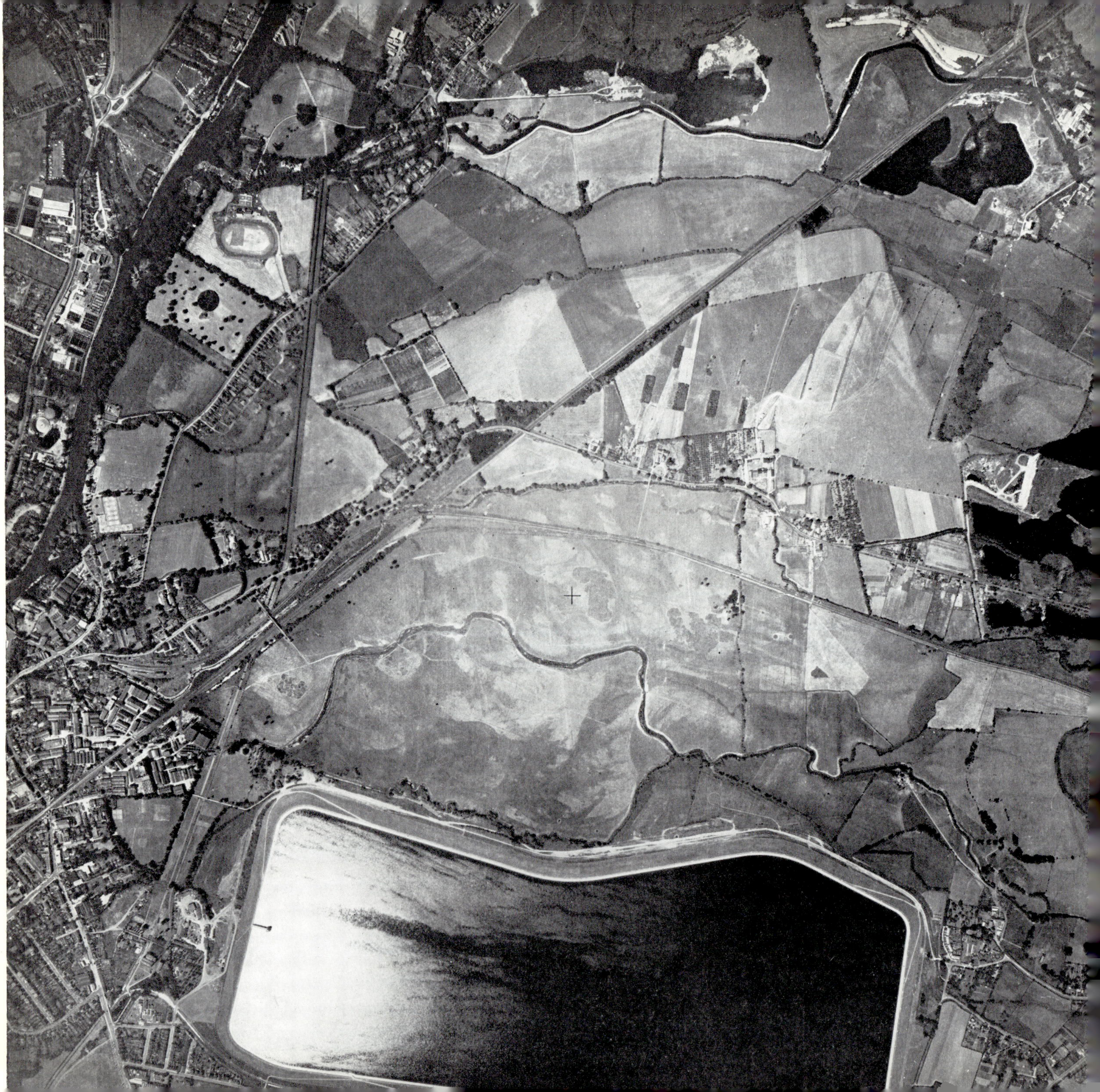

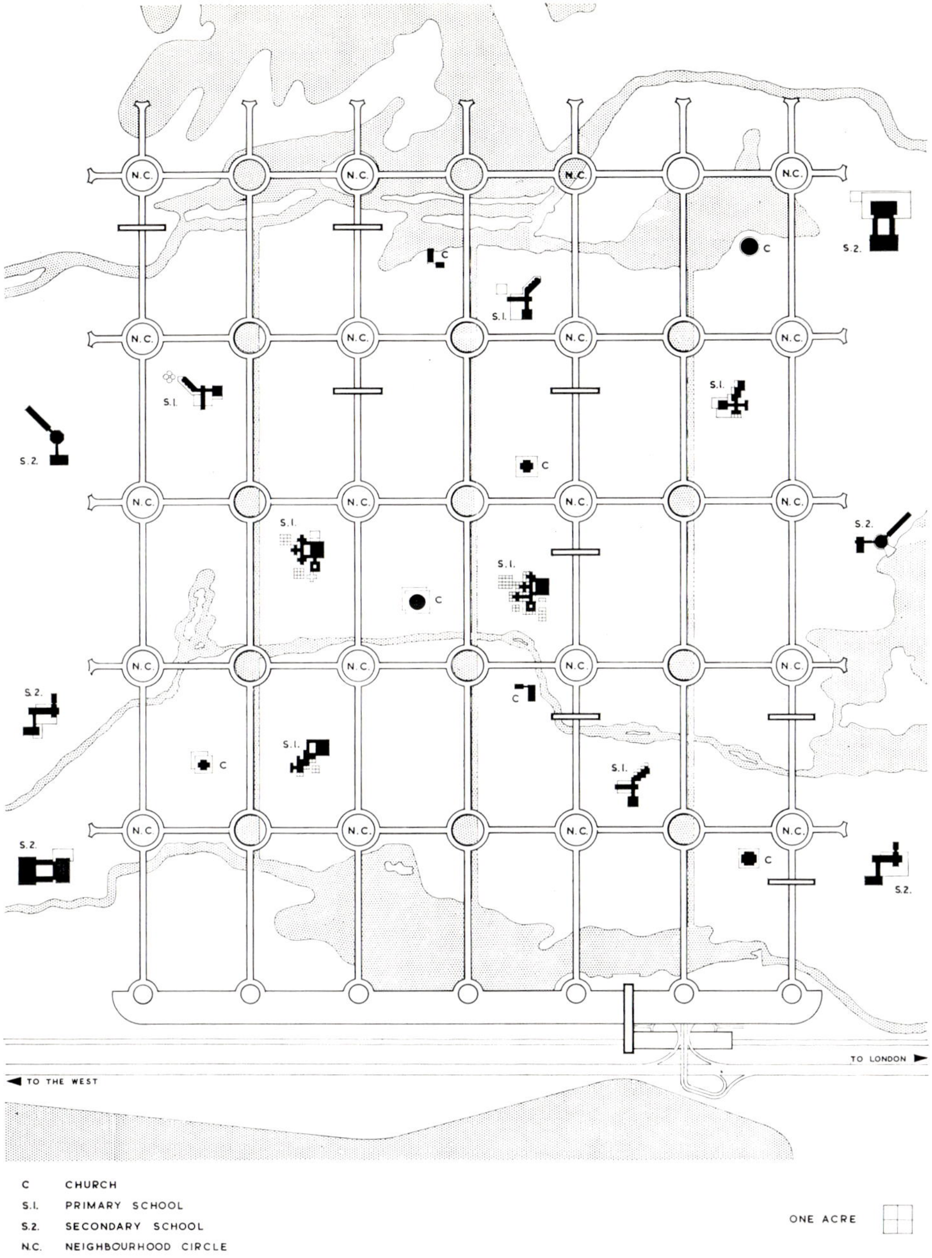

113 **The Grid of Motopia applied to the site.** The existing site can be located by Staines Reservoir to the south, and the rivers and gravel pits. All dwellings and commerce are contained within the grid; all churches, schools, sports clubs and similar activities, are contained within the ground landscape. New forest planting runs parallel to the rivers. The site chosen is in the Green Belt round London and is therefore an exercise only.

◀ 112 **Air view of site.** The only major adjustments were the diversion of the railways. The rivers and water-logged gravel pits have been developed.

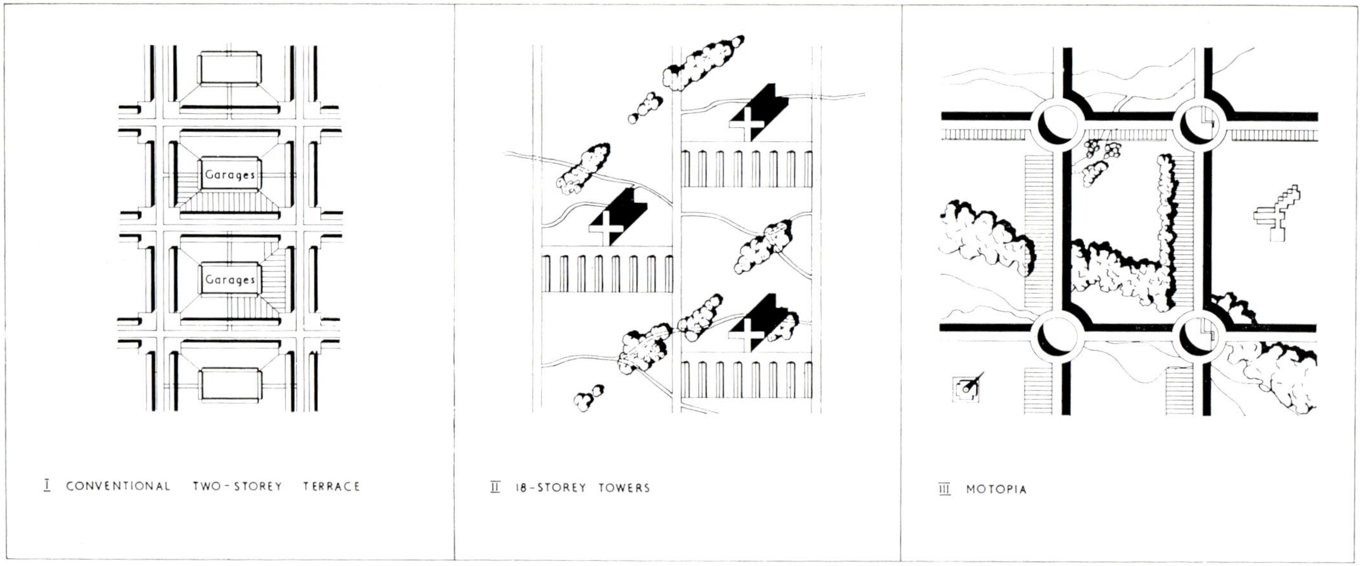

114 **Theory of use of land.** The diagram represents three methods of housing at a density of 30 persons per acre, based on the Motopian grid of approximately 800 ft × 1,200 ft. The conventional is suited to English climate and characteristic; and includes terrace and semi-detached houses, some with attached garages; there is no open space. The towers are foreign in climate and characteristic but give more freedom to landscape; there are no private gardens and the garages sterilize much of the open space.

115 **The continuous landscape beneath the grid** ▶

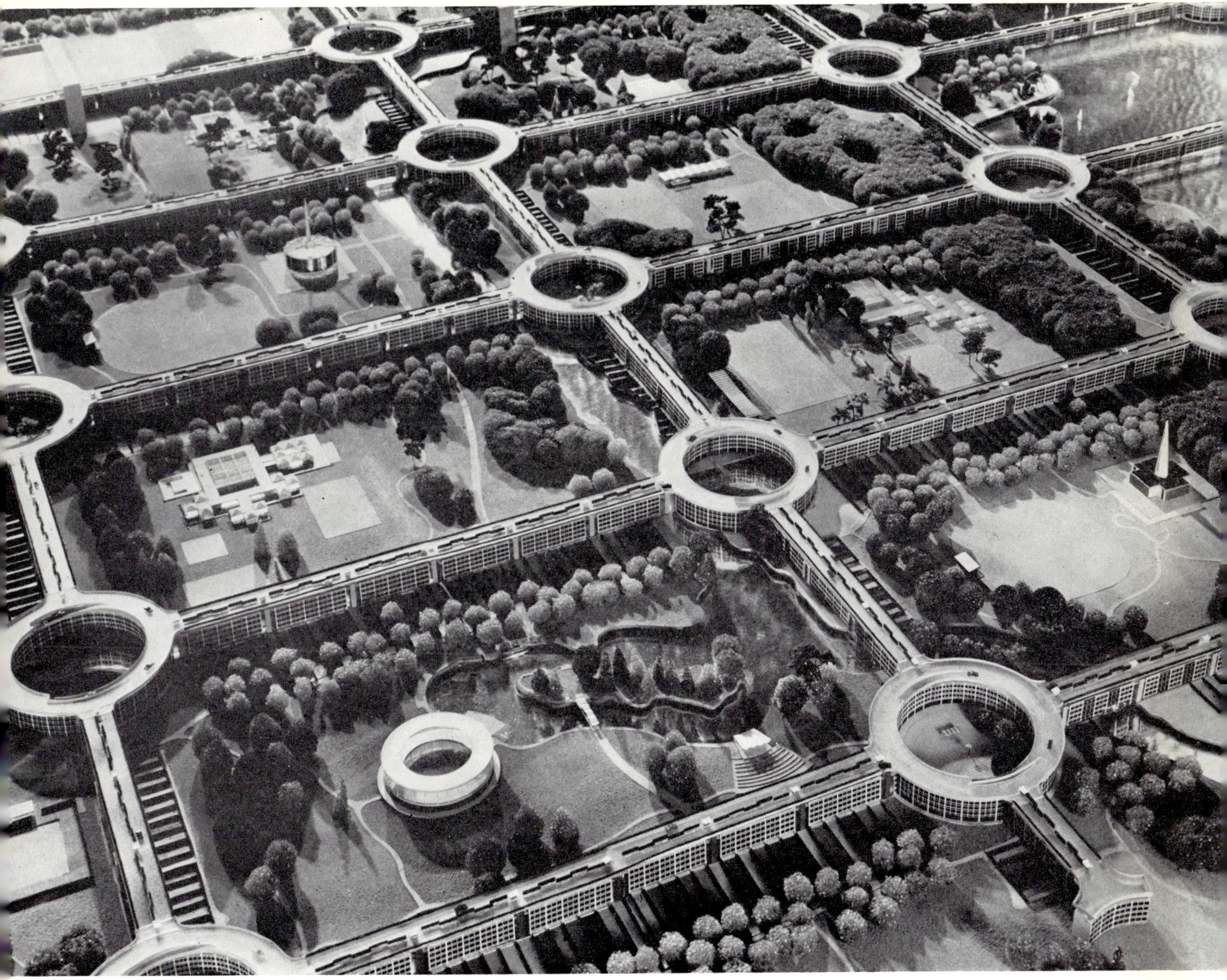

116 **Ground and Typical Floor Plan of Circle and Terrace.** Shown diagrammatically. The shaded areas are dwellings. Round the circles on the ground floor are shops, etc.

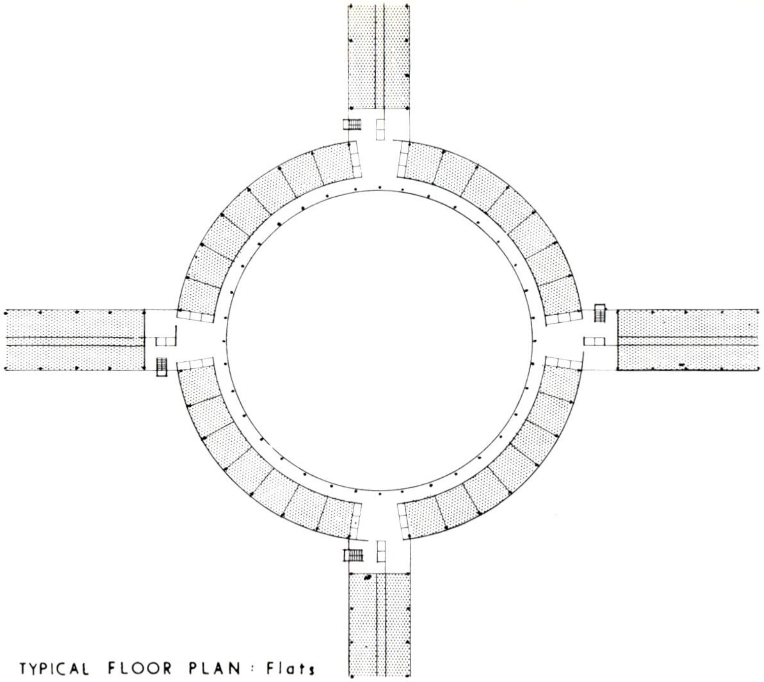

TYPICAL FLOOR PLAN : Flats

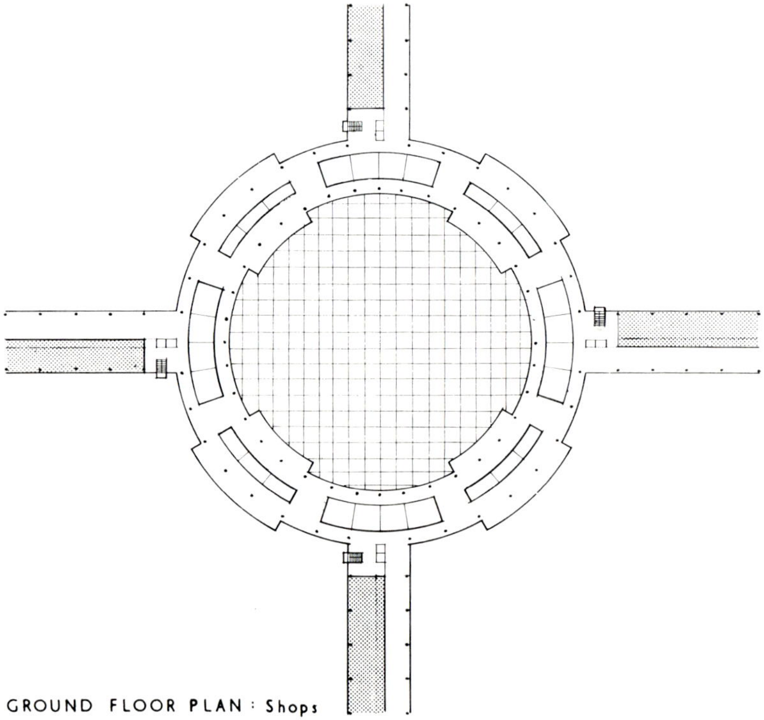

GROUND FLOOR PLAN : Shops

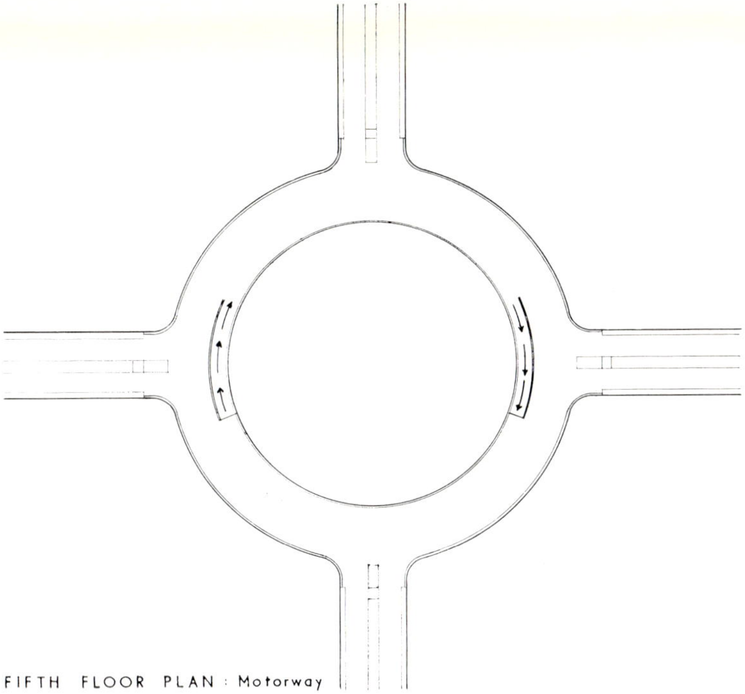

FIFTH FLOOR PLAN : Motorway

117 **Motorway and Mews Road.** The peak load flow of cars along the residential roads is comparatively small and from west to east or vice-versa. The north-south flow is negligible. The total width is 40 ft, and the ramps are 10 ft wide, headroom 8 ft, and a rise of 1 in 10. Stop sign and good visibility at one-way exit from mews roads.

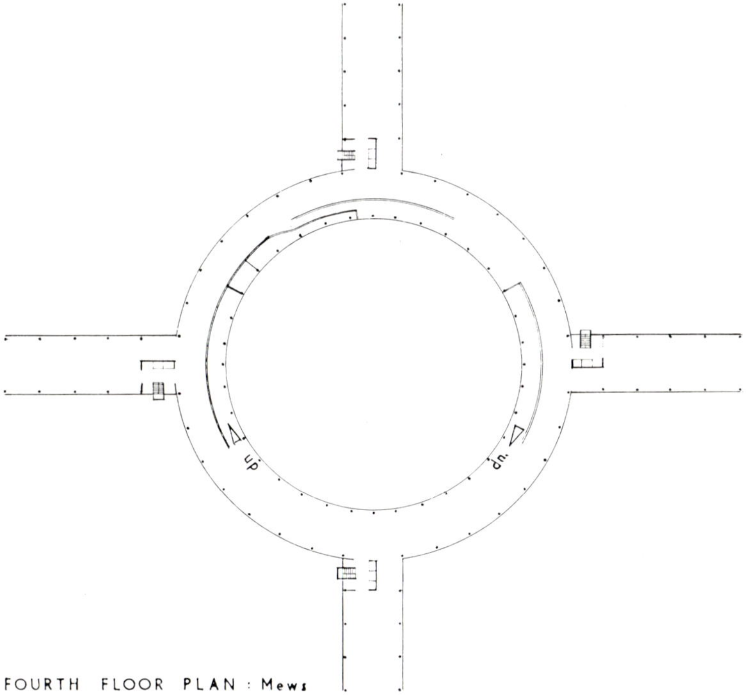

FOURTH FLOOR PLAN : Mews

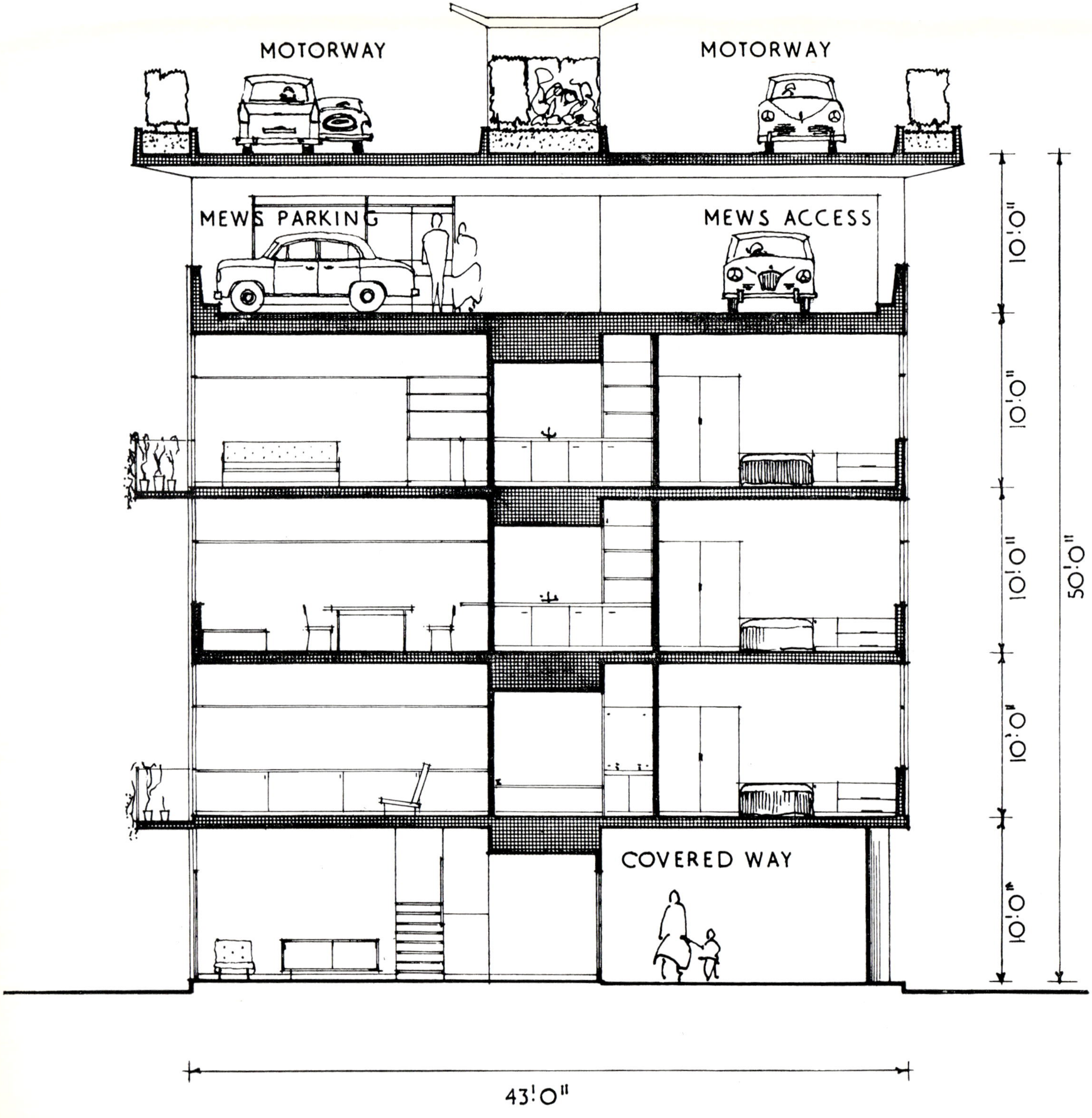
MOTORWAY
MOTORWAY
MEWS PARKING
MEWS ACCESS
COVERED WAY
10'0"
10'0"
10'0"
10'0"
10'0"
50'0"
43'0"

118 **Section of a Residential Terrace.** This is the section upon which the economy of Motopia is based. There is no problem of structure nor of transmission of sound. The real problem lies in suppressing or concealing the two roadways as an element of architecture. If, for example, the mews road were to be the same width as the motorway above, the roads would become the dominating feature and the idea of the landscape would collapse.

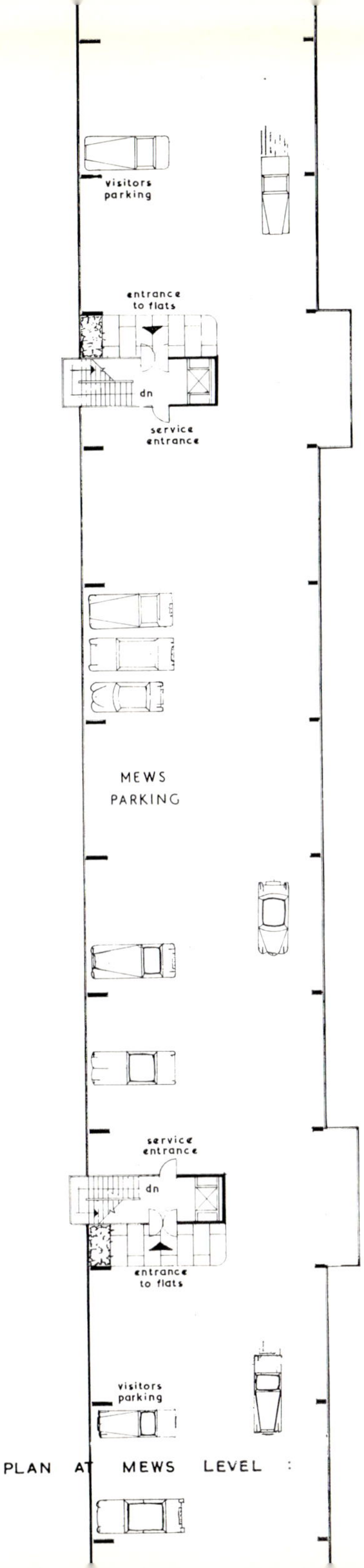

119 **Plan of a Mews Road.** This road lies immediately below the motorway, and is reached by ramps in the adjoining circles. The available width is 42 ft. The grid is 21 ft. There is parking space of one car per dwelling, together with standing space for visitors and service cars. The traffic flow is one-way and limited to 15 m.p.h.

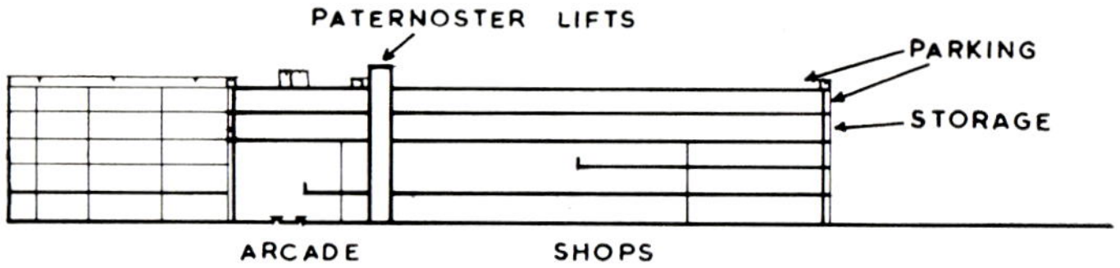

120 a and b **Town Centre.** This linear shopping street is approximately one mile in length, and consists of shops and storage, places of entertainment, and double decker roof parking for 6,000 cars. Continuous pedestrian lifts called paternosters, used extensively in Germany, ply between car parks and arcade. Moving bands (used first in the Paris Exhibition 1889) convey passengers along the full length, since there are no buses. The arcade is totally enclosed and air-conditioned. The shops are on two levels, the upper being served by a balcony. Opposite the shops is a continuous view of the lakes and public parks of the eastern rectangles. The circles under the glass domes are meeting places and cafés extend their tables into the public thoroughfare.

The centre is designed to serve a population of more than five times that of Motopia itself. The town public transport is water bus, which stops at the circles. The external transport is the electric railway that has been diverted from its present course, and public road buses (and in due course helicopter buses which would land on the roof).

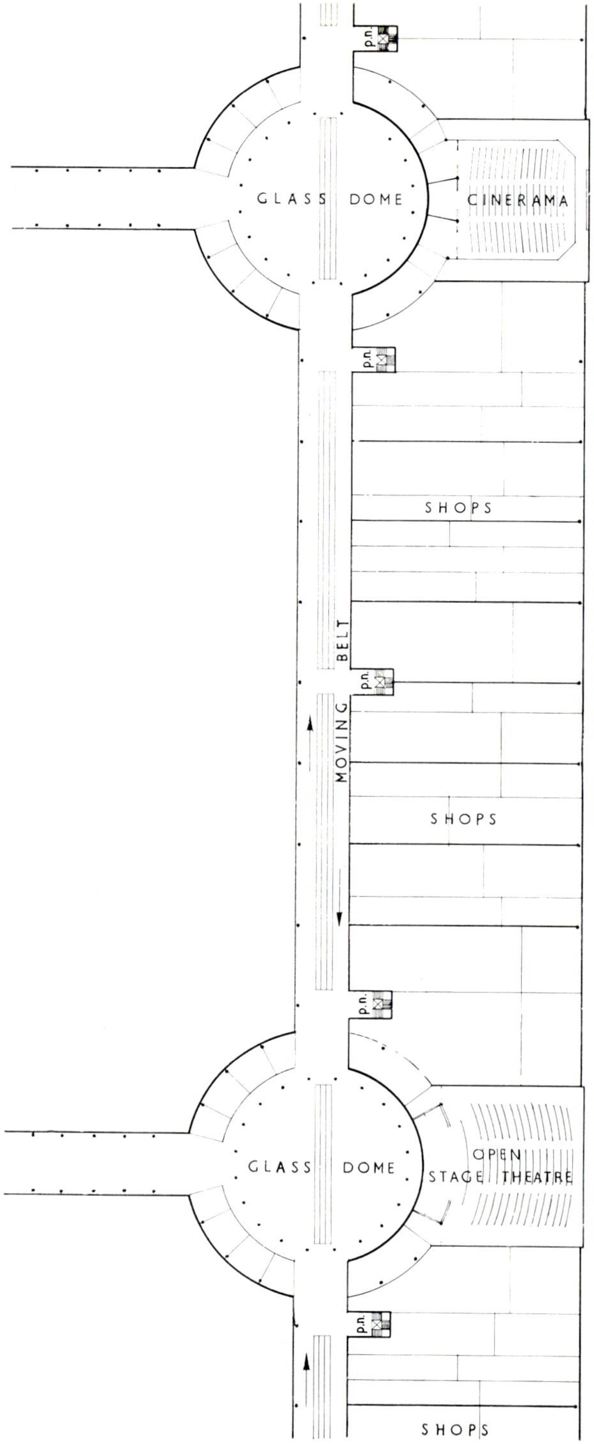

121 **General View of Town Centre.** The entrance fly-over crosses the car park above the railway station and ascends to roof level. Branches serve the railway and rear of shops. The tall block contains the civic centre at the top and administrative and private offices below. A second entrance towards the west would seem desirable.

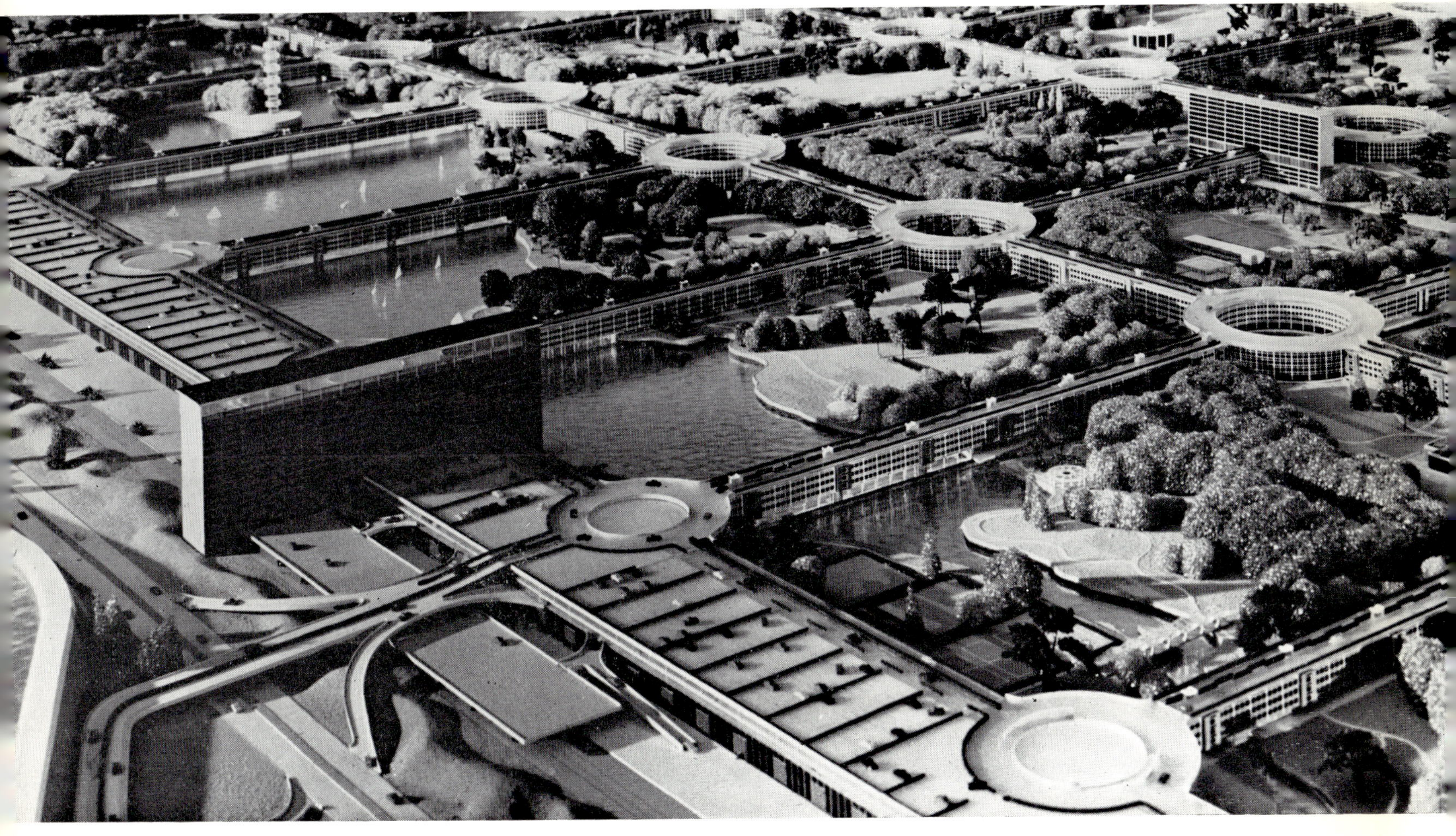

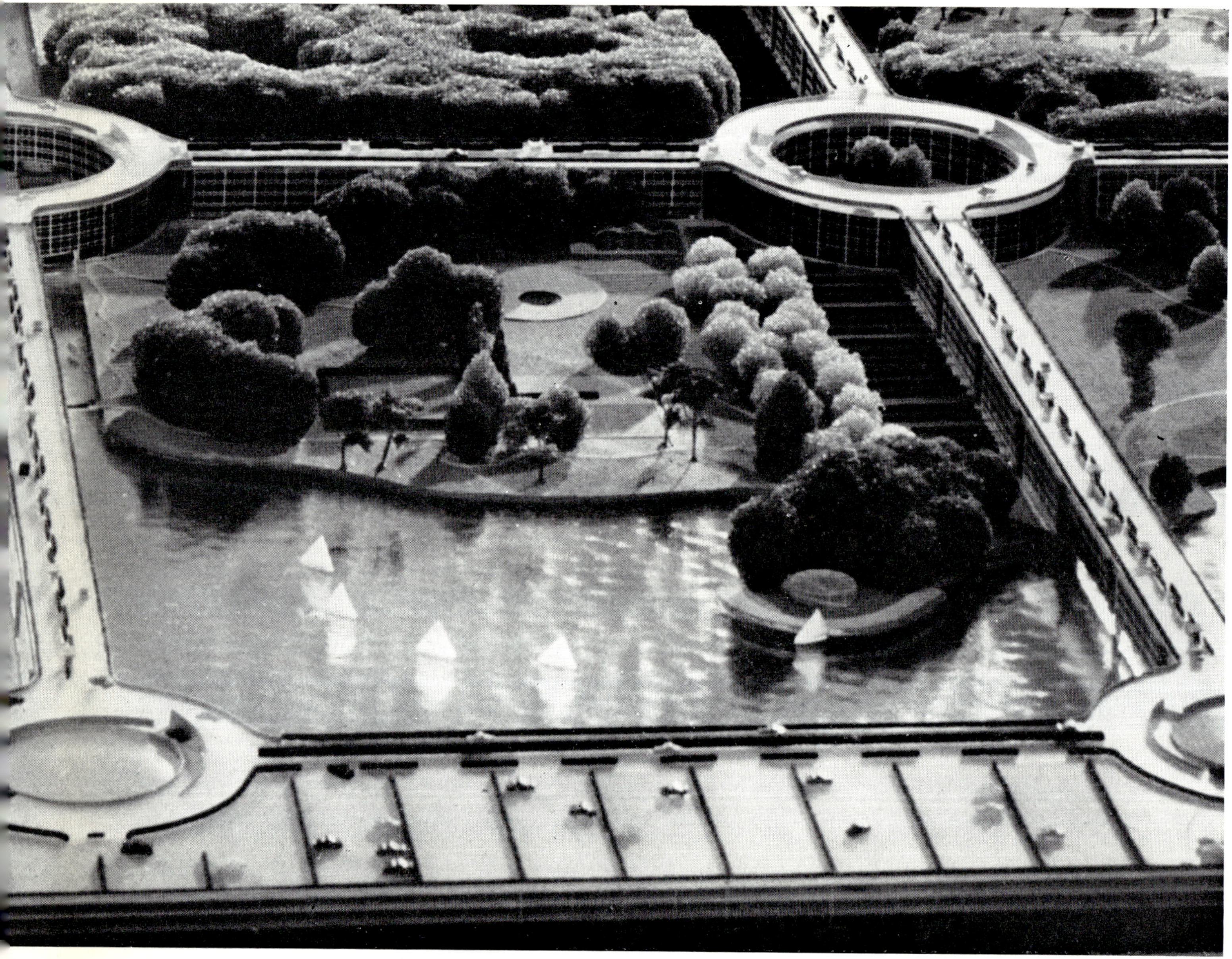

122 **Town Centre.** Central Gardens.

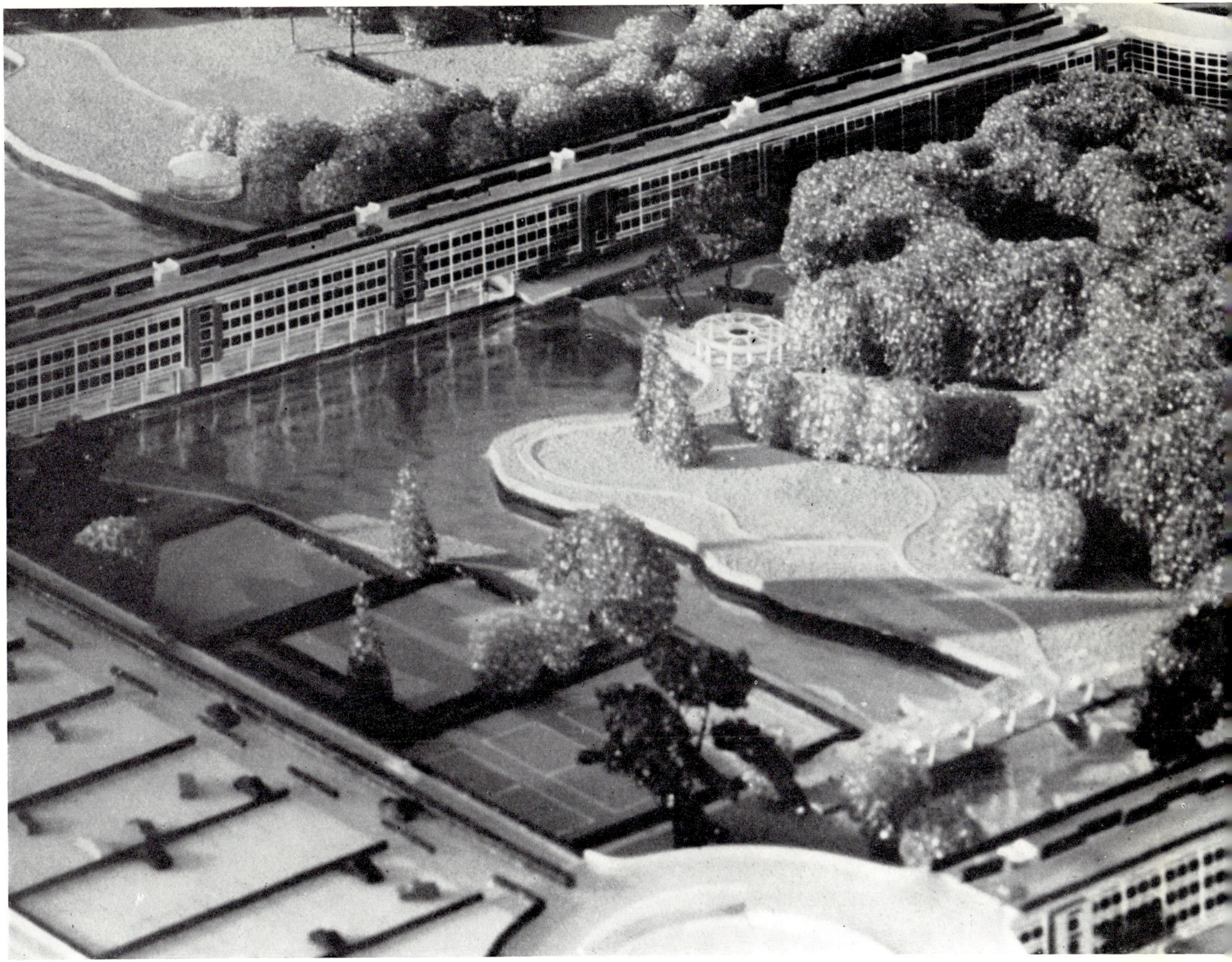

123 **Town Centre.** Public tennis courts and the glass bridge.

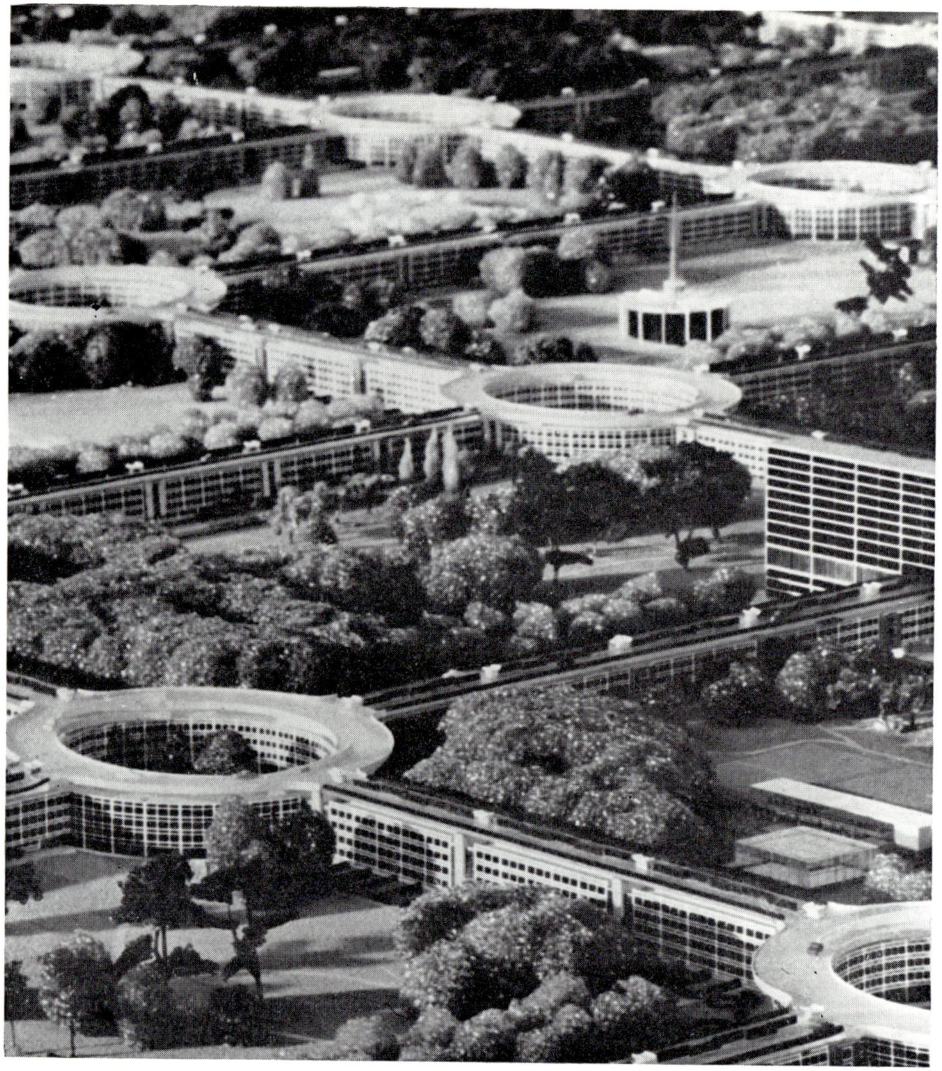

124 **The Church.** General view showing how the shape of a church contrasts with the terraces and the landscape.

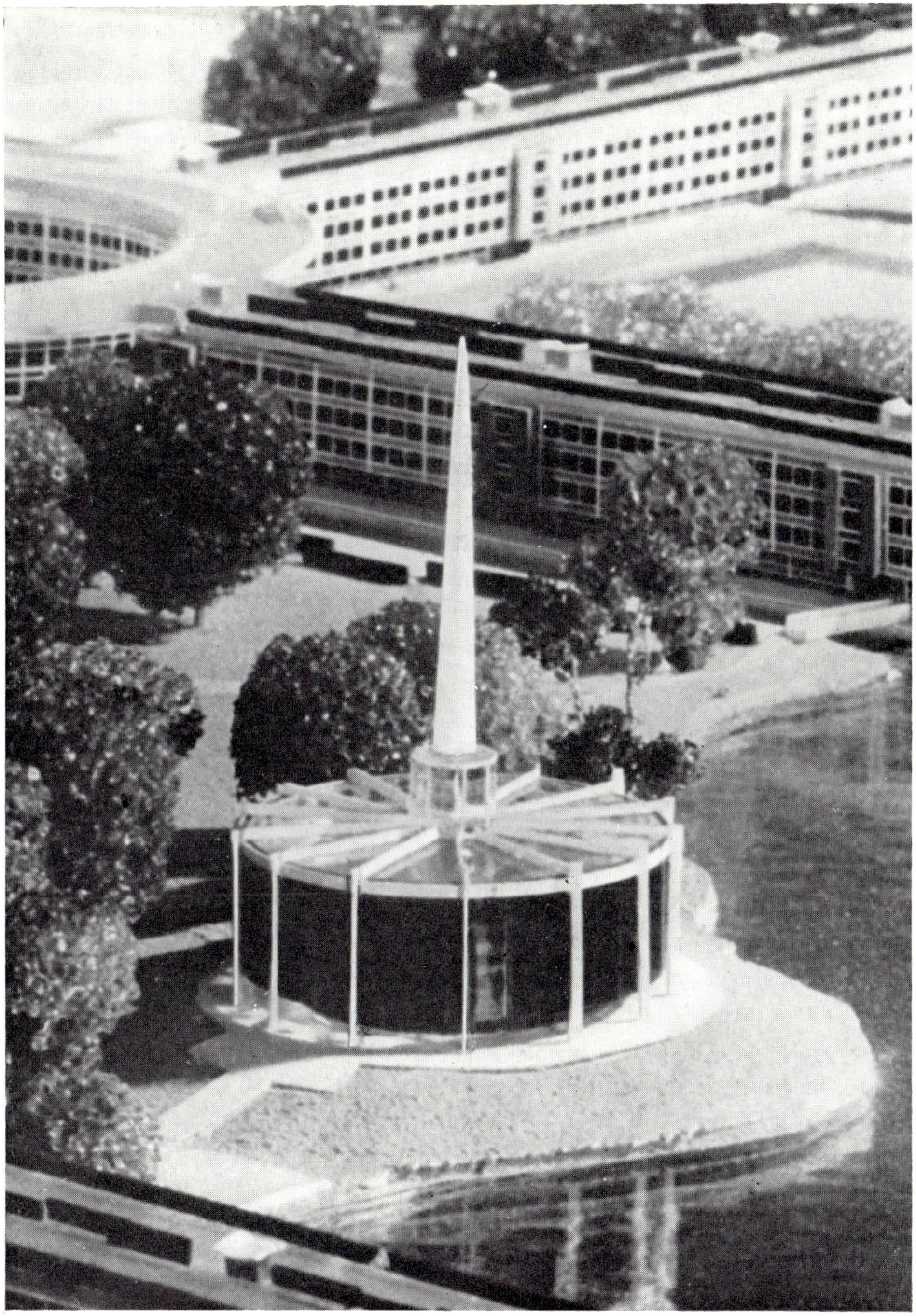

125 **The Church.** Detail of a church, showing the symmetry of the design. In this example the walls are opaque but the roof is of glass and will be seen by passing motorists. The spire is a television aerial and is illuminated; it is anticipated that services and sacred plays may come to be televised for local congregations.

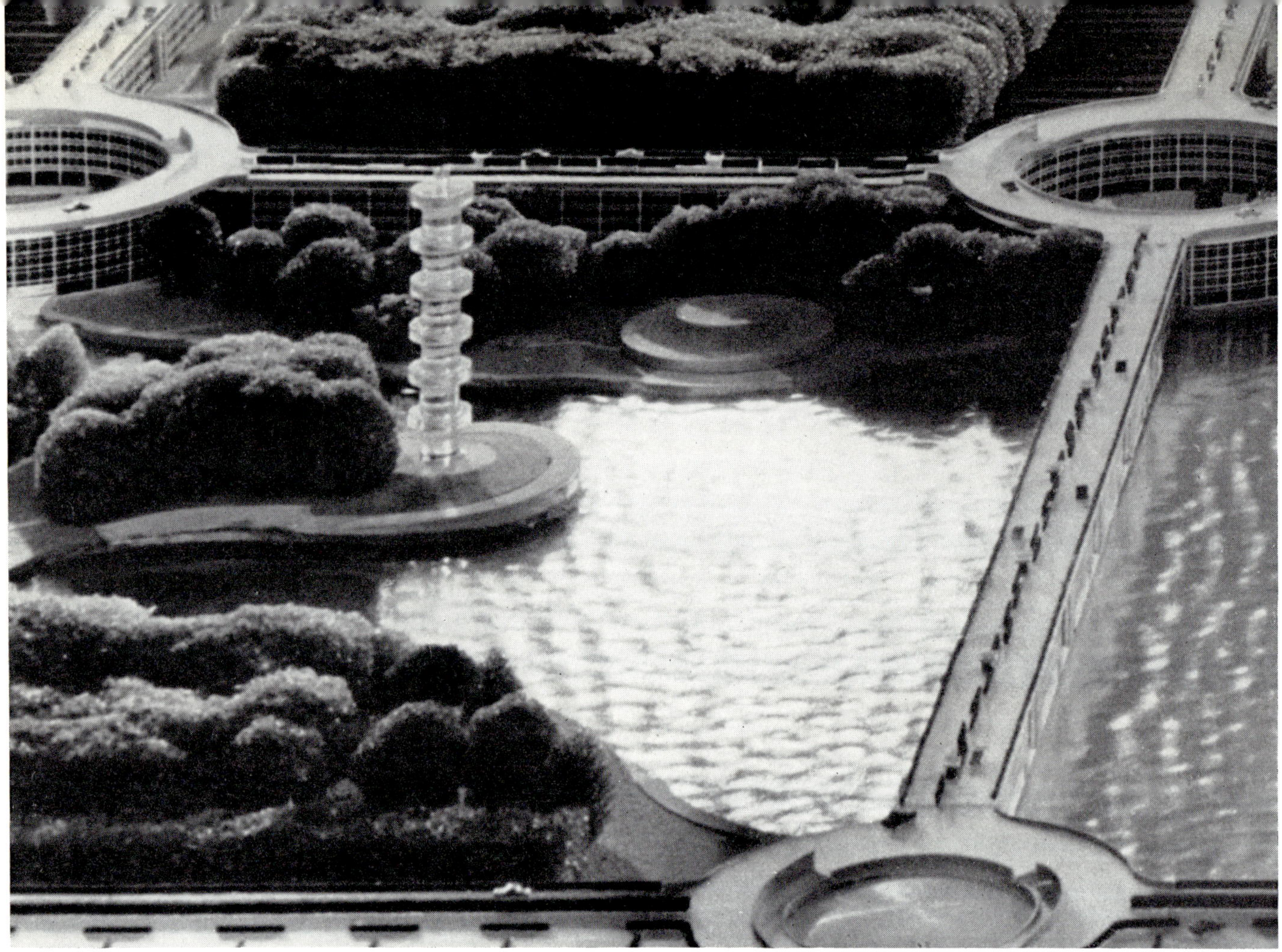

126a **The Glass Television Pagoda.** Each floor contains a café tuned to a different wave length.

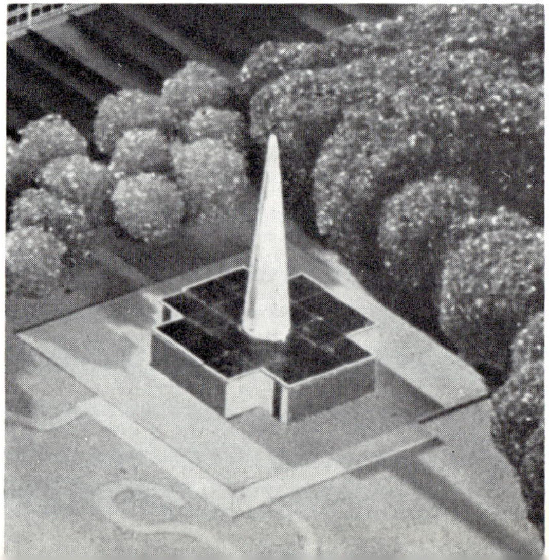

126b Detail of another church. The design varies from that shown in Plate 125, since the ceiling is opaque and the walls are transparent.

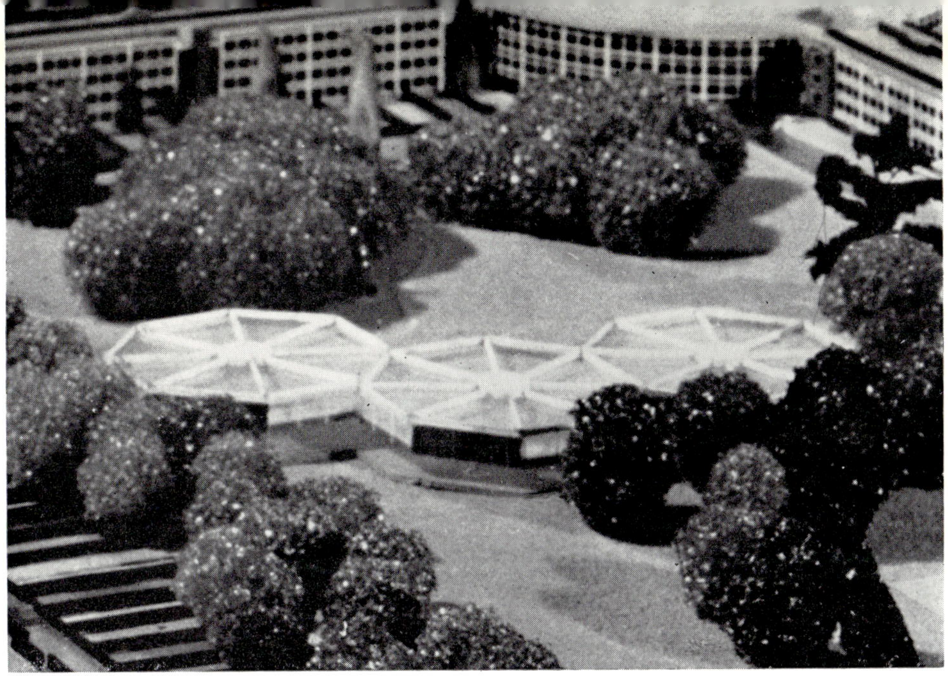

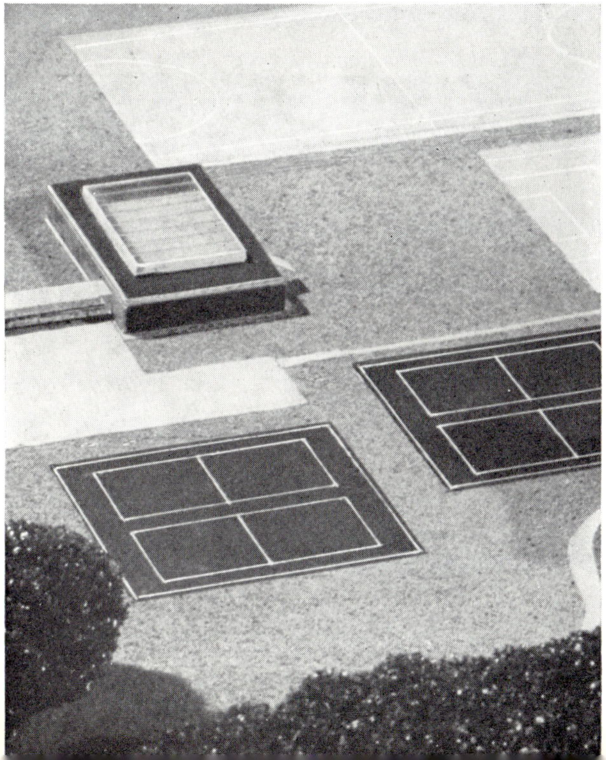

127 a and b **The School.** In contrast to the shape of the churches, which in principle varies very little from one to another, the schools are wholly different and have an organic design based on their function. These two examples are contrasting and each has made an environment peculiar to itself.

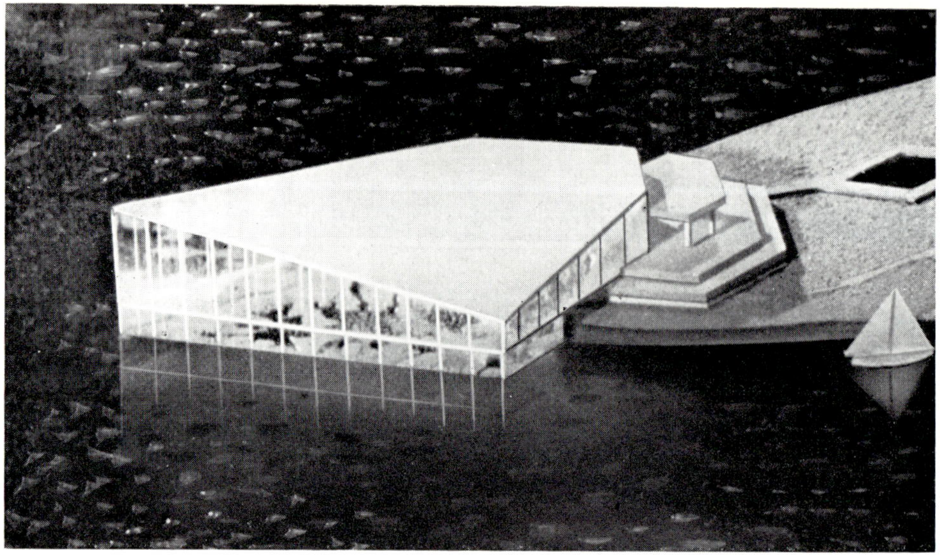

128a and b **The Yacht Club.** These are two of the principal clubs, which form a strong feature of the social life of the town.

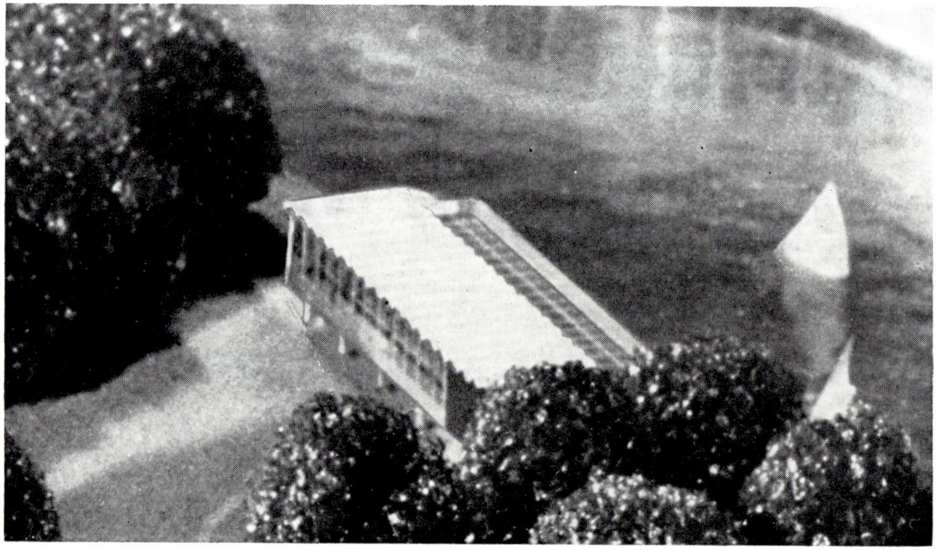

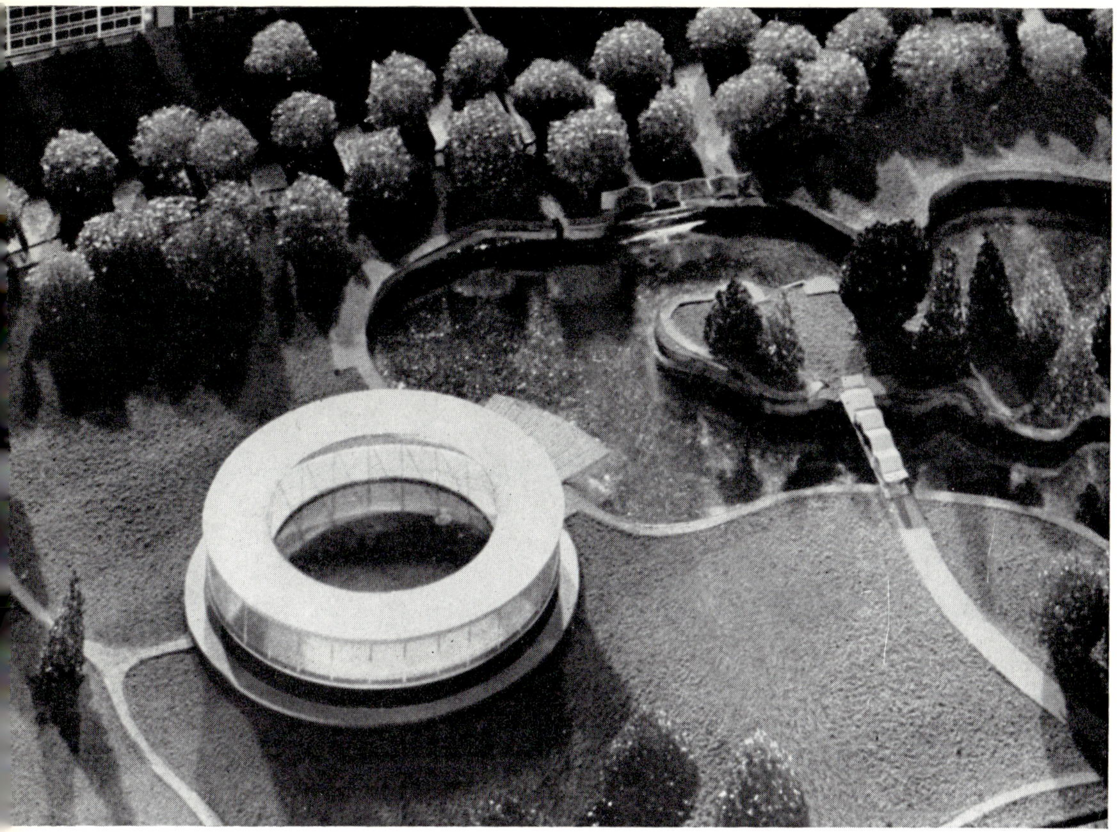

129a **A small Sports Arena** planned to receive visitors by water if necessary.

129c **A Shelter**

:9b **An open-air Theatre**

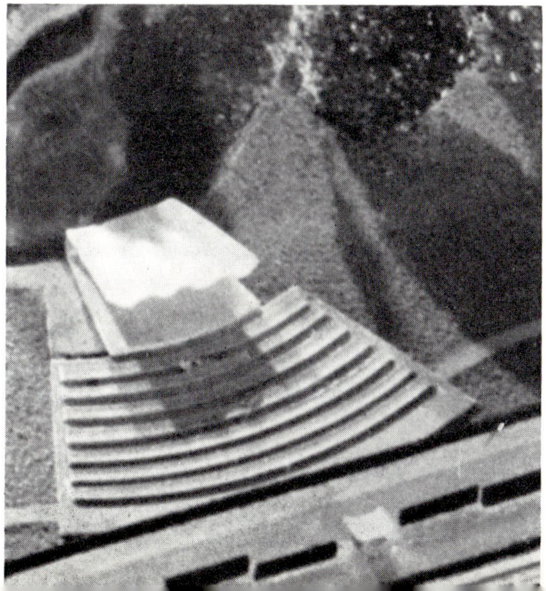

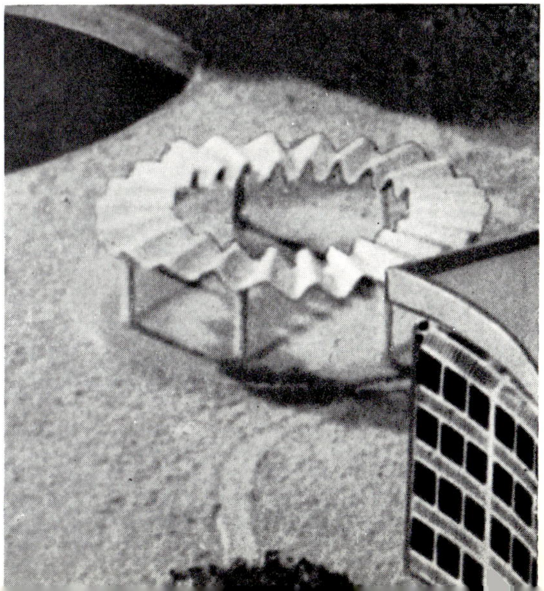

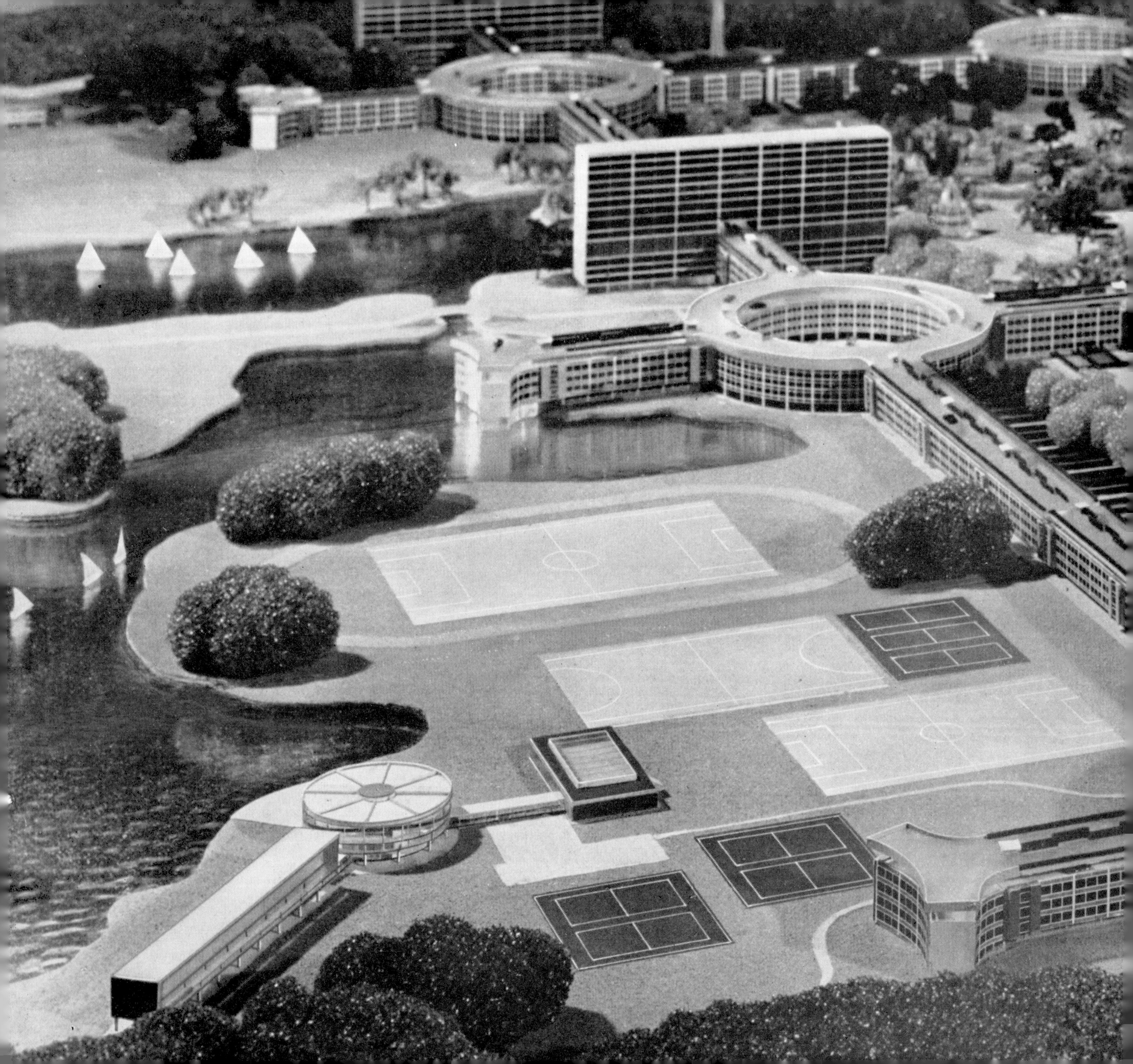

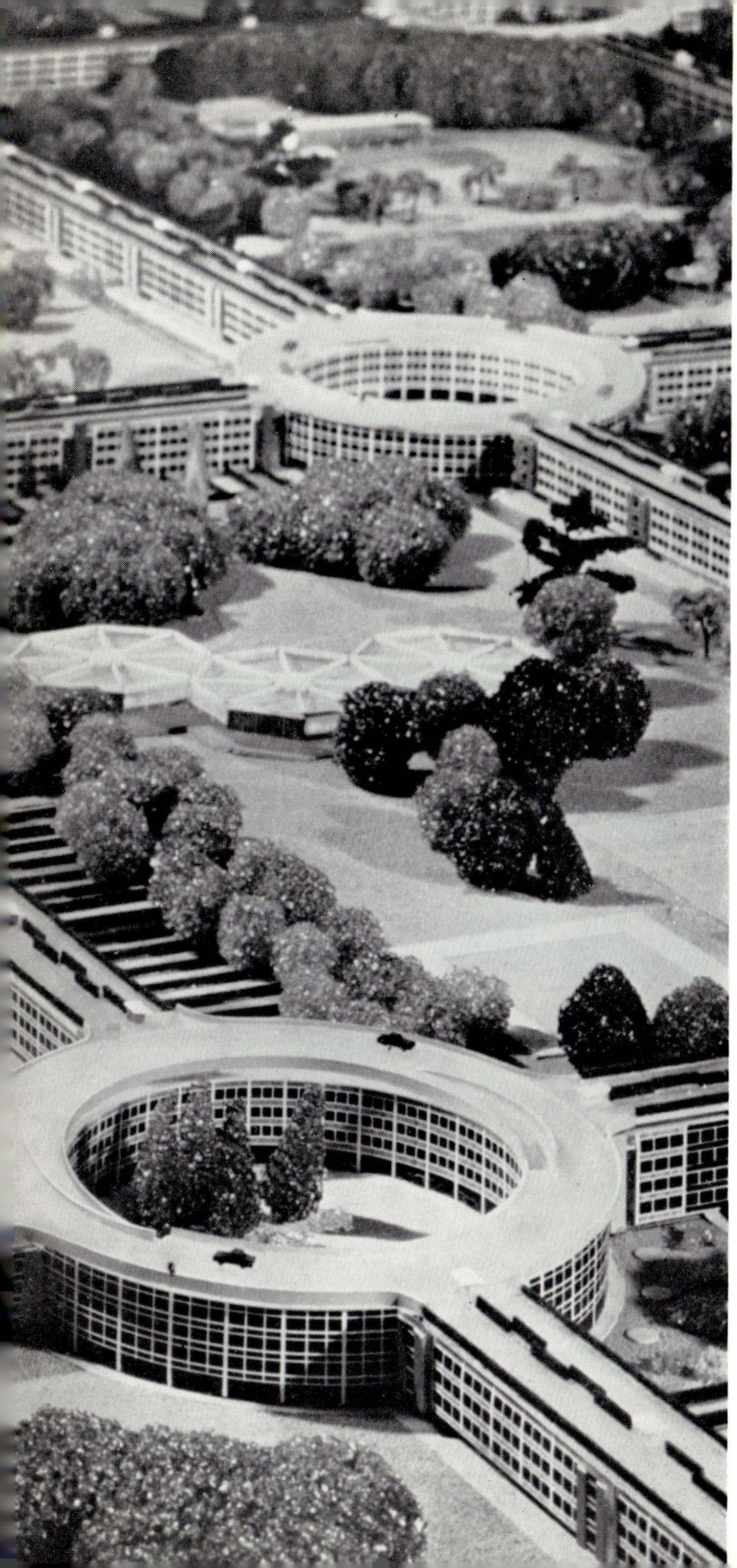

130 **Typical detail of the perimeter of Motopia.** Helicopters would not be allowed overhead and must land on the projecting bays, to fold up their wings and thereafter to use the normal roads. Car parking for the tall flats is on two floors at terrace rooftop level.

131 **Another detail of the perimeter.** These two separate views show the variety that has been given by the landscape. Here are schools and sports clubs with their playing fields, and the boating lakes made from existing waste gravel quarries. Perhaps the most important element in the landscape is the forest tree, which normally is too large for urban development.

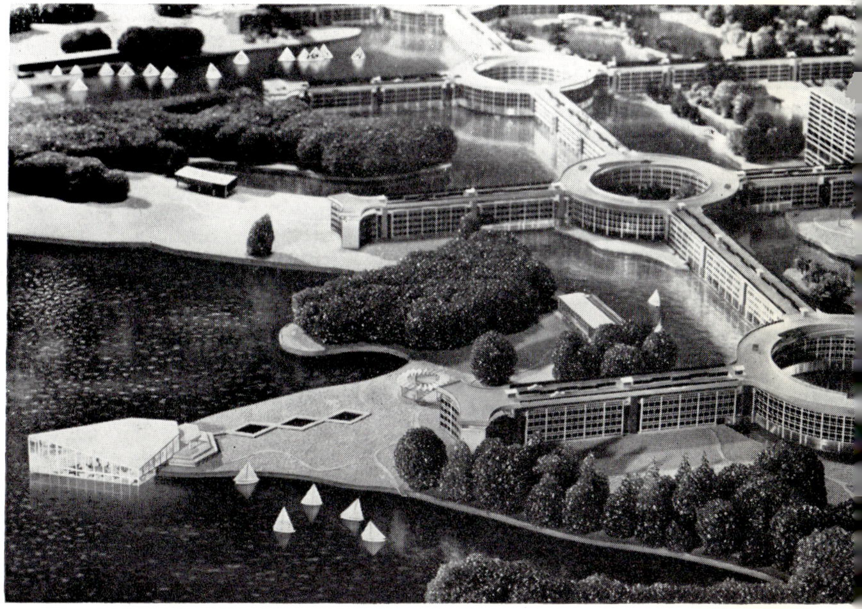

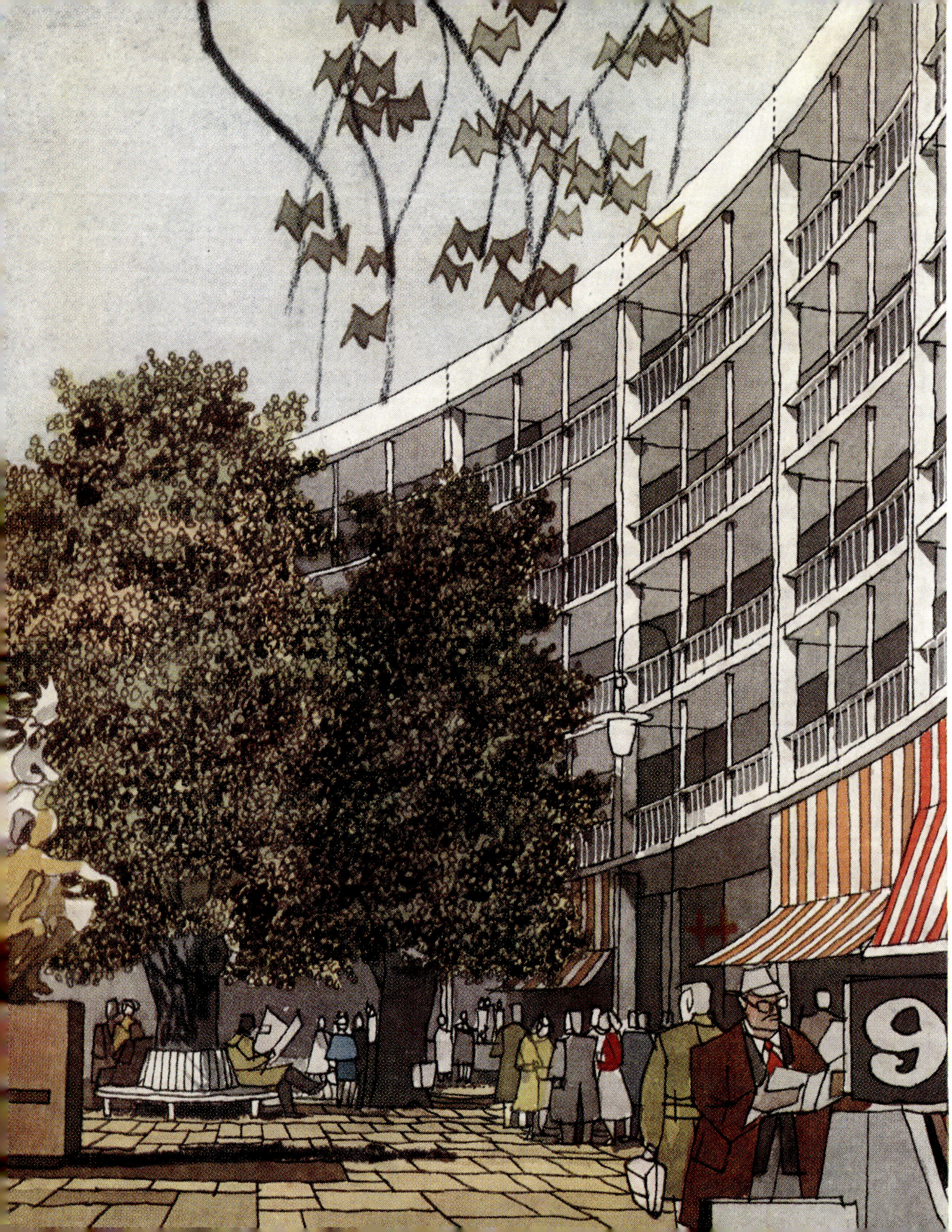
9

INDEX OF ILLUSTRATIONS